Lectures on Neoclassical Production Economics

Lectures on Neoclassical Production Economics

Robert G. Chambers

OXFORD
UNIVERSITY PRESS

OXFORD
UNIVERSITY PRESS

Oxford University Press is a department of the University of Oxford.
It furthers the University's objective of excellence in research, scholarship,
and education by publishing worldwide. Oxford is a registered trade mark of
Oxford University Press in the UK and in certain other countries.

Published in the United States of America by Oxford University Press
198 Madison Avenue, New York, NY 10016, United States of America.

CIP data is on file at the Library of Congress.

ISBN 9780197817728

DOI: 10.1093/9780197817759.001.0001

Printed by Marquis Book Printing, Canada

The manufacturer's authorized representative in the EU for product safety is
Oxford University Press España S.A. of El Parque Empresarial San Fernando de Henares,
Avenida de Castilla, 2 – 28830 Madrid (www.oup.es/en or product.safety@oup.com).
OUP España S.A. also acts as importer into Spain of products made by the manufacturer.

MIX
Paper | Supporting responsible forestry
FSC® C103567
FSC www.fsc.org

To my "big" sisters, Christy and Ellen.

Contents

Preface

Almost four decades ago, I published *Applied Production Analysis: A Dual Approach.* I based that book on lectures for graduate students of agricultural economics at the University of Maryland (UMD).

Several years after it appeared, I began teaching an undergraduate course on production economics. That presented a dilemma. Several then-existing books targeted the advanced undergraduate production-economics audience. But their content was outdated. On the other hand, I had written a book that I (guardedly) felt was up-to-date but written at an inappropriate level for my undergraduate audience. I couldn't ask students to purchase outdated books or one that they couldn't understand.

My compromise was to design a lecture-based course without a text that attempted to convey the intuitive essence of my graduate book. "Chalk and talk" was the delivery mechanism. Students seemed to like the course, but a common complaint was the lack of a text. My consistent answer was that a text appropriate for the course did not exist, which was true. Another common complaint was my failure to post Powerpoint@ slides online. The latter always met with smiling resistance. Slides, of course, would have made lecture preparation simpler. They would have also helped the less regular class attendees pass the course. But being the product of a liberal arts program who only turned to economics as a graduate student, I remain convinced that "chalk and talk" from an informed and engaged instructor dominates slide-based instruction.

For two decades, a dynamic equilibrium persisted. The lecture content evolved, but the presentation format remained stable. CoVid proved the disequilibrating event. Not only could I not rely on "chalk and talk," but lectures had to be online. Slides were *de rigueur.* Once I developed them (Beamer@), the next step was natural. This book is the result.

Acknowledgments

I would like to thank the generations of UMD students who took AREC 405. Perhaps without knowing it, you taught me more than I taught you. I deeply appreciate the chance to have met, interacted with, and learned from each of you. I want to give a particular shout-out to the Mr. and Ms. Lates of those classes. You know who you are.

Any professional reading this book will know that I learned from many, many teachers. Because of the way the book is designed, I cite few of them, but their influence percolates throughout the discussion. Those ideas that are mine were molded by them. I acknowledge my debt and thank them for opening so many happy professional doors. I also thank Rolf Färe, John Quiggin, Rulon Pope, Jorge Holzer-Bilbao, Simo Pieralli, Daniel Voica, Shuo Wang, Youpei Yan, and Valentin Zelenyuk for collaboration, drafting assistance, teaching assistance, or reading earlier drafts of this book. Three very insightful reviewers for Oxford University Press gave very valuable comments. I didn't always follow their advice, but I took it seriously, and it changed the final form of the book.

I close by thanking my family and friends for their support and love. (That *includes* the humans, the dogs, and the horses.) That support and love made the difference.

Introduction

Students in economics are introduced to broad concepts in early ECON classes and are expected to master them for more advanced study. Two such concepts are *supply* and *demand*. Suppliers are individuals who sell goods or commodities in market exchanges, and demanders are the buyers. These two forces are illustrated using a "scissors diagram" with a downward-sloping demand curve and an upward-sloping supply curve.

This book is a guide to the fundamental economic model behind the supply blade of the demand and supply scissors. Known as the "the theory of the producer" or "production economics," it describes the economic behavior of individuals who "make" commodities to sell in a market. "Make" means both physical production of a commodity (for example, growing wheat) and delivery of a service (for example, providing a taxi ride).

This book emerged from an undergraduate production economics class at the University of Maryland. My intent is to distill the essence of that theory in a form that will be accessible to anyone with a rudimentary class in microeconomics and the usual doses of high school and first-year university mathematics. The essential ideas are due to others, and no claim is made to originality.

I have tried to make the discussion rigorous but accessible. To that end, I have avoided calculus-grounded arguments. Many years of teaching have convinced me that grounding economic concepts in calculus terms promotes mechanical thinking that inhibits reasoning about the nuances of economic behavior. So while the calculus makes cameo appearances, it never assumes a supporting, let alone a starring, role. Instead, the argument relies on a geometric approach, grounded in convex analysis, that is more basic and more rigorous. The key ideas are conveyed with pictures, but they are rooted in results that I trace to R. T. Rockafellar's *Convex Analysis* and J. J. Moreau's *Fonctionnelles Convexes* that form the basis of much of modern optimization theory (Rockafellar, 1970; Moreau, 1962). In no small way, much of what I write here repeats arguments and analysis made in my book *Competitive Agents in Certain and Uncertain Market*, which was intended for a graduate-student audience, in a form that I hope is digestible to advanced undergraduate students in economics (Chambers, 2021).

Lectures on Neoclassical Production Economics. Robert G. Chambers, Oxford University Press.
 DOI: 10.1093/9780197817759.003.0001

Another characteristic of the discussion is that it takes a "constructive" approach to production economics. It starts with simple concepts that reflect common axioms in modern production theory. Then it constructs representations of a technology by postulating the existence of observations on inputs and outputs and imposing those axioms on the data.

We start with a general discussion of economic models. The takeaway message is that economic models do not depict reality. Instead, they are intellectual tools, organized around the principle of abstraction, that assist thinking about reality. Models have realistic kernels, but they contain unrealistic elements.

Three chapters on the different ways economists model the production of goods and services follow. I first introduce and discuss the notion of the "technology" (Chapter 2). And then after discussing production and input-requirement functions (Chapter 3), I treat input sets and output sets (Chapter 4).

Four chapters on the neoclassical producer model follow. Each examines producer behavior from a different perspective. But all assume, without apology, that producers are profit seekers operating in a competitive environment. That means self-interest motivates their behavior and that they cannot affect the prices at which they buy or sell. Chapter 5 introduces the profit-maximization problem and rudimentary tools for its analysis. Chapters 6, 7, and 8, respectively, treat cost functions, revenue functions, and profit functions. Chapter 9 treats duality theory and shows that the path taken in the preceding four chapters is reversible. If producer behavior is consistent with accepted economic principles, there must exist a technology underpinning it that is consistent with the technology model developed in Chapters 2 through 4. So, in a way, Chapter 9 justifies Chapter 2–4's focus on the model of the technology.

Chapters 10 and 11 cover function representations of the technology that I refer to as distance functions. They are better suited to studying multiple-input, multiple-output producer behavior than the production and input-requirement functions developed in Chapter 3. Chapter 12 closes the book by examining the consequences of relaxing key assumptions underlying the first eleven chapters and the canonical model introduced in them.

I have set off sections and exercises that I believe require "more-than-average" thought with an asterisk (*).

1
Models in Economics

1.1 The Role of Models in Economics

Parables are stories meant to convey a *moral*. They are simple so that the listener can grasp the moral easily. Good economic *models* are similar to parables. They identify a problem and strip it of unnecessary detail to focus on its essence. Thus, economic models are *abstract* rather than realistic. Abstraction promotes analysis, but it also makes economic models *as if* in nature. The principle isn't that models are realistic but that valuable lessons are learned by pretending *as if* they are.

As children, we learn something about transportation by playing with toy cars and something about cooking by playing with toy kitchens. Both a toy car and a toy kitchen are models. Both convey information about their realistic counterparts. And just as children enjoy playing with toys, they learn from them. Economists try to design their models so that they, too, learn real-world lessons from them.

Economic models assume verbal, mathematical, and visual (read graphical) forms. Often, they mix all three, and the forms are *always* interchangeable. Mathematical arguments translate into plain English. If they don't, something's wrong. By the same token, a verbal economic argument should be expressible mathematically. Economists illustrate their verbal and mathematical arguments using two- or three-dimensional graphs. Examples with which you may be familiar include *demand* and *supply curves.* Just as mathematical arguments translate into words, these pictures translate into either words or mathematics.

Economists use mathematics and graphs as *tools* to promote precision, to ensure logical reasoning, to promote intuition, and to facilitate generalization from simpler to more complex settings. Neither the mathematics nor the graphs are *ends* in themselves. They have no innate economic content. That only comes from the *extramathematical interpretations* that we, as economists, attach to the mathematical objects.[1]

[1] The peculiarly apt phraseology *extramathematic interpretation* is due to Fishburn (1972).

Lectures on Neoclassical Production Economics. Robert G. Chambers, Oxford University Press.
 DOI: 10.1093/9780197817759.003.0002

Mathematical symbols also provide a "shorthand" that replaces (harder to write) strings of words. Once a symbol is defined, it can be used with other symbols to construct meaningful (and precise) sentences. Graphs illustrate concepts phrased in either verbal or mathematical terms in the belief that the adage, "a picture is worth a thousand words," is correct.

In working with a model, it's crucial to stay within its confines. Results must trace to an element or elements of your model. They cannot emerge from factors implicitly imported into your reasoning. If your model cannot capture behavior you wish to explain, consider changing or adapting it to incorporate elements that might explain the phenomenon.

1.2 Thought Experiments and Models

Albert Einstein often illustrated complex reasoning using simple *thought experiments.* For example, in *Relativity: The Special and General Theory,*[2] he used images of a moving railway carriage, a man standing on the railway carriage, a man on a railway platform, and lightning strikes to explain his *Special Theory of Relativity* (Einstein, 1920). His thought experiments are examples of a rhetorical method that uses models spelled out in imaginary settings to convey an argument.

Thought experiments are important in economics, and most conceptual models are designed to be used with them. Typically, they are hypothetical. The reader is asked to imagine a plausible situation and then to make inferences about how individuals behave in that setting. Their importance in economics emerges from the difficulty that economists have in conducting *controlled experiments.* From your high school science classes, you know that a *controlled experiment* is one in which all possible sources of variation for the outcome except one (the treatment) are held fixed.

Thinking about the complexity of the settings in which social transactions occur reveals the difficulty of achieving such control in studying them. Physicians, sociologists, psychologists, neuroscientists, and economists strive to execute such experiments, but the outcomes are often problematic. And with good reason. Imagine, for example, how two balls moving toward one another react as they strike. A bit of physics gives the answer. Now imagine the same setting when the two balls can think and control their trajectory. What happens then? Social scientists study problems that are similar to those physicists study in that they can involve physical interactions, but they differ

[2] Einstein intended this book for the general reader.

in that those interactions involve thinking individuals. True control becomes difficult, if not impossible.

1.3 Some Simple Mathematical Background

Many readers may find repeated mentions of "mathematics" daunting. *Math anxiety*[3] is a common affliction that haunts many students from elementary school on. Having suffered it, I can empathize. But if you suffer it, please take a deep breath and read on. For while these lectures contain many mathematical symbols, that doesn't mean that the underlying ideas are unfamiliar or something to which you cannot attach an everyday meaning. All can and will be explained in verbal and pictorial terms. While we strive to maintain formal correctness, the focus is on the intuition that lies behind the symbols and not on the symbols themselves. So where most economics texts for advanced undergraduates freely use the calculus, these lectures avoid it precisely because so many find it impenetrable and unintuitive.[4] Still, math statements percolate throughout each of the lectures. My reasons for using mathematics are two: First, I believe in the following sentiment

> *. . . plus nous avançons dans la connaissance de l'univers, plus il nous apparaît fondè sur des lois mathèmatiques. (Le Tellier, 2020)*[5]

And second, much of what needs to be said requires some math notation and arguments.

Some, perhaps many, may find the notion that human behavior can be depicted using mathematics repellent because it conflicts with the belief that humans exercise free will. Such arguments merit serious thought, but a detailed discussion of them would turn what is intended as an introduction to an area of economics into a philosophy tome. But if you are so inclined, I would ask that you consider several points.

[3] This is particularly true for readers from the United States, where all too many believe that math is only accessible to the Sheldon Coopers of the world and not to regular people. And because so many feel this way, innumeracy is tolerated to an extent that illiteracy is not. Often it's rooted in experiences with teachers who, in addition to being sufferers themselves, project their own discomfort with rudimentary concepts into feelings of inadequacy upon the part of the student. On the other hand, there are those who simply suffer math antipathy, which is perfectly understandable.

[4] I also believe it promotes mechanical thinking about economics that tends to retard rather than promote a deeper intuitive understanding.

[5] . . . the more we understand the laws of the universe, the more it seems that they are based on the laws of mathematics (my translation)

The physical reality in which we operate is described by mathematical principles to an astonishing degree of accuracy. Many things we now understand to be true about it were discovered as a consequence of mathematical argument. For example, Einstein's general theory of relativity predicted the existence of the phenomenon that we call *black holes* roughly fifty years before humans coined the term and observed direct evidence of them. Why would inhabitants of that reality be exempt from such description? Saying that human behavior is amenable to mathematical representation is not the same as saying humans are mindless automatons. Indeed, the field of mathematics known as *optimization* is devoted to finding the best choice from an array of alternatives. And, more prosaically, how does one explain humanity's obvious affinity for straight lines? We see them everywhere, from reforested land to footpaths between two objects, despite Kent's famous admonition that "Nature abhors a straight line." You need not be Hari Seldon to believe in the usefulness of mathematics in the study of human behavior.[6]

Regardless of how you feel about such matters, this is an economics book, not a math one. You should be able to understand the fundamental story by skipping the math and just reading the words. However, that's akin to the golfer who avoids certain clubs. It gets you through the round and may even lower your score. But you'll still have the weaknesses in future rounds.

Because mathematical concepts and symbols are used, you need to know what they mean when you encounter them. Therefore, we now introduce a few concepts and a list of symbols. The list's intent is to provide a convenient reference for later discussion and reference.

The most basic concept is a *set*, which is defined as *a collection of objects.* What those objects are can vary. Familiar examples include a set of tools, a set of silverware, or a dozen apples. Each set meets the criterion of having objects in it. Perhaps more complicated, but still familiar, examples include the set of integers and the set of rational numbers.[7] Objects in the set are referred to interchangeably as *members* or *elements* of the set.

We denote sets by the symbol $\{\cdot\}$. Here, and in all that follows, the symbol $\cdot$ is a stand-in for an argument to be filled in later. The set definitions we use in these lectures have three parts: *the name of the set, a description of the kind of*

[6] William Kent was an eighteenth-century English landscape architect. Hari Seldon is a fictional psychometrician who is the hero of Isaac Asimov's *Foundation* (Asimov, 1951).

[7] Integers are the whole numbers such as 1,2,3 and a rational number is one that can be expressed as a ratio of two integers.

objects that are in the set, and *a qualifying statement about those objects.* For example, the expression

$$O = \{\text{oranges: the oranges are edible}\}$$

is to be read as "*O* is the set of oranges such that (a colon, :, is the math symbol for the words *such that*)[8] the oranges are edible." Here the name of the set is *O*, the kind of objects in the set are oranges, and the qualifier is that the oranges be edible. Similarly,

$$RO = \{\text{oranges: the oranges are inedible}\}$$

would be be read as *RO* is the set of oranges that are inedible.

If all the elements of set *A* also belong to set *B*, then *A* is a *subset* of *B*, which we denote by $A \subset B$. For example, if $B = \{$ *all apples*$\}$ and $A = \{$*golden apples*$\}$ then $A \subset B$. The *intersection* of sets *A* and *B*, denoted $A \cap B$, consists of the set of elements that they have in common. For example, if $A = \{red,\ white,\ blue\}$ and $B = \{white,\ black,\ yellow\}$, then $A \cap B = \{white\}$. Unless assumed otherwise, the order in which elements of a set appear is arbitrary. Therefore, $A = \{red,\ white,\ blue\}$ and $B = \{red,\ blue,\ white\}$ are the same set, denoted $A = B$. Alternatively, $A \subset B$ and $B \subset A$ implies that $A = B$.

Associated with the notion of a set is that of the *empty set*, which is defined as the set with nothing in it. You might reasonably ask why we are interested in a set that has nothing in it. My best answer is that we often encounter situations that involve physical or (currently) technical impossibilities. And to tell complete economic stories, we need to account for them. The notion of an empty set lets us. The notation for the empty set is Ø, which resembles a zero with a backslash drawn through it. The convention is that Ø belongs to all sets.

1.4 Common Symbols

We now list, for convenient later reference, symbols used in these lectures. We haven't yet told you what they all mean, but that will come later.

- $\{\cdot\}$, set
- Ø, the empty set

[8] Many writers use |, vertical slash, in place of :.

- $\subset$, is a subset of, $A \subset B$ reads A is a subset of B
- $\cap$, intersection, $A \cap B$ is the intersection of sets A and B
- x, a single input or a vector of inputs
- w, a single input price or a vector of input prices
- y, a single output or a vector of outputs
- p, a single output price or a vector of output prices
- $wx = \sum_n w_n x_n$, the sum of all input prices times the input values
- $py = \sum_m p_m y_m$, the sum of all output prices times the output values
- $\exists$, there exists
- :, such that
- $\geq$, greater than or equal to
- $\leq$, less than or equal to
- =, equal to or "*is*"
- $\equiv$, is defined as or is equivalent to
- (a, b), all real numbers x such that $a < x < b$
- $[a, b]$, all real numbers x such that $a \leq x \leq b$
- ΔA, the change in A
- $\Rightarrow$ *or* $\Downarrow$, implies. For example, $A \Rightarrow B$ is to be read as A implies B. Alternatively (and more completely), $A \Rightarrow B$ is translated as: If A is true, then B is true.
- $\Leftrightarrow$, two statements are equivalent. For example, $A \Leftrightarrow B$ is to be read as A and B are equivalent, or as A implies B and B implies A.
- for vectors x and y, $x \geq y, x \neq y$, every element of x is at least as large as the corresponding element in y and one element of x is strictly larger than its corresponding element in y. For example, $(0, 0)$ and $(0, 1)$ both satisfy $(0, 0) \geq (0, 0)$ and $(0, 1) \geq (0, 0)$ but only $(0, 1) \geq (0, 0), (0, 1) \neq (0, 0)$.
- $\in$, belongs to or is a member of. For example, $\hat{a} \in A$ is to be read as $\hat{a}$ belongs to A, or $\hat{a}$ is a member of A
- $\notin$, does not belong to or is not a member of. For example, $\hat{a} \notin A$ is to be read as $\hat{a}$ is not a member of A.y
- T, a technology set
- $f(x)$, a production function
- $e(y)$, an input-requirement function
- $X(y)$, an input set
- $Y(x)$, an output set
- $\bar{X}(y)$, an isoquant
- $\bar{Y}(x)$, a transformation curve
- $\bar{\mathcal{P}}(\pi, p, w)$, isoprofit hyperplane
- $\mathcal{P}^+(\pi, p, w)$, isoprofit (upper) half space
- $\mathcal{P}^-(\pi, p, w)$, isoprofit lower half space

- $\bar{C}\,(c, w)$, isocost hyperplane
- $C^{+}\,(c, w)$, isocost (upper) half space
- $C^{-}\,(c, w)$, isocost (lower) half space
- $\bar{\mathcal{R}}\,(r, p)$, isorevenue hyperplane
- $\mathcal{R}^{+}\,(r, w)$, isorevenue (upper) half space
- $\mathcal{R}^{-}\,(r, w)$, isorevenue (lower) half space
- $\pi(p, w)$, a profit function
- $c(w, y)$, a cost function
- $R(p, x)$, a revenue function
- $\bar{T}$, a dual technology set
- $\bar{c}(w, y)$, a dual cost function
- $\bar{R}(p, x)$, a dual revenue function
- $I(x, y)$, disposable surplus
- $I^{g}(x, y)$, an (input) distance function
- $O^{g}(y, x)$, an (output) distance function
- $\bar{I}^{g}(x, y)$, a dual (input) distance function
- $\bar{O}^{g}(y, x)$, a dual (output) distance function
- $X^{g}(y)$, a g input efficient set for y
- $Y^{g}(x)$, a g output efficient set for x

2
The Producer and the Technology

2.1 Producers

In this chapter, we study individuals who make (*produce*) goods or services to sell in markets. We refer to them interchangeably as *producers*, *decisionmakers*, or *firms*. A handy example is a farmer producing agricultural commodities (for example, wheat, corn, soybeans, hogs, and beef). But feel free to substitute your own examples to suit your experience and intuition. The more you think in familiar terms, the more you will understand.

We make basic assumptions about what motivates producers and about the setting in which they make decisions. **These assumptions are maintained throughout much of the book.** You don't need to agree with them or even find them believable. But the analysis that follows often assumes that they hold.

The first assumption is that producers are *small* or *perfectly competitive* relative to the markets that they face. Small means that they take the prices at which they buy and sell market items as *given by the market*. Producers cannot manipulate prices, they are *price-takers*. The second assumption is that producers are *self-interested* individuals who seek to maximize their profit from producing and selling commodities.

In other economics classes, you may have encountered situations where producers can manipulate prices (for example, monopoly or monopsony). These lectures aren't about them. We treat a situation similar to what one faces on entering a *Starbucks@* or *McDonalds@*. You do not bargain with a barista over the price of a cappucino. Either you pay the stated price or you don't get the cappucino. Same here: a producer doesn't negotiate the price of an input or the selling price of the product.

The profit-maximizing assumption can be controversial. Many argue that individuals are not motivated solely by self-gain. Others argue that producers should not behave selfishly. I make no argument either for or against those positions. *But* these lectures are about individuals who, when faced

Lectures on Neoclassical Production Economics. Robert G. Chambers, Oxford University Press.
 DOI: 10.1093/9780197817759.003.0003

with a market setting, maximize profit. If producers maximize profit, what prevents them from making it infinitely large? Our answer is what we call the *Technology*, which is the subject of the rest of this chapter.

2.2 The Technology Set Introduced

The *Technology* describes the possibilities for producing *outputs* using *inputs*. *Inputs*, which we denote by x, are commodities or goods used to produce something. For example, in making a cake, the inputs include its raw ingredients, your time and effort, heat from the oven, and so on. *Outputs*, denoted by y, are the commodities produced (for example, the cake). We characterize the *feasible* possibilities as a set that contains *inputs* and *outputs* and that is common to all producers. Producers cannot affect that set. So, it is not unlike market prices. Producers take it as given and then react to it in making their production decisions. You might think of this set as given by *Nature*.

The mathematical definition is

$$T = \{(x, y) : x \text{ can produce } y\}$$

Here T is a notational stand-in for the *Technology*. The expression (x, y) tells us that the members of the set are inputs and outputs, and the qualifying statement is that "x can produce y." Expressed in words: *The technology is the set of inputs and outputs such that the outputs can be produced using the inputs.*[1] So, saying that "x and y belong to T," written in symbols as $(x, y) \in T$, is the same as saying "x can produce y." Or, in symbols, $(x, y) \in T \Leftrightarrow x$ can produce y. (Recall that $\Leftrightarrow$ translates into words as "is equivalent to.")

Thus, the technology contains all feasible combinations of inputs and outputs. This way of thinking of the technology contrasts with everyday usage of the word *technology*. For example, you may have heard individuals speak of the *technology for growing corn* or the *technology for producing steel*. This is sensible given most dictionary definitions of technology. But it's *not* how we use the term. Our usage of the term includes all such notions in a common set from which any producer can choose. So, instead of saying the *technology for growing corn* we use the phrasing the *process for growing corn* or *the technical process for growing corn*.

[1] Having introduced and defined the term, in the following we refer to the technology using lower-case letters.

2.3 The Technology Is a "Model"

T contains many possibilities, most of which are complex. That's true for even simple choices. Think of what's involved in producing a wooden pencil. Its obvious inputs include wood, pencil lead, an eraser, and a piece of metal or plastic to hold the eraser in place. Each of these inputs has itself been produced or processed. The productive process stretches further back. It quickly becomes apparent that keeping track of all such activities becomes complex. Faced with such complexity, we need a *model.* This chapter details the production model used in these lectures. We construct it by imposing assumptions (restrictions) upon T. We strive for a model that captures the economic essentials of production, but that remains parsimonious.

First, we must clarify how we think about x and y. We have said that they are inputs and outputs but not how we measure them. We assume they can be represented as *real numbers.* Because we are interested in cases that may involve multiple inputs and multiple outputs, we let x be a nonnegative N-dimensional vector

$$x = (x_1, x_2, \ldots, x_N),$$

where x_n stands for the *nth* input to the production process. Similarly, y stands for a nonnegative M-vector

$$y = (y_1, y_2, \ldots, y_M),$$

and y_m for the *mth* output produced. M and N are integers and typically differ. In the following, to avoid mathematical jargon, we often refer to $x's$ and $y's$ that are vectors as *bundles* and not as vectors. The concepts are interchangeable.

Real numbers are familiar, so it's easy to gloss over this assumption. But familiar or not, they are abstract and a bit mysterious. They represent the completion of the rational numbers. Or, put another way, they are the set of rational numbers augmented by the numbers (the irrational numbers) that fall in between the rational numbers to form the continuum. Mathematicians developed the notion of an irrational number because physical phenomena exist that we cannot measure exactly without them. *Pi* (usually written π) that gives the ratio of a circle's circumference to its diameter is one example. Another is the length of the diagonal of a square. By the Pythagorean Theorem the length of the diagonal for a square with 90-foot sides is $\sqrt{2} \times 90$ feet. And, regardless of the units used to measure the square's sides, the diagonal's length remains $\sqrt{2}$ times that length. That means that we cannot devise a discrete system of measuring the lengths of diagonals and the sides. It's as if Nature demands the existence of an irrational number, $\sqrt{2}$, to measure length.

In thinking about inputs and outputs, it's important to remember that T is defined in terms of *all* possible inputs and outputs. In particular, x contains all possible inputs to a production process and y contains all the possible outputs. To give an example, think of a farmer who grows corn on a parcel of land. If asked to list the associated inputs, one might respond land, labor, fertilizers and pesticides, capital equipment, and fuel. That list, in fact, encompasses the inputs most often considered in empirical studies of farmer behavior, but it is incomplete. Corn growth also depends upon other factors, including natural moisture, natural radiation, the presence or absence of a pest infestation, and the organic content of the soil. In short, anything that affects corn growth is included in x. x even includes factors that inhibit production, such as pests.

What's true for x is true for y. When we write y, we mean all outputs. For the corn grower that extends the list beyond corn to include air pollution emitted by burning fuel, soil runoff as a result of plowing, fertilizer and pesticide leakage into the environment, noise pollution from running capital equipment, and so on. Again the list contains both desirable outputs and nondesirables such as pollution, noise, and runoff. All belong in T.

We emphasize the higher dimensional nature of x and y because most of our discussions are in simpler terms. For example, our graphical illustrations are two- (sometimes three-) dimensional. So, when we discuss the interaction of inputs and outputs, it will be rare for us to illustrate a production process that contains more than one or two outputs and one or two inputs. That doesn't mean that other dimensions are not important. Instead. it manifests our visual perception of the world as three-dimensional and reading surfaces as two-dimensional. In drawing such pictures, we assume that *all other things are held constant.*[2]

As you read, please keep in mind that our model of T assumes a deterministic setting. We do not treat situations where producers make decisions in the presence of uncertainty about the outcomes of those decisions. This is unrealistic, but we are trying to build a tractable model and not to replicate reality. And, as unrealistic as it is, it's a common assumption in even the most advanced economic analyses. No one believes that uncertainty is unimportant. But treating uncertainty makes even the simplest production problems complicated. We also assume that T satisfies a *regularity condition*:[3] T is a

[2] In economics jargon, the Latin phrase *ceteris paribus* is often used in place of "all other things held constant."

[3] In a more formal setting, the regularity condition would be listed as a separate (the sixth) assumption. I have avoided this to maintain the focus on what I regard as the more important restrictions.

closed set and $\{y : (x, y) \in T\}$ is bounded for all x finite. If you have a smattering of math knowledge, you may know what this means. If you don't, the regularity condition's primary role is to simplify the definition of maxima and minima in what follows.

2.4 Assumptions on T

Our restrictions on T mix five assumptions. We list them in mathematical form and then explain each in the subsections that follow. A good way to view these assumptions is as a menu of alternative properties T may possess. Each assumption may be reasonable in some settings but not in others.

Assumptions on T

1. $T \neq \emptyset$ (T is nonempty);
2. $(x, y) \in T \Rightarrow (x', y) \in T$ for $x' \geq x$ (free disposability of inputs (FDI));
3. $(x, y) \in T \Rightarrow (x, y') \in T$ for $y' \leq y$ (free disposability of outputs (FDO));
4. If $(x^0, y^0) \in T$ and $(x^1, y^1) \in T$ then $\lambda(x^0, y^0) + (1 - \lambda)(x^1, y^1) \in T$ for all $\lambda \in (0, 1)$ (T is a *convex* set).
5. $(0, y) \notin T$ if $y \geq 0$ and $y \neq 0$ (no free lunch (NFL)) and $(0, 0) \in T$ (no fixed costs (NFC)).

2.4.1 T Is Nonempty

$T \neq \emptyset$, which is read as "T is not an empty set," is easy to justify. It means that we assume that an x and a y exist such that x can produce that y. Because we live in a world where things are produced, it's plausible.

Nonemptiness of T is a good place to start illustrating our model of T. In all the illustrations that follow, we assume that you understand the traditional $x - y$ axis representation of the Cartesian coordinate system (coordinate plane). We refer to the $x - y$ axis representation interchangeably as (x, y) *space* and the (x, y) *plane.*

In Figure 2.1, we label the vertical axis as y and let it measure output. We use the horizontal axis to measure input and label it as x. Because there are only two dimensions, the figure is a stylized representation of our ideas. Various interpretations exist. It can illustrate a hypothetical technology where one input produces a single output, how one output and one input covary while holding all others fixed, or, in a macroeconomic spirit, the behavior of

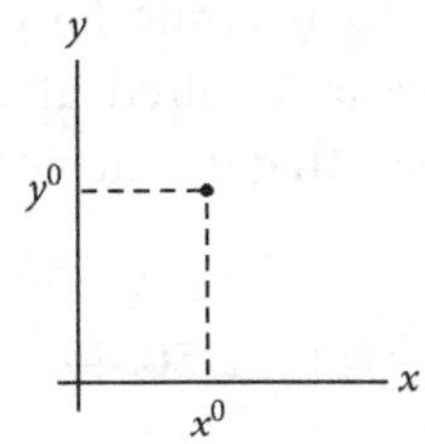

Figure 2.1 *T* not the empty set

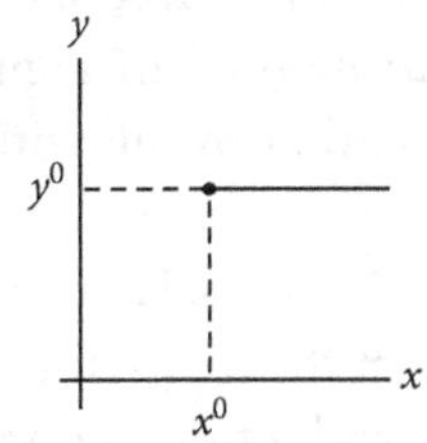

Figure 2.2 Free disposability of inputs

an "aggregate input" and an "aggregate output." Nonemptiness of T means that at least one feasible point exists in (x, y) space. It's illustrated by the point (x^0, y^0).

2.4.2 Free Disposability of Inputs

Free disposability of inputs (FDI) requires that if x can produce y, any input *bundle* that is at least as large as x in all its N dimensions can produce that same y. This assumption strikes many as intuitive. And in many cases it is. For example, if a farmer can produce 75 bushels of wheat with one hired hand, it seems reasonable that the farmer could continue to produce 75 bushels of wheat if another hired hand were added. In fact, intuition would suggest that the farmer could produce more than 75 bushels. Intuition might also suggest that if the farmer increased the other inputs devoted to wheat production, producing 75 bushels of wheat remains feasible.

Starting from the feasible point, (x^0, y^0), depicted in Figure 2.1, FDI requires that all points to its right holding output at y^0 are feasible (illustrated in Figure 2.2). Note the logical force of the assumption. Nonemptiness of T ensures that one feasible input–output bundle exists. Adding FDI ensures that an infinity of feasible input–output combinations exists.

This intuition has its limits. To illustrate, let's use our farmer example. Suppose that the farmer's inputs are land, hired labor, fertilizer, and seed and that the output is wheat. Let's also say that the farmer's input usage to produce that 75 bushels is

$$x = (1, 1, 50, 40),$$

which stands for 1 unit of land, 1 unit of hired labor, 50 units of fertilizer, and 40 units of seed. (You are free to choose "units" to suit your intuition.) Now, what do you believe happens if land, hired labor, and seed remain constant but fertilizer increases *without bound*? In Figure 2.2, if the horizontal axis measures fertilizer, we illustrate that by allowing x to run off the edge of the page and on to infinity.

FDI requires that producing 75 bushels of wheat remains feasible. But this counters reality. It is well known that applying *too much* fertilizer is destructive rather than productive. Production economists call this phenomenon *congestion*. It happens because increasing one input while holding others constant eventually overwhelms the other inputs with which it cooperates. Another simple example comes from holding land, fertilizer, and seed constant at $(1, 50, 40)$, respectively, and allowing hired labor to grow toward infinity. Sooner rather than later, those extra workers get in each other's way. Congestion is a general phenomenon common to many different production processes. The aphorisms that one can "get too much of a good thing" or that "too many cooks can spoil the broth" capture the intuitive essence of congestion.

So, if FDI counters physical reality, why use it? The answer is that it is an acceptable approximation in many practical instances. Think of our farmer. Because the farmer knows the technology, the farmer will know about congestion and will not operate in regions of T where it exists. It's hard to imagine a producer applying destructive inputs. If they do, they soon go out of business. Therefore, while we know congestion can occur, we may lose little to no explanatory power in using FDI in examining producer behavior. As always, models are "as if" devices.

2.4.3 Free Disposability of Output

Free disposability of output (FDO) requires that if x can produce y, it can also produce any output bundle, y^*, whose elements, y^*_m, $m = 1, 2, \ldots M$, are no larger than the corresponding element in y. For example, suppose that 1 acre of land and 1 unit of hired labor can produce 40 bushels of corn and 40 bushels

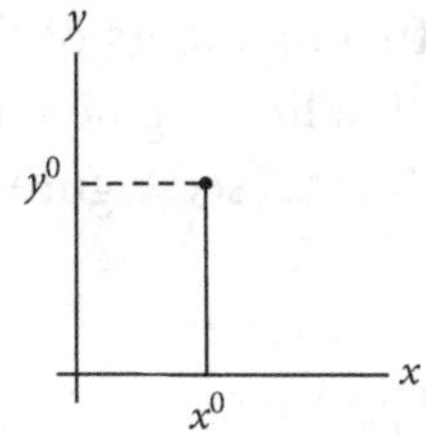

Figure 2.3 Free disposability of output

of soybeans. Then, FDO requires that 1 acre of land and 1 unit of hired labor can produce 40 bushels of corn and 0 bushels of soybeans, 0 bushels of corn and 40 bushels of soybeans, 30 bushels of corn and 30 bushels of soybeans, and so on. Producers can *dispose of (throw away) outputs* without changing input use or the production of other outputs. Figure 2.3 illustrates the impact of imposing FDO on the nonempty T depicted in Figure 2.1. If (x^0, y^0) is feasible, FDO requires that all the points on the line segment connecting (x^0, y^0) and $(x^0, 0)$ belong to T.

Some production processes exist for which FDO is implausible. An important counterexample is offered by processes that involve the production of *undesirable outputs*. For example, farming that involves tilling land generates soil erosion. Soil erosion is undesirable because it pollutes water resources and wastes a valuable resource, the soil. If FDO were true, farmers could hold all inputs and crop production constant and reduce soil erosion. In fact, FDO requires that soil erosion could be eliminated. But soil erosion occurs. Is it that farmers have a pathological need to pollute or to waste valuable resources? No, FDO is implausible in this setting because reducing erosion requires diverting resources from crop production. If production processes generate undesirable outputs, the rule of thumb is that resources will have to be diverted from the production of desirables to remediate the problem.

2.4.4 *T* Is a Convex Set

Diminishing marginal returns is a fundamental concept in economics. Its essence is that one receives smaller marginal returns or benefits as one works harder or consumes more. In producer theory, its most common manifestation is *diminishing marginal productivity*. The consumer analogue is *diminishing marginal utility*.

Assuming that T is a convex set is the way that economists ensure that T is consistent with diminishing returns. A set is *convex* or satisfies *convexity* if any weighted average of any two members of the set also belongs to the set. Geometrically, a set is convex if a line segment connecting any two elements of the set lies entirely within the set (see Figure 2.4). The math names for the expression

$$\lambda\left(x^0, y^0\right) + (1 - \lambda)\left(x^1, y^1\right)$$

for $\lambda \in (0, 1)$ are the *convex combination* of $\left(x^0, y^0\right)$ and $\left(x^1, y^1\right)$ or the *line segment* connecting them. Thus, another way to define a set as being convex is to require that all the convex combinations of the elements of the set belong to the set. Familiar examples are the set of real numbers $(-\infty, \infty)$ and the (x, y) coordinate plane.

Let $\left(x^0, y^0\right)$ and $\left(x^1, y^1\right)$ in Figure 2.5 be two feasible input–output bundles. Convexity requires that $\lambda\left(x^0, y^0\right) + (1 - \lambda)\left(x^1, y^1\right) \in T$ for all $\lambda \in (0, 1)$. For example, setting $\lambda = \frac{1}{2}$ gives

$$\left(\frac{x^0 + x^1}{2}, \frac{y^0 + y^1}{2}\right) \in T, \qquad (2.1)$$

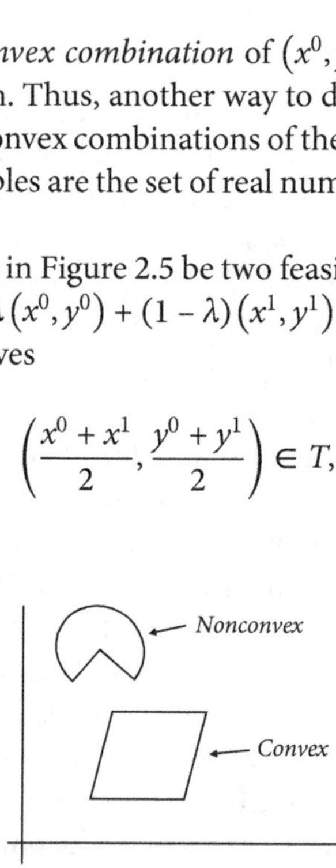

Figure 2.4 Convex and N nonconvex sets

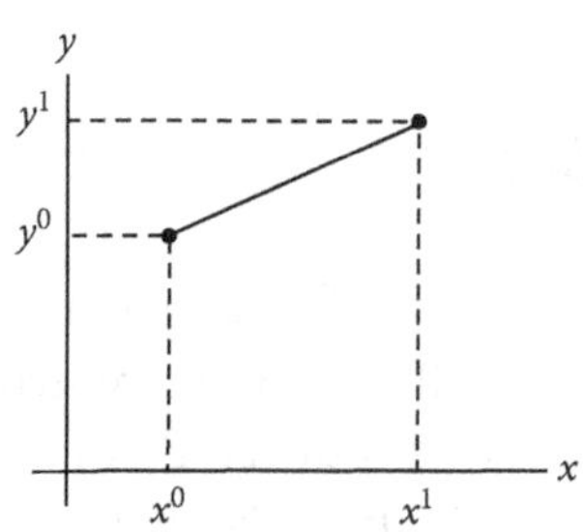

Figure 2.5 Convexity and *T*

which is the simple average of (x^0, y^0) and (x^1, y^1) that Figure 2.5 illustrates as falling halfway between them on the connecting line segment. Taking $\lambda = \frac{3}{4}$ gives

$$\frac{3}{4}(x^0, y^0) + \frac{1}{4}(x^1, y^1) \in T \tag{2.2}$$

that corresponds to the point falling midway between $\left(\frac{x^0+x^1}{2}, \frac{y^0+y^1}{2}\right)$ and (x^0, y^0) on that line segment. Repeating this argument for all $\lambda \in (0, 1)$ shows that all the points on the line segment connecting $(x^0, y^0) \in T$ and $(x^1, y^1) \in T$ must belong to T.

Invoking convexity exposes some mental puzzles associated with working with real numbers. For example, it's sensible to think of an automobile as the output of a production process. But how does one interpret

$$\frac{1+2}{2} = 1.5$$

automobiles? Is $\frac{1}{2}$ of an automobile meaningful, other than as junk? We don't provide an answer. The answers exist, and you are encouraged to seek them out. What's important is that you realize such questions exist.

2.4.5 No Free Lunch and No Fixed Costs

No free lunch (NFL) requires that an input bundle with all inputs equal to 0 cannot produce an output bundle that contains any positive elements, that is, one with at least one $y_m > 0$. Producing an output requires using some inputs. NFL is hard to contradict. In essence, it repeats the *Law of the Conservation of Mass*: matter can be neither created nor destroyed. In thinking about NFL, it helps to remember that when we say that "we make a product," we do not mean that we "create" it. Instead, we mean that we transform an existing mass of matter in the form of inputs into other forms. NFL ensures that a point such as $(0, y^0)$ in Figure 2.6 cannot be feasible. NFC (no fixed costs), which is also referred to as *Inaction is possible*, permits the producer to choose to do nothing. Combining NFL and NFC ensures that points on the vertical axis above the origin cannot be feasible, while the origin remains in T.

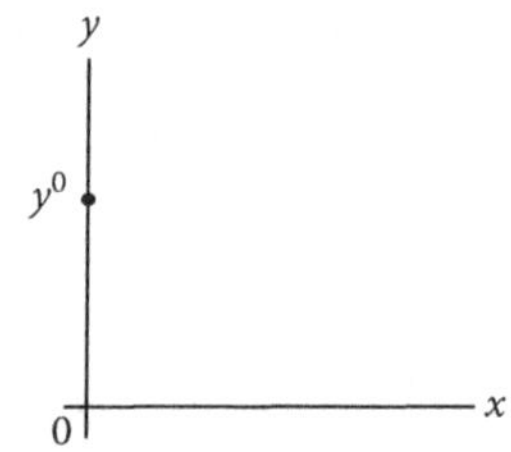

Figure 2.6 Violation of No Free Lunch

2.5 The Canonical Technology

We say that T is a *canonical technology* if it satisfies all five assumptions. We use a distinct term for such a technology to emphasize that production processes exist that do not satisfy all five assumptions. Calling it *canonical* signals that it's a standard or familiar representation.

Our visual illustration of its construction highlights a key point: one can use observed data on inputs and outputs to build a set, call it $\hat{T}$, that satisfies all five assumptions. That has important implications. First, because such a $\hat{T}$ always exists, we cannot use observed data to falsify the five assumptions. That does not mean that they are correct or that we can verify them. Rather, we cannot rule them out using real-world data. Second, observed data can be used to construct a "canonical technology." Our *model* is not just a conceptual toy; it has empirical content and can be used to study observed phenomena.

To demonstrate the construction, we assume that we are given two data points (x^0, y^0) and (x^1, y^1), as illustrated in Figure 2.7. (Thus, nonemptiness is satisfied.) Invoking convexity incorporates all points on the solid line segment connecting these two points into the technology. Imposing FDO on each point on this line segment (including its endpoints) ensures that all points lying below it and on or above the horizontal axis belong to T. Applying FDI to the result includes all points lying below a horizontal line emanating from (x^1, y^1) (toward the right) and on or above the horizontal axis. Adding assumption 5 includes $(0, 0)$. Convexity includes the line segment connecting $(0, 0)$ and (x^0, y^0). FDO includes the area below that line segment. The result, as built up from (x^0, y^0) and (x^1, y^1), is illustrated by Figure 2.7. (In Exercise 2, you are asked to revisit this construction using an alternative approach to developing T.)

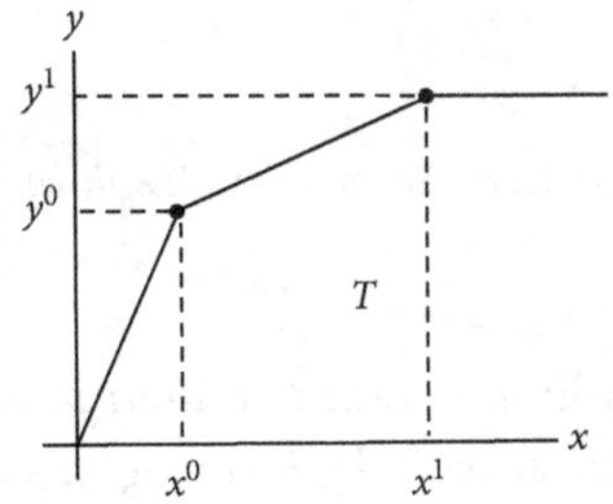

Figure 2.7 The Canonical Technology

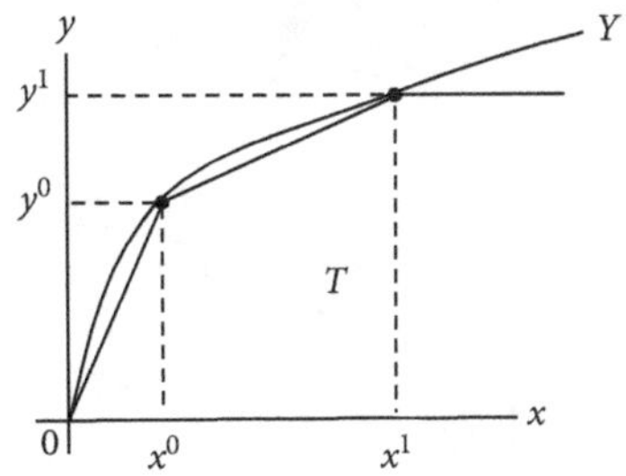

Figure 2.8 A smooth canonical technology

Figure 2.7 was constructed using only two data points and our assumptions. That accounts for its *polygonal* appearance.[4] You should not infer, however, that the canonical technology must be polygonal. Figure 2.7 ensures that we do not rule that out, but other forms are allowed. For example, Figure 2.8 illustrates T as the area below the smooth curve emanating from the origin labeled OY, which includes the points (x^0, y^0) and (x^1, y^1). You can verify that the technology illustrated in Figure 2.8 satisfies our five assumptions. Observing (x^0, y^0) and (x^1, y^1) is consistent with both the technology illustrated in Figure 2.7 and the technology in Figure 2.8. But the technology shown in Figure 2.8 includes points not included in the technology illustrated in Figure 2.7. One interpretation of the technology in Figure 2.7 is as a *conservative approximation* to a technology consistent with the technology illustrated in Figure 2.8 (and possibly others) that has been constructed using observed (x^0, y^0) and (x^1, y^1) and our five assumptions.

[4] A *polygon* is a figure in the coordinate plane with a finite number of sides. Special cases are triangles, rectangles, and squares.

2.6 Exercises

Exercise 1. *Figure 2.9 depicts a technology. Explain which of the properties it satisfies.*

Exercise 2. *Assume that you are given two data points* (x^0, y^0) *and* (x^1, y^1) *as illustrated in Figure 2.5. Construct* T *by invoking in succession free disposability of inputs, convexity, free disposability of outputs, and no free lunch and no fixed costs. Compare and contrast your result with Figure 2.7.*

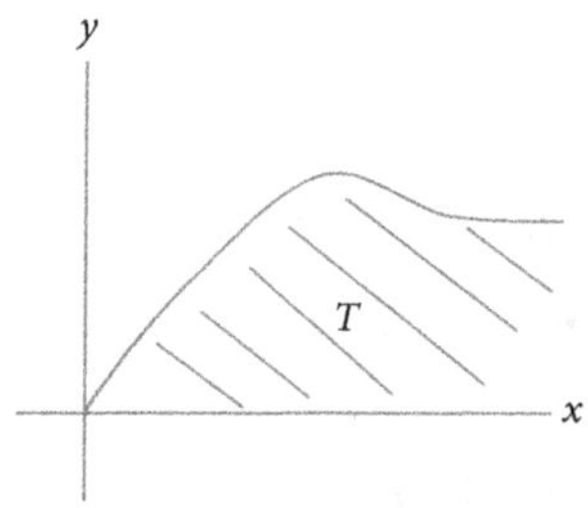

Figure 2.9 Exercise 1

3
Production and Input Requirement Functions

3.1 Introduction

So far, we have discussed the technology as a set of inputs and outputs. Many readers, however, will have encountered the technology represented as a *production function*. Some may have also encountered an *input-requirement function*. This chapter shows how to derive these functions from T and how our basic assumptions regarding T affect their properties.

Figure 3.1 depicts a single-input, single-output, canonical technology, T, as everything on or below the curve OY.[1] Such a technology is unrealistic. The same is true for single-input, single-output production processes. We study them because they provide the core economic intuition on producer behavior and give us a nice format for showing how the notion of the technology is incorporated into economic analyses.

We first study the *production function* for a single-output, single-input production process, visualized as the curve 0Y in Figure 3.1. Then we study the *input requirement function*, visualized as 0X in Figure 3.2. We conclude the chapter by looking at the (slightly) more general cases of a multiple-input, single-output production process and a single-input, multiple-output production process.

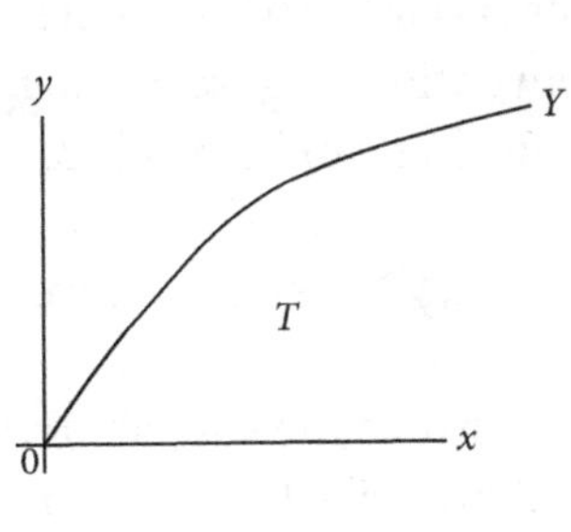

Figure 3.1 Canonical Technology

[1] Figure 3.1 is derived from Figure 2.8 in Chapter 2.

Lectures on Neoclassical Production Economics. Robert G. Chambers, Oxford University Press.
 DOI: 10.1093/9780197817759.003.0004

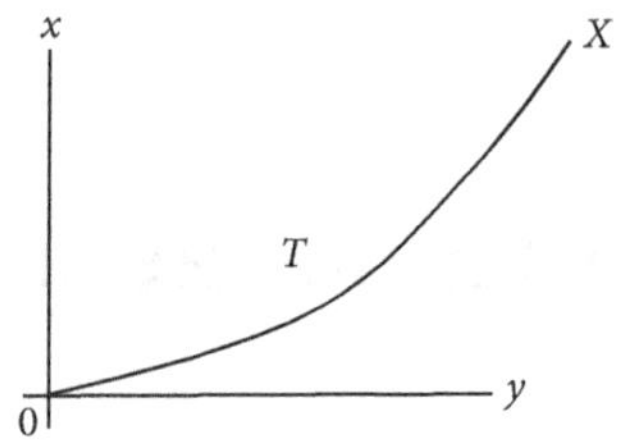

Figure 3.2 Canonical *T* in Input Dependent Form

But first, a few words on viewing phenomena from different perspectives.

3.2 A Parable on Perspective

When three blind men were confronted with, to them, an unknown beast called an *elephant,* they decided to identify its nature by examining it by touch. The first man, who touched its side, declared it to be a wall. The second, who touched its ear, declared it to be a fan. And the third, who felt its tail, proclaimed it a snake. (Source: Apocryphal)

The moral of this parable isn't that production economists should act as blind men. Rather, it's that examining things from different perspectives conveys different information. Think, for example, what you do when you are handed an unfamiliar object. Do you turn it over to look at it from all sides? We can draw insight from doing the same thing, metaphorically speaking, with our model of T.

By convention, ordered pairs graphed in the real plane measure the *independent variable* along the horizontal axis (labeled x in Figure 3.1) and the *dependent variable* along the vertical axis (labeled y in Figure 3.1).[2] This shows that the independent variable drives or determines the dependent variable. So, following this convention, Figure 3.1 suggests that choosing x fixes the range of possible outputs that can be produced. Our definition,

$$T = \{(x, y): x \text{ can produce } y\},$$

written in the *active voice* with x as the subject, reinforces that intuition. But it can be useful to view technologies treating y as the independent variable and x as the dependent variable. This approach involves switching axes in

[2] We should say the *convention outside of economics* because economists violate this rule when they graph demand and supply curves.

depicting T. Figure 3.2 illustrates that T is now represented as everything on or above the curve 0X. This changes the visual perspective on T, but not the substance of T. We rephrase the definition of T in the *passive voice* as

$$T = \{(x, y): y \text{ can be produced by } x\},$$

Examining T from different perspectives is a recurring theme in these chapters. In the present chapter, its manifestations are the production function and the input-requirement function. Later chapters extend these concepts to encompass more general technologies and decision settings.

3.3 Production Function (Single-Input, Single-Output Case)

Definition 1 (The Production Function). *The production function for input level x, $f(x)$, is the maximum output that can be produced using x.*

The mathematical version is

$$f(x) \equiv \max\{y : (x, y) \in T\}.$$

(Recall that $\equiv$ translates as *is defined*.) Here and elsewhere, we interpret $\max\{\cdot\}$ as an instruction to choose the maximum (largest) element contained in the set $\{\cdot\}$. In this instance, that set is all the output levels that can be produced using x, that is,

$$\{y : (x, y) \in T\} = \{y : \ x \text{ can produce } y\}.$$

One locates $f(x)$ in Figure 3.1 by choosing x on the horizontal axis and then locating the largest (highest) y in T that x can produce. Using this procedure for all x in Figure 3.1 gives the curve 0Y as the *graph* of input-output pairs, $(x, f(x))$, falling on the production function for T. For the single-input, single-output technology, you can think of the graph of the production function as the *upper boundary* for T.

To appreciate an economist's interest in $f(x)$, consider the simple economic problem involving a producer who is endowed with a fixed amount of x (assumed nonconsumable). How would the producer use that x? One plausible alternative is to convert it into as much y as possible via T. $f(x)$ achieves that.

We now investigate how the basic assumptions about T affect $f(x)$.

T Is not Empty

$T \neq \emptyset$ means that at least one (x, y) is feasible. Thus, *at least one x exists for which $f(x)$ is well defined.* Here's the reasoning. If T is not empty, take any $(x, y) \in T$. If that y is the only output that x can produce, then $y = f(x)$. If other output levels can be produced using x, the largest of them is $f(x)$. Thus, $f(x)$ must exist for at least one x if $T \neq \emptyset$, as desired.

T is not empty, however, *does not imply that $f(x)$ is well defined for all x.* The reasoning here is that $T \neq \emptyset$ *is satisfied even if only one feasible input-output bundle exists.* (Imagine a T that has a single point in it.) The production function is well defined for that x, but what about other values of x?[3]

We state the conclusion in math terms as:

- $T \neq \emptyset \Rightarrow \exists\ x$ such that $f(x)$ is well defined.

In words, T not equal to the empty set implies that there exists an x for which $f(x)$ is well defined.[4]

Free Disposability of Inputs

If free disposability of inputs (FDI) holds, then $(x, y) \in T \Rightarrow (x', y) \in T$ for $x' \geq x$, or, in words, increasing x does not result in a lower y. To determine its consequences, first find the production function for x, $f(x)$. By the definition of $f(x)$, x must be able to produce $f(x)$ so that $(x, f(x)) \in T$. Now substitute $f(x)$ for y in the statement of FDI to get

$$(x, f(x)) \in T \Rightarrow \left(x', f(x)\right) \in T$$

for $x' \geq x$. Because $f(x)$ can be produced using x', it cannot be true that the *maximum output* for x' can be less than $f(x)$. It must be that $f(x') \geq f(x)$. We conclude that FDI implies that the production function is *nondecreasing* in the input,

- $FDI \Rightarrow f(x') \geq f(x)$ for $x' \geq x$ (nondecreasing in x).

The intuitive idea is that increasing input use causes maximum output, $f(x)$, to increase. So, the graph of $f(x)$ has positive slope as x changes. 0Y in

[3] We can use mathematical conventions ("tricks") to circumvent this problem. For example, one such trick is to set $f(x)$ to a tiny nonnegative number. That solves the mathematical problem, but it makes for problematic intuition. For example, if we set $f(x) = 0$ in such instances, that implies that the physical input disappears, leaving the unhappy suggestion that T violates the Law of the Conservation of Mass.

[4] A minor mathematical aside: here we are invoking the regularity condition of closed T to ensure the existence of a well-defined maximum.

Figure 3.1 illustrates an $f(x)$ with positive slope. While that intuition is correct, it is not precise. Under FDI, an increasing $f(x)$ is possible, but it is not required. What FDI requires is that $f(x)$ not fall as input rises or that the graph of $f(x)$ not have a negative slope.

Remark 1. *Understanding the difference between the intuitive meaning of a statement and its precise meaning is important. But your primary focus should be the intuition. Once possessed, you can refine it to be more precise. The terminology "increasing" and "nondecreasing" in an input offers a good example. The first term means that as the input increases, output goes up. The second means that it does not go down. Going up is a special case of not going down, as is staying constant. But the "intuition" here is that output increases.*

Free Disposability of Output

Under free disposability of output (FDO),

$$(x, y) \in T \Rightarrow (x, y') \in T$$

for $y \geq y'$. For any $(x, y) \in T$, the definition of $f(x)$ ensures that $f(x) \geq y$. On the other hand, $(x, f(x))$ must belong to T. Applying FDO requires that x can also produce any y less than or equal to $f(x)$, so that $f(x) \geq y$ implies that $(x, y) \in T$.

Thus, if FDO applies, knowing $f(x)$ lets one construct T. But if one knows T, one can construct $f(x)$ for single-output technologies. We, therefore, conclude that under FDO $f(x)$ and T convey the same information. That is,

- $FDO \Rightarrow \; (x, y) \in T \Leftrightarrow f(x) \geq y$,

which translates as: the statements that $(x, y) \in T$ and that $f(x) \geq y$ are equivalent. The production function, $f(x)$, is a *function representation of* T.[5]

T *Is a Convex Set*

Convexity requires that the weighted averages of two feasible points must be feasible. In mathematical form,

$$(x^o, y^o) \in T \text{ and } (x', y') \in T \Rightarrow \lambda(x^o, y^o) + (1 - \lambda)(x', y') \in T$$

for $\lambda \in (0, 1)$.

[5] Many, if not most, elementary texts define the "technology" by the production function without invoking or recognizing FDO. For simple enough cases, that gives a workable model. But the approach becomes more problematic as more general production processes are considered.

To investigate the consequences for $f(x)$, choose $y^o = f(x^o)$ and $y' = f(x')$. Both $(x^o, f(x^o))$ and $(x', f(x'))$ fall on the graph of $f(x)$, the curve 0Y in Figure 3.1. Imposing convexity ensures that all weighted averages of $(x^o, f(x^o))$ and $(x', f(x'))$ belong to T. These weighted averages are illustrated in Figure 3.3 as the points on the line segment connecting $(x^o, f(x^o))$ and $(x', f(x'))$. Pick any $\lambda \in (0, 1)$ and define

$$\hat{x} = \lambda x^o + (1 - \lambda) x',$$

which we illustrate in Figure 3.3 as falling between x^o and x'. We seek

$$f(\hat{x}) = f(\lambda x^o + (1 - \lambda) x').$$

Convexity implies that $(\hat{x}, \hat{y}) \in T$, where

$$\hat{y} = \lambda f(x^o) + (1 - \lambda) f(x').$$

(See Figure 3.3.) It must be true, therefore, that the largest output that $\hat{x}$ can produce, $f(\hat{x})$, cannot be smaller than $\hat{y}$. Therefore,

$$\begin{aligned} f(\lambda x^o + (1 - \lambda) x') &= f(\hat{x}) \\ &\geq \hat{y} \\ &= \lambda f(x^o) + (1 - \lambda) f(x') \end{aligned}$$

In Figure 3.3, either $\hat{y} = f(\hat{x})$ or $(\hat{x}, f(\hat{x}))$ lies above $(\hat{x}, \hat{y})$. If it's the latter, the graph of $f(x)$ passes above the line segment connecting $(x^o, f(x^o))$ and $(x', f(x'))$. Because our choice of λ was arbitrary, the same argument applies for all $\lambda \in (0, 1)$. That yields the conclusion:

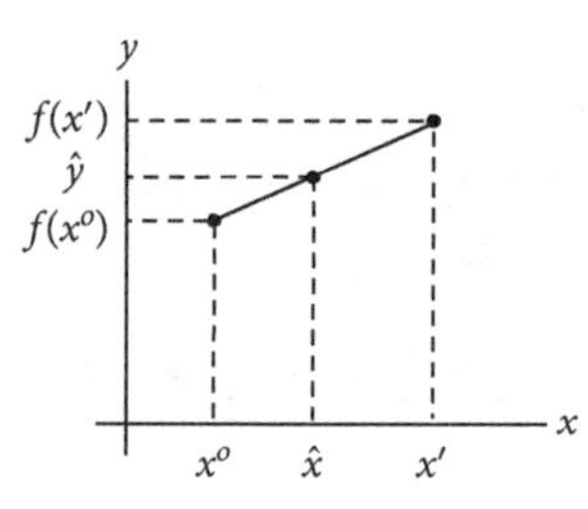

Figure 3.3 Convexity and the Production Function

- Convexity $\Rightarrow f(\lambda x^o + (1-\lambda)x') \geq \lambda f(x^o) + (1-\lambda)f(x')$ for $\lambda \in (0,1)$.

$f(x)$ is a *concave function* of x.[6] The curve 0Y in Figure 3.1 depicts the graph of an increasing and concave function of x. The positive slope comes from FDI, and the behavior of the slope as x varies is a consequence of convexity. In Figure 3.1, the slope of 0Y gets flatter as x increases. This is a characteristic of concave functions.[7] Thus, together FDI and convexity (speaking loosely) require that the *production function increases at a decreasing rate as x increases* and manifests the *law of diminishing returns*. We defer a more complete discussion of diminishing returns until after we discuss the consequences of NFL (no free lunch) and NFC (no fixed cost) for $f(x)$.

No Free Lunch and No Fixed Cost

NFL requires that $(0,y) \notin T$ if $y \geq 0$ and $y \neq 0$. For the single-output case, we rewrite that as $(0,y) \notin T$ if $y > 0$. A positive output cannot be produced using zero input. $f(0)$ cannot be greater than zero. Adding NFC requires that $(0,0) \in T$, leading to the conclusion that $f(0) = 0$. Thus,

- *NFL* and *NFC* $\Rightarrow f(0) = 0$

NFL and NFC imply that the graph of the production function emanates from the origin, again as illustrated in Figure 3.1 by the curve 0Y.

3.4 Average Products, Marginal Products, and the Law of Diminishing Returns

We use the production function to define and investigate the concepts of *average product* and *marginal product*.

Definition 2 (Average Product). *The average product at input level $\hat{x}$ is the ratio of $f(\hat{x})$ to $\hat{x}$.*

In equation form,

$$AP(\hat{x}) \equiv \frac{f(\hat{x})}{\hat{x}},$$

[6] A function $h(z)$ is defined to be concave in z if $h(\lambda z^o + (1-\lambda)z') \geq \lambda h(z^o) + (1-\lambda)h(z')$ for $\lambda \in (0,1)$.

[7] More precisely, a concave function's slope does not increase as x increases.

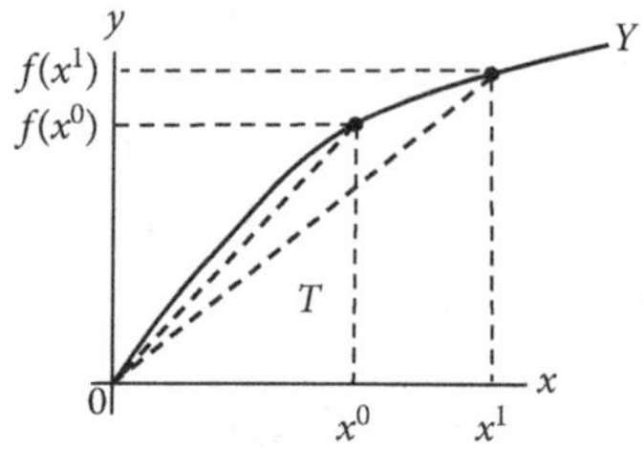

Figure 3.4 Average Product

where AP stands for average product. Because $f(x)$ changes as x varies, the average product is a function of x. In Figure 3.4, $AP\left(x^0\right)$ is the vertical distance $0f\left(x^0\right)$ divided by the horizontal distance $0x^0$, which equals the slope of the dotted line segment connecting the origin, 0, and $\left(x^0, f\left(x^0\right)\right)$.

In Figure 3.4, $AP\left(x^0\right) > AP\left(x^1\right)$. The average product falls as x increases. You can experiment with modifications of Figure 3.4 to convince yourself that this is true for the canonical technology. Economists call this phenomenon a *diminishing average product* or *diminishing average returns.* It is a consequence of imposing convexity on T, and it implies that $f(x)$ grows, in percentage terms, at a slower rate than x

Definition 3 (Arc Marginal Product). *The arc marginal product is the ratio of the change in the value of $f(x)$ to the change in x as x varies.*

A standard way to write this definition is

$$MP(x) \equiv \frac{\Delta f(x)}{\Delta x}$$

where MP stands for marginal product and capital Greek delta (Δ) denotes change. Starting at $\left(x^0, f\left(x^0\right)\right)$ and moving to $\left(x^1, f\left(x^1\right)\right)$, we calculate that ratio in Figure 3.4 as

$$\frac{\Delta f(x)}{\Delta x} = \frac{f\left(x^1\right) - f\left(x^0\right)}{x^1 - x^0},$$

which is given by the slope of the line segment connecting $\left(x^0, f\left(x^0\right)\right)$ and $\left(x^1, f\left(x^1\right)\right)$ (not drawn) in Figure 3.4.

On the Meaning of 'Marginal'

The adjective *marginal* recurs repeatedly in economic discussions. Its use in the English literature was popularized by Alfred Marshall, who attributed it to a German term used by Johann Heinrich von Thünen. The *Oxford English Dictionary* offers the following definition (among others):

> **Of or relating to the extra cost, revenue, or utility involved in or deriving from the production or consumption of one additional unit of a product.**

We paraphrase this definition to suit our discussion, as follows:

> **Of or relating to the extra production deriving from the use of one additional unit of a input.**

Note that the statement "one additional unit" leaves unspecified the units in which x and y are measured. Think of our agricultural illustrations, and let y stand for corn and x for land. Is corn measured in bushels or in metric tons? Do we measure land in acres, hectares, square miles, or square kilometers? Units matter. Change the units and the measures change. The overwhelming tendency in economics is to interpret "marginal" changes as involving "tiny" units so that $x^1 - x^0$ is practically zero (infinitesimally small).

Speaking in "tiny-units" terms, the marginal product *often* has a simple *geometric interpretation.*

Definition 4 (Marginal Product). *The marginal product at x^0 is the slope of the line segment tangent to the graph of $f(x)$ at $\left(x^0, f\left(x^0\right)\right)$.*[8]

Figure 3.5 illustrates the marginal products for x^0 and x^1. The respective marginal products are given by the slope of the tangent line segments $MP\left(x^0\right)$ and $MP\left(x^1\right)$. Observe in Figure 3.5 that $MP\left(x^0\right) > MP\left(x^1\right)$ and that the slope of $f(x)$ decreases as x increases. Thus, $f(x)$ exhibits a *diminishing marginal product* in x.

A diminishing marginal product means that x becomes less effective in promoting extra output growth as its use grows. Hence, successively applying the same dose of x produces less output with each dose, a phenomenon

[8] For those with a calculus bent, take the $lim\left(x^1 - x^0\right) \longrightarrow 0$.

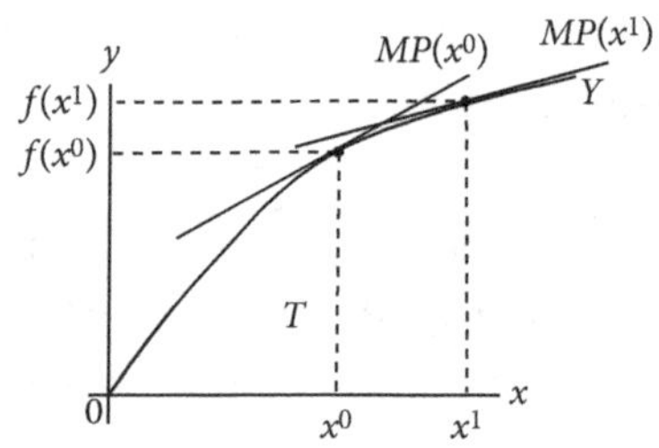

Figure 3.5 Marginal Product

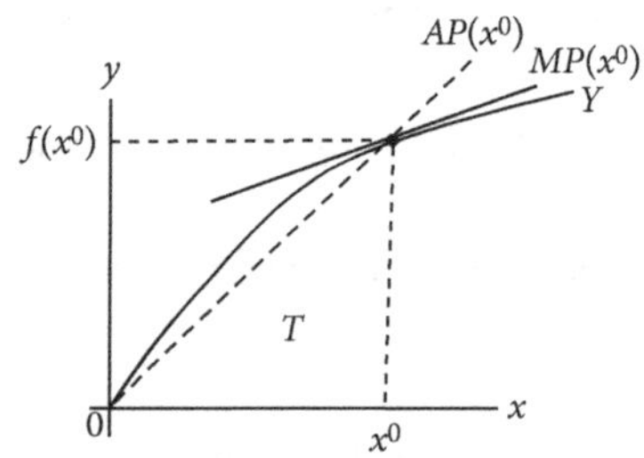

Figure 3.6 Average Product and Marginal Product

that economists have observed as *eventually occurring* for many production processes.[9]

The production functions depicted in Figures 3.4 and 3.5 exhibiting both a *diminishing average product* and a *diminishing marginal product* are a consequence of imposing convexity on T. Figure 3.6 illustrates another consequence of convexity. There $AP\left(x^0\right)$ and $MP\left(x^0\right)$ are depicted together, and it is apparent that

$$AP\left(x^0\right) \geq MP\left(x^0\right).$$

Experimenting with Figure 3.6 confirms that this inequality holds for all x for a canonical technology.

Defining the marginal product as the slope of the line segment tangent to the graph of the production function is problematic if its graph is "kinked." Figure 2.7 in Chapter 2 illustrates such a "kinked" production function. At either $\left(x^0, y^0\right)$ or $\left(x^1, y^1\right)$, the graph of $f(x)$ for the illustrated T has multiple (literally an infinity) tangent line segments. The multiple tangencies manifest the difference, for example, between the arc marginal products calculated at

[9] von Thünen was among the first to document it empirically, and he did it in the early nineteenth century using German farming data.

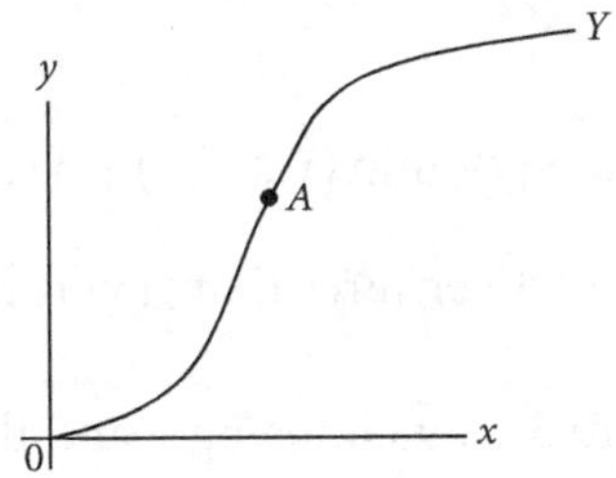

Figure 3.7 Variable Returns to Production

(x^1, y^1) for increases and decreases in x. For increases, the arc marginal product is zero, but for decreases it is the slope of the line segment connecting (x^0, y^0) and (x^1, y^1).[10]

You may have encountered production functions that look different than $f(x)$ in Figure 3.1. Many discussions depict the production function as resembling the curve labeled 0Y in Figure 3.7, which violates convexity. Under FDO, T includes all points falling on or below 0Y. Connect a point such as A and the origin with a straight-line segment (not drawn). If T were convex, points on the line segment should fall in T. But they don't. Hence, this technology is not convex. You will also note that for the technology in Figure 3.7 both $AP(x)$ and $MP(x)$ first increase and then decrease. (You are asked to verify this visually in Exercise 3.) Production processes like the ones shown in Figure 3.7 are said to exhibit *variable returns* to distinguish them from convex ones. We reconsider variable returns in Chapter 12.

3.5 Input-requirement Function (Single-Input, Single-Output Case)

Definition 5 (Input-requirement Function). *The input-requirement function for output level y is the smallest input that can produce y.*

The mathematical definition is:

$$e(y) \equiv \min\{x : \ x \text{ can produce } y\}.$$

Here and elsewhere, the expression $\min\{\cdot\}$ is an instruction to choose the smallest (minimal) element in the set $\{\cdot\}$. If T satisfies FDO, Definition 5 is

[10] In analytic terms, at (x^1, y^1) the left-hand derivative and right-hand derivative of $f(x)$ differ, so that the function is not differentiable.

equivalent to

$$e(y) \equiv \min\{x : f(x) \leq y\}.$$

Here we use the fact that FDO ensures that $f(x)$ is a function representation of T.

We locate $e(y)$ in Figure 3.2 by choosing y and then locating the smallest (lowest) x in T that can produce y. This gives the curve 0X as the graph of the input-output pairs $(e(y), y)$ that lie on the input-requirement function for T.[11]

A thought experiment reveals why an economist might be interested in $e(y)$. Consider a self-interested producer, facing a single-input, single-output technology, who is contractually obligated to deliver a fixed amount of y. How much x would that producer use in producing that output?

We now develop the consequences of our basic assumptions for $e(y)$.

T *Is not Empty*

We have:

- $T \neq \emptyset \Rightarrow \exists\, y : e(y)$ is well defined.

In words, T not equal to the empty set implies that there exists a y such that its input-requirement function, $e(y)$, is well defined. We demonstrate using arguments that parallel our earlier demonstration that $T \neq \emptyset$ implies the existence of at least one well-defined production function. Recall that if T is not empty, at least one feasible input-output pair, (x, y), must exist. If that x is the smallest that can produce y, then $x = e(y)$. If it's not, $e(y)$ will be smallest that can produce that y. That shows that one y exists for which $e(y)$ is well defined. But just as $T \neq \emptyset$ did not imply the existence of a production function for all x, $T \neq \emptyset$ does not imply the existence of an input-requirement function for all y. And, again, the reason is that $T \neq \emptyset$ is satisfied if only one feasible input-output pair exists.

Free Disposability of Inputs

The consequence of imposing FDI for $e(y)$ is that

- $FDI \Rightarrow \; x \geq e(y) \Leftrightarrow (x, y) \in T,$

[11] Because Figure 3.2 depicts output, y, on the horizontal axis and x on the vertical axis, it is more *conventional* to refer to the points on the graph of the input-requirement function as output–input pairs and write them as $(y, e(y))$ in place of $(e(y), y)$. In an attempt to avoid confusion, we adhere here to the convention maintained elsewhere in this discussion of listing inputs first and outputs second.

which reads as *FDI* implies that $x \geq e(y)$ and $(x, y) \in T$ are equivalent statements. Thus, *FDI* ensures that $e(y)$ is a *function representation of* T so that knowing it is equivalent to knowing T. In Figure 3.2, this consequence validates the interpretation of T as all points lying on or above 0X. To verify, choose $(x, y) \in T$. Then, by the definition of $e(y)$, $x \geq e(y)$. On the other hand, because $(e(y), y) \in T$, FDI requires $x \geq e(y) \Rightarrow (x, y) \in T$.

Free Disposability of Output

FDO implies that $e(y)$ is a nondecreasing function of y, or

- $FDO \Rightarrow e(y) \geq e(y')$ for $y \geq y'$

To verify this claim, find $e(y)$ for y. Then because FDO requires that

$$(x, y) \in T \Rightarrow (x, y') \in T$$

for $y \geq y'$ substituting $e(y)$ for x gives

$$(e(y), y) \in T \Rightarrow (e(y), y') \in T$$

for $y \geq y'$. Because $e(y)$ can produce y', the smallest x that can produce y' cannot be larger than $e(y)$, which establishes the desired property. Figure 3.2 captures this consequence by depicting the graph of $e(y)$ (the curve 0X) with a positive slope. Strictly speaking, that graphical depiction means that $e(y)$ is increasing in y, which is permitted but not required by FDO. What FDO rules out is the graph of $e(y)$ having a negative slope.

Convexity

The slope of OX in Figure 3.2 increases as y increases. The positive slope is a consequence of FDO. The increasing positive slope is a characteristic of a *convex function*[12] and is a consequence of imposing convexity on T. In mathematical terms,

- Convexity $\Rightarrow e(\lambda y^o + (1-\lambda) y') \leq \lambda e(y^o) + (1-\lambda) e(y')$

for $\lambda \in (0, 1)$. Convexity of T thus implies that $e(y)$ is a *convex function of* y. The demonstration parallels our earlier demonstration that imposing

[12] A function $h(z)$ is defined to be convex in z if $h(\lambda z^o + (1-\lambda) z') \leq \lambda h(z^o) + (1-\lambda) h(z')$ for $\lambda \in (0, 1)$. Another way of saying this, which you can verify yourself, is that $h(z)$ is convex if $-f(z)$ is concave.

convexity on T implies that $f(x)$ is concave in x. (As such, we leave it to the reader to carry out the visual illustration of the arguments in Exercise 4.)

Pick y^o and y' and find $e(y^o)$ and $e(y')$. We seek $e(\lambda y^o + (1-\lambda)y')$ for $\lambda \in (0,1)$. If T is convex,

$$(e(y^o), y^o) \in T \text{ and } (e(y'), y') \in T \Rightarrow (\lambda e(y^o) + (1-\lambda)e(y'), \lambda y^o + (1-\lambda)y') \in T$$

for $\lambda \in (0,1)$. Thus, because $\lambda y^o + (1-\lambda)y'$ can be produced using $\lambda e(y^o) + (1-\lambda)e(y')$, the smallest input that can produce $\lambda y^o + (1-\lambda)y'$ cannot be greater than $\lambda e(y^o) + (1-\lambda)e(y')$, so that

$$e(y^o) + (1-\lambda)e(y') \geq e(\lambda y^o + (1-\lambda)y'),$$

as required.

A cautionary remark is in order. We use the same adjective *convex* to describe two different mathematical objects. One is a *convex set*, and the other is a *convex function*. The concepts are related, and both involve taking weighted averages. (See Exercises 5 and 6.) But they describe different mathematical objects that correspond to different, albeit related, economic concepts.

The economic implication of convexity is that increasing output by the same amount requires increasingly larger doses of x. This is, so to speak, the "flip side" of a diminishing marginal product and is a precursor to the notion of *increasing marginal cost* developed in Chapter 6.

No Free Lunch and No Fixed Cost

For the single-output case, NFL requires that $(0, y) \notin T$ if $y > 0$. That requires that $e(y) \neq 0$ for $y > 0$. The minimal input required to produce a positive output cannot be zero. NFC, on the other hand, requires that $(0,0) \in T$, allowing us to conclude that $e(0) = 0$. This is illustrated by the graph of the input-requirement function, $0X$, emanating from the origin in Figure 3.2 and never intersecting the horizontal axis for $y > 0$.

3.6 Multiple-Input, Multiple-Output Technologies

The production function is well defined for both single-output and multiple-input technologies. On the other hand, in a multiple-input setting, the definition of an input-requirement function becomes somewhat problematic. When multiple inputs exist, $x_1, x_2, \ldots, x_N$, we can define an input-requirement function for one of the N inputs. It would be the minimum amount of that input required to produce a fixed output bundle *given that the other N-1 inputs are held constant.* But selecting the input to be minimized is arbitrary. Thus, N distinct input-requirement functions are available. Analogous arguments suggest that in the single-input, multiple-output, $y_1, \ldots, y_M$, setting, the production function is somewhat problematic. while the input-requirement function is well defined.

Treating either single-output, multiple-input production functions or single-input, multiple-output input-requirement functions necessitates adjusting jargon and graphical illustrations. Figure 3.8 illustrates a single-output, two-input technology as the manifold $0AB0$ emanating from the origin. Curve OB depicts the graph of the production function in (x_1, x_2, y) space associated with $(x_1, 0, f(x_1, 0))$. It traces out how production varies with x_1 holding the second input at 0. The curve OA is the graph of the production function over $(0, x_2, f(0, x_2))$.[13]

When viewed in a multiple-input setting, we can interpret curves such as $0Y$ in Figure 3.1 as depicting how $f(x)$ varies with a single input while holding other inputs constant. In the three-dimensional case, that entails, for example, projecting the graph of $f(x_1, x_2)$ from (x_1, x_2, y) space parallel to the x_2 axis onto the (x_1, y) plane. So, for example, Figure 3.1 could be interpreted as fixing $x_2 = 0$ and portraying OB in Figure 3.8. More generally, however, the choice of which inputs and where to hold them constant is arbitrary.

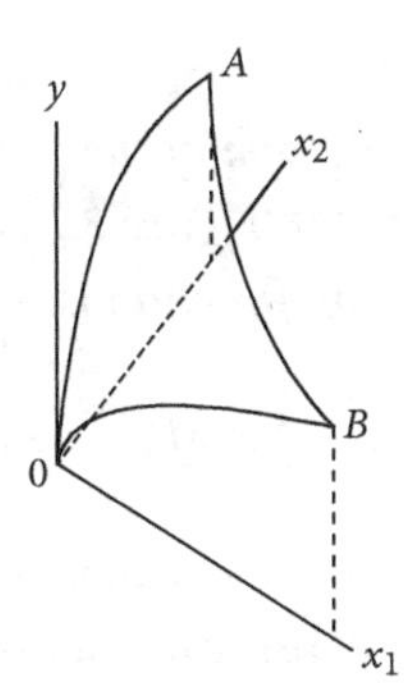

Figure 3.8 Production Function with Two Inputs

[13] For illustrative purposes, we assume that neither x_1 nor x_2 is *essential* in production.

To distinguish the single-input, single-output from its multiple-input counterpart, we also modify jargon slightly and replace "product" with productivity. Thus, the *average productivity of* x_1, with x_2 held constant at $\hat{x}_2$ is

$$\frac{f(x_1, \hat{x}_2)}{x_1}.$$

The *marginal productivity of* x_1 with x_2 held constant at $\hat{x}_2$ is

$$\frac{\Delta f(x_1, \hat{x}_2)}{\Delta x_1}.$$

The graphical descriptions of these productivities are as before except that the graph of $(x_1, f(x_1, \hat{x}_2))$ or its appropriate generalization when there are more than two inputs, which is now called *the productivity response contour for* x_1 *with* $x_2 = \hat{x}_2$, or a *productivity contour*, replaces the graph of the single-output, single-input production function. Parallel adjustments are needed to accommodate the single-input, multiple-output, input-requirement function.

3.7 Exercises

Exercise 3. *Demonstrate visually that the technology depicted in Figure 3.7 exhibits initially increasing and then decreasing average products and marginal products. What characterizes the input level where AP(x) reaches its maximum?*

Exercise 4. *Develop a graphical illustration of the consequences of convexity of T for an input-requirement function.*

Exercise 5. * *By Definition 1, the graph of the production function, $f(x)$, in (x, y) space for the technology illustrated in Figure 3.1 is the curve labeled 0Y. That T is convex, and the resulting production function is* concave. *That is,*

$$f(\lambda x^o + (1-\lambda)x') \geq \lambda f(x^o) + (1-\lambda) f(x')$$

for $\lambda \in (0,1)$. *This algebraic notion of concavity can be linked more intuitively to the geometric notion of a convex set using the notion of* hypograph *of the function,* $f(x)$. *The* hypograph *of the function consists of the points in (x, y) space falling on or below the graph of $f(x)$, that is,*

$$\textit{hypograph of } f \equiv \{(x, y) : f(x) \geq y\}.$$

In Figure 3.1, the hypograph consists of the points on or below the curve 0Y.

This notion offers a geometric definition of a concave function that reveals its link to set convexity. Namely, $f(x)$ is concave if and only if its hypograph is a convex set. *Show that if*

$$f(\lambda x^o + (1-\lambda)x') \geq \lambda f(x^o) + (1-\lambda)f(x')$$

for $\lambda \in (0,1)$, *then hypograph of* f *is a convex set.*

Exercise 6. * *A function,* $e(y)$, *is convex if and only if its* epigraph *is a convex set, where*

$$\textit{epigraph of } e \equiv \{(y,x) : e(y) \leq x\},$$

consists of all the points on or above the graph of $e(y)$. *Show that if the epigraph of* $e(y)$ *is a convex set, then*

$$e(\lambda y^o + (1-\lambda)y') \leq \lambda e(y^o) + (1-\lambda)e(y')$$

for $\lambda \in (0,1)$.

4

Input Sets and Output Sets

4.1 Introduction

Chapter 4 treats a single-input, single-output technology that provides an unrealistic, but simple, setting for examining production relationships. The emphasis, respectively, is on how input availability drives the output produced and how output needs drive input use. That analysis yields the concepts of a production function, an input-requirement function, an average product, and a marginal product. Each is basic to the way economists think about production relations.

Because it is unrealistic, it is natural to generalize. The last section of Chapter 3 briefly discussed two generalizations: a single-output, multiple-input technology and a multiple-output, single-input technology. Figure 4.1 depicts the graph in (x_1, x_2, y) space of a production function for a canonical single-output, two-input technology as the manifold $0AB0$. Figure 4.2 depicts the graph of the input-requirement function for a canonical single-input, two-output input-requirement function by the manifold $0CD0$. It is understood that all points falling below $0AB0$ and above $0CD0$ belong to the respective T.

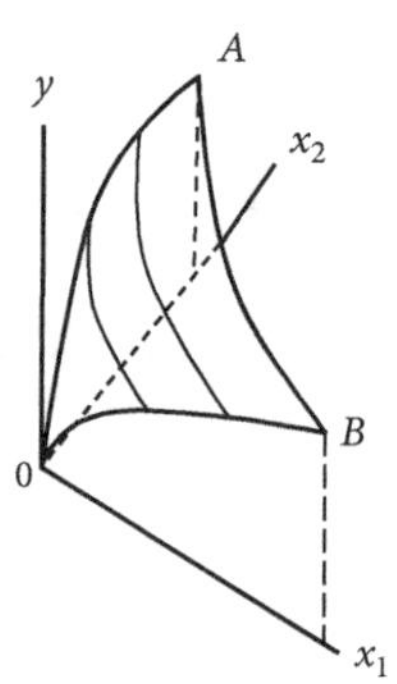

Figure 4.1 Two-input production function

Lectures on Neoclassical Production Economics. Robert G. Chambers, Oxford University Press.
 DOI: 10.1093/9780197817759.003.0005

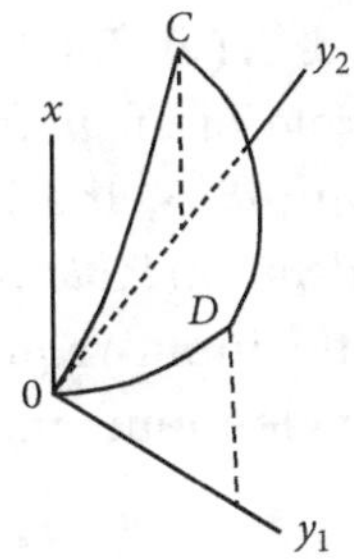

Figure 4.2 Two-output input-requirement function

We make no claims for realism for either of these technologies. Indeed, both are best viewed as simple models that illustrate different aspects of production technologies. For example, in Figure 4.1 the surface $0B$ depicts the graph in (x_1, x_2, y) space of the productivity contour for x_1 (holding $x_2 = 0$). The surface $0A$ plays a similar role in (x_1, x_2, y) space for the productivity contour for x_2 (holding $x_1 = 0$). More generally, any point on the manifold $0AB0$, say $(\hat{x}_1, \hat{x}_2, \hat{y})$, will fall on two productivity contours: one for x_1 (holding $x_2 = \hat{x}_2$) and one for x_2 (holding $x_1 = \hat{x}_1$). Marginal productivities and average productivities are available for all such points using the methods described in Chapter 3. Figure 4.2 lets us examine the interplay between the single input and the two outputs.

What Figure 4.1 and Figure 4.2 also capture, but that we have not yet discussed, is the interplay between inputs (the surface AB in Figure 4.1) and the interplay between outputs (the surface CD in Figure 4.2). This chapter studies these interactions. As before, we typically illustrate our ideas using the real plane. But, unlike Chapter 3, the analysis presented here is for technologies with multiple inputs and multiple outputs.

4.2 Input Sets

Definition 6. *The input set, $X(y)$, for y is the set of inputs that can produce the output vector y.*

We write $X(y)$'s definition mathematically as

$$X(y) \equiv \{x : x \text{ can produce } y\},$$

or

$$X(y) \equiv \{x : (x, y) \in T\}.$$

We emphasize two aspects of $X(y)$. First, $X(y)$ depends upon the output bundle, y, that plays the role of an *independent variable.* Once fixed, it determines the *dependent variables*, the inputs. Now, however, instead of determining a *single dependent variable, y* determines a *set of independent variables.*[1] $X(y)$ resembles the input-requirement function. If y changes, $X(y)$ responds. And in the single-input, multiple-output case under free disposability of inputs (FDI)

$$X(y) = \{x : x \geq e(y)\},$$

so that $e(y)$ forms the lower boundary for $X(y)$.

The second notable aspect of $X(y)$ is that it satisfies the equivalence relations

$$x \in X(y) \Leftrightarrow (x, y) \in T \Leftrightarrow x \text{ can produce } y.$$

These equivalences are key to determining the implications of the five basic assumptions for input sets, $X(y)$, that offer a new visual perspective on T.

T *Not Empty*

$T \neq \emptyset$ means that at least one feasible (x, y) bundle exists. Because that x can produce that y, $X(y)$ for that y is not empty. That establishes that one nonempty $X(y)$ exists. Hence,

- $T \neq \emptyset \Rightarrow \exists\, y : X(y) \neq \emptyset.$

In words, T not equal to the empty set means a y exists for which $X(y)$ is not the empty set. It does not mean, however, that $X(y) \neq \emptyset$ for all possible y.

On the meaning of ≥ and ≤

This chapter's focus is on comparing points in the coordinate plane. But instead of following the usual convention of labeling the horizontal axis x and the vertical axis y, we label the horizontal axis as x_1 and the vertical axis as x_2 in one instance and as y_1 and y_2 in another. We now compare input and output bundles, and we must be careful in interpreting the symbols ≥ and ≤. When we compare two real numbers, a and b, the meaning is clear. Then $a \geq b$ means that a is not smaller than b. Similarly, $a \leq b$ means that a is not larger b. Our ability to make such comparisons changes, however, when we move to bundles (vectors) of inputs or outputs. To take an example,

[1] Some writers call $X(y)$ a *correspondence*, whereas others use the term *set-valued function*.

suppose that $x^A = (4 \text{ rakes}, 2 \text{ shovels})$ and $x^B = (2 \text{ rakes}, 4 \text{ shovels})$. Can one meaningfully say that either $x^A \geq x^B$ or that $x^B \geq x^A$? The answer is no, because A has more rakes than B but less shovels. So, all points in the coordinate plane (or its higher-dimensional generalizations) cannot be ranked (ordered) relative to one another using either $\geq$ or $\leq$. $\geq$ and $\leq$ are examples of *partial orderings* of the coordinate plane. It's not important that you remember this term because we don't use it again. But is important to remember that our ability to compare points in the coordinate plane using $\geq$ and $\leq$ is limited. That, in turn, means that properties of T that hinge upon $\geq$ or $\leq$ only convey information about T in limited regions of the coordinate plane.

Free Disposability of Inputs

FDI requires that

$$(x, y) \in T \Rightarrow (x', y) \in T$$

for $x' \geq x$. Using the equivalence relation $(x, y) \in T \Leftrightarrow x \in X(y)$, we rewrite this as:

- $FDI \Rightarrow \; x \in X(y) \Rightarrow x' \in X(y)$ for $x' \geq x$.

FDI requires that if x is in the input set for y, then any x' greater than or equal to x belongs to the input set for y.

We illustrate using Figure 4.3. Let the point illustrated as x belong to $X(y)$. FDI requires that any x' at least as large as x, depicted visually by any point to the northeast of x, also belongs to $X(y)$.

Convexity

Convexity means that T, when viewed as a set in (x, y) space, is convex. (In geometric terms, any two points that belong to T can be connected by a straight line segment that lies entirely within T.) When we consider input sets,

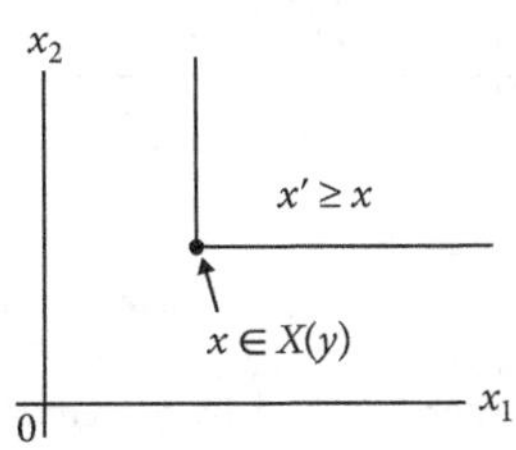

Figure 4.3 FDI and $X(y)$

we work in input, x, space with output, y, playing the role of an independent variable. For this discussion,[2] we simplify by holding y constant. Keeping y fixed, we see that the original definition of convexity becomes

$$(x^o, y) \in T \text{ and } (x', y) \in T \Rightarrow (\lambda x^o + (1-\lambda)x', y) \in T$$

for $\lambda \in (0,1)$. (Note that $\lambda y + (1-\lambda)y = y$.) Applying the equivalence relation $(x, y) \in T \Leftrightarrow x \in X(y)$ gives:

- *Convexity* $\Rightarrow x^o \in X(y)$ and $x' \in X(y) \Rightarrow \lambda x^o + (1-\lambda)x' \in X(y)$ for $\lambda \in (0,1)$.

We translate this into words as convexity implies that if x^o and x' belong to the input set for y, $X(y)$, then any weighted average of x^o and x' also belongs to $X(y)$. More simply, convexity implies that $X(y)$ is a convex set. This holds for all y.[3]

Figure 4.4 illustrates the consequences of imposing FDI and convexity on $X(y)$. We build the illustration as follows. First, assume that points x^o and x' belong to $X(y)$. Then impose convexity to obtain that any weighted average of these two points, illustrated by the line segment $x'x^o$ connecting them, also belongs to $X(y)$. Finally, use FDI to obtain that any points to the northeast of the points on the line segment $x'x^o$ also belong to $X(y)$.

Free Disposability of Output

When there are multiple outputs, not all output bundles, y and y', can be ranked (ordered) using $\geq$. FDO only restricts production possibilities when two output bundles can be ranked using $\geq$. For those bundles that can be

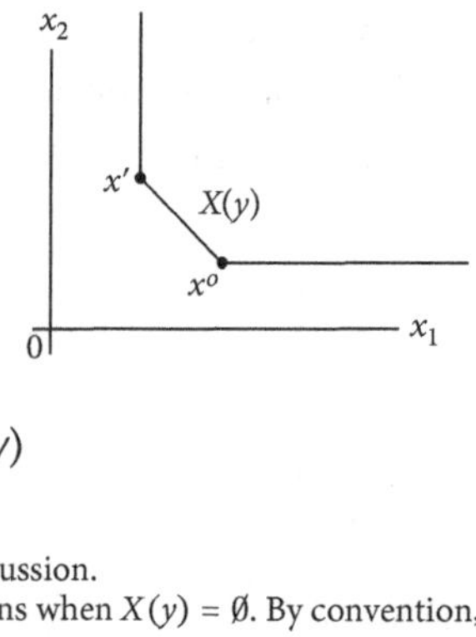

Figure 4.4 Convexity and $X(y)$

[2] See Section 4.6 for further discussion.

[3] You might wonder what happens when $X(y) = \emptyset$. By convention, $\emptyset$ is convex.

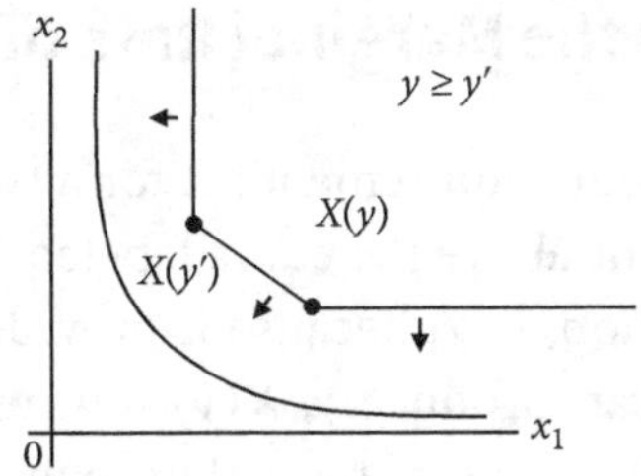

Figure 4.5 Free disposability of Output and $X(y)$

ranked, $y \geq y'$, FDO requires that $(x, y) \in T \Rightarrow (x, y') \in T$. Using the equivalence relation $(x, y) \in T \Leftrightarrow x \in X(y)$ gives

- $FDO \Rightarrow x \in X(y) \Rightarrow x \in X(y')$ for $y \geq y'$.

Or, in words, if x is in the input set for y, $X(y)$, it remains in the input set for y', $X(y')$, for $y \geq y'$. Hence, every member of $X(y)$ must belong to $X(y')$, which we write in symbols as

- $FDO \Rightarrow X(y) \subset X(y')$ for $y \geq y'$.

FDO implies that the input set for y, $X(y)$, is a *subset* of $X(y')$ for $y \geq y'$. Figure 4.5 depicts this property as the boundary for $X(y)$ shifting towards the origin as y decreases to y'.

The input set *expands* (includes more elements) as y decreases. But FDO is also satisfied, if moving to y' from y leaves $X(y)$ unchanged, that is, $X(y') = X(y)$. Strictly speaking, FDO rules out the input set getting smaller (having fewer elements) as output decreases.

No Free Lunch, No Fixed Cost

NFL requires $(0, y) \notin T$ if $y \geq 0$ and $y \neq 0$ and *NFC* requires $(0, 0) \in T$. Using the equivalence relation $(x, y) \in T \Leftrightarrow x \in X(y)$, we write these as

- $NFL \Rightarrow 0 \notin X(y)$ if $y \geq 0$ and $y \neq 0$,
- $NFC \Rightarrow 0 \in X(0)$.

In visual terms, NFL says that the origin, 0, cannot belong to an input set for an output bundle, y, that contains a positive output. You cannot make something from nothing. NFC, on the other hand, says that nothing can produce nothing.

4.3 Isoquants and the Marginal Rate of Substitution

Figure 4.6 depicts the input-requirement set for a two-input canonical technology as everything on or above the curve labeled $\bar{X}(y)$. $\bar{X}(y)$ resembles the input-requirement function, $e(y)$ because it provides a lower boundary for the input bundles that can produce y, $X(y)$. But unlike $e(y)$, it contains a collection of points in the (x_1, x_2) plane rather than a single real number.

We call the curve $\bar{X}(y)$ the *isoquant* for y. Isoquant is a portmanteau word peculiar to economics. It combines *isos* from Greek meaning "equal or like" with *quantity* from English to connote "same quantity."[4] Our use here captures the intuitive idea that all points on the curve represent input combinations that can produce the same y. Economists have a special interest in $\bar{X}(y)$ because it gives the set of input bundles from which self-interested producers will choose to produce y if they pay to purchase inputs. Consider, for example, point A in Figure 4.6. Because it's in $X(y)$, it can produce y. But so can A^0, which uses the same amount of x_2 but less of x_1. Similarly, A^1, uses the same amount of x_1 but less of x_2 than A. A self-interested individual who has to pay for inputs would choose either A^0 or A^1 over A. Points lying along curve segment A^0A^1 use less of both x_1 and x_2 than A to produce y.

Definition 7. *An input vector, x, belongs to the* isoquant *for y, $\bar{X}(y)$, if and only if $x \in X(y)$ and any proportional shrinkage of x in the direction of the origin does not belong to $X(y)$.*

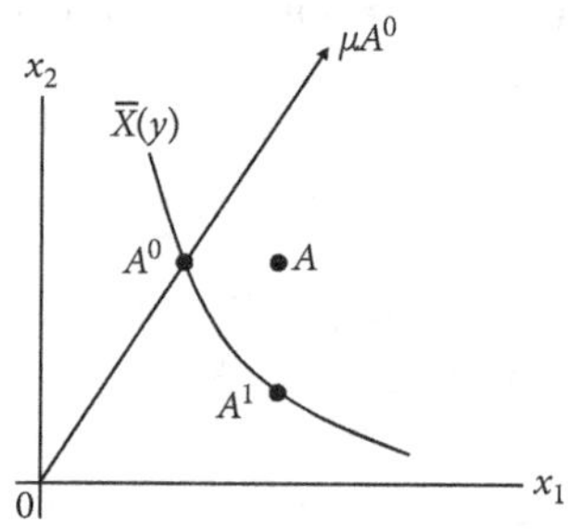

Figure 4.6 An Isoquant for a Canonical Technology

[4] Historians of economic thought debate who to credit for the notion of an isoquant. It parallels utility theory's indifference curve, which is attributed to F. Y. Edgeworth, 1881. *Mathematical Psychics: An Application of Mathematics to the Moral Sciences.* G. Kegan Paul. But ithe terminology apparently originates with the Norwegian term *isokvant* used in R. Frisch's lecture notes circa 1927.

Phrased in mathematical terms, that definition becomes

$$\bar{X}(y) \equiv \{x \in X(y) : \lambda x \notin X(y) \ \texttt{for} \ \lambda \in (0,1)\}.$$

To visualize, take point A^0 in Figure 4.6. It belongs to $X(y)$. Consider the ray from the origin that passes through A^0. That ray is described in symbols as μA^0 where μ represents any positive real number, that is, $\mu \in (0, \infty)$ $(0 < \mu < \infty)$. A^0 corresponds to $\mu = 1$. Points beyond A^0 on the ray correspond to $\mu > 1$, and points between the origin and A^0 correspond to $0 < \mu < 1$. Because A^0 lies in $X(y)$ and any movement along the ray toward the origin moves out of $X(y)$, it belongs to the isoquant. You can use a parallel argument to convince yourself that so does A^1. On the other hand, A can be moved toward the origin without taking it out of $X(y)$. Thus, it does not belong to $\bar{X}(y)$.

As depicted in Figure 4.6, the isoquant has a negative slope. That is a consequence of FDI, which rules out a positive slope. It also resembles an upturned bowl that faces toward the northeast. That characteristic is a consequence of convexity. Note that any two points on $\bar{X}(y)$ can be connected by a straight line segment that is contained in $X(y)$.

Figure 4.7 depicts an isoquant for a three-input canonical technology in (x_1, x_2, x_3) space as the manifold $ABCA$. The curve CA depicts $\{(x_1, x_3) : (x_1, 0, x_3) \in \bar{X}(y))\}$, AB depicts $\{(x_1, x_2) : (x_1, x_2, 0) \in \bar{X}(y))\}$, and BC depicts $\{(x_2, x_3) : (0, x_2, x_3) \in \bar{X}(y))\}$

A fundamental tenet of economics is that self-interested individuals respond to changing or evolving market conditions by altering their economic activities. Therefore, if prices change, producers respond by adjusting their behavior to accommodate those price changes. In particular, if certain inputs become more expensive, producers will find their use less attractive

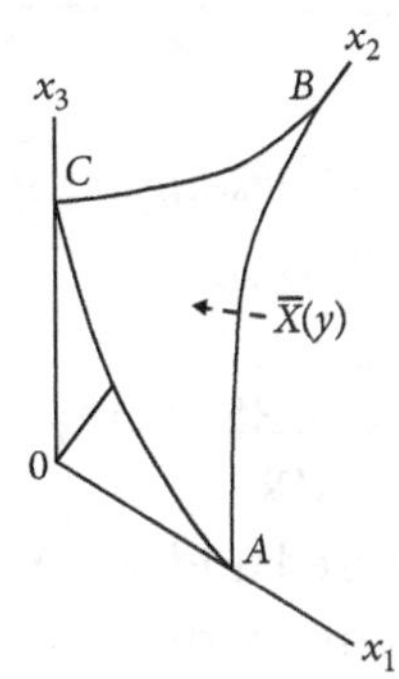

Figure 4.7 Isoquant for a three-input technology

and may attempt to find more attractive input combinations to produce y. Economists refer to such behavior as producers *substituting* some inputs for others.

To grasp what's involved, let's assume that the producer is at A^0 in Figure 4.6. If that input bundle becomes unattractive, does the producer have alternative ways to produce y? The answer is yes, any input bundle in $X(y)$ will also produce y. And, of those alternatives, the ones on $\bar{X}(y)$ are the most attractive. So, suppose that the producer moves along the isoquant to A^1 from A^0. Making that move involves the producer using less of x_2 and more of x_1, while holding y constant. Speaking economics, x_1 *has been substituted for* x_2 in the production of y.

To measure the degree to which inputs substitute for one another, economists use the following definition:

Definition 8. *The* marginal rate of substitution *(MRS) of input x_1 for input x_2 is the rate at which marginal changes in x_1 are substituted in $\bar{X}(y)$ for marginal changes in input x_2 while holding output y and all other inputs constant.*

Before we offer a visual interpretation of this definition, a few comments are in order. First, inputs 1 and 2 act as placeholders here. For a multiple-input technology, one can define an MRS between, say, inputs k and j by replacing x_1 and x_2 with, respectively, x_k and x_j. Second, when we speak of an MRS, we are talking about how two, *and only two*, inputs interact as all other inputs and output are held constant. Third, "rate" when used in economic discussions always signals a ratio comparison. And fourth, under FDI, the MRS can never be positive. It can be 0 or even $-\infty$, but not positive.[5]

Presuming, as in our discussion of marginal products, that marginal is interpreted as involving "tiny" changes in x_1 and x_2 gives the visual definition for the MRS:

Definition 9. *The marginal rate of substitution at x is given by the slope of the line segment tangent to the isoquant at x.*

Figure 4.8 illustrates with the MRS at A^0 given by the slope of the dotted line segment $MRS(A^0)$ and the MRS at A^1 given by the slope of the dotted line segment $MRS(A^1)$. As required under FDI, both slopes are negative, and (when viewed from the perspective of the x_2 axis) $MRS(A^1)$ has a flatter slope

[5] Some (perhaps most) authors define the MRS as the negative of our definition to avoid dealing with negative numbers. To preserve simplicity and to avoid confusion, we do not follow that convention.

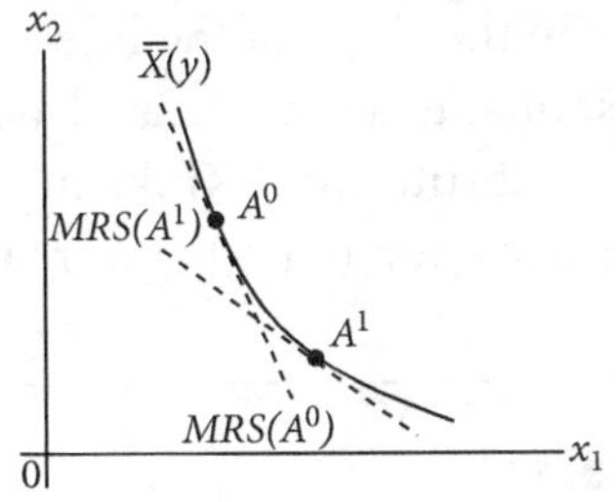

Figure 4.8 Diminishing Marginal Rate of Substitution

than $MRS(A^0)$. This flattening of the isoquant is referred to as the technology exhibiting a *diminishing marginal rate of substitution* and is yet another consequence of imposing convexity upon T.

To interpret this phenomenon, consider a thought experiment that involves the producer decreasing x_2 successively by the same amount while replacing the lost production potential by increasing x_1. Viewed this way, the MRS measures the change in x_1 needed to balance the x_2 decrease. For each successive increment that the producer decreases x_2, the principle of a diminishing marginal product suggests each matching decrease in y is larger. (See, for example, the single-output technology in Figure 4.1). But that same principle means that larger and larger doses of x_1 are needed to balance the losses in y. So, x_1 becomes an increasingly poorer substitute for x_2 as you move from, say, A^0 to the southeast along $\bar{V}(y)$ in Figure 4.8. The visual manifestation of becoming a poorer substitute is a flattening of the isoquant. If you reverse the thought experiment and reason in terms of decreasing x_1 while increasing x_2 (moving to the northwest from A^0), a parallel argument shows that larger and larger incremental doses of x_2 will be needed to balance successive decreases in x_1 of the same size.

Just as the notion of a marginal product presents difficulties when the graph of the production function is kinked, so too does the MRS notion when the isoquant is kinked. Take, for example, Figure 4.4. Working from the northwest to the southeast, we see that the isoquant for that $X(y)$ consists of the vertical line segment that emanates from x', the line segment connecting x' and x^o, and the horizontal line segment emanating from x^o. Along the vertical line segment, x_2 can be decreased without requiring any balancing adjustment in x_1. The rate at which x_1 substitutes for a tiny decrease in x_2 of the amount φ is $\frac{-\varphi}{0}$, which equals $-\infty$ by convention. The portion of $\bar{X}(y)$ lying on the line segment $x'x^o$ has a negative (but finite) slope, and the horizontal portion has slope 0. Thus, any line segment with slope between $-\infty$ and the slope of the line segment $x'x^o$ will be tangent to the isoquant at x'. Similarly, any line segment with slope between the slope of the line segment $x'x^o$ and 0 will be tangent at x^o. Kinks in isoquants are associated with multiple (an infinity) different marginal rates of substitution.[6] Kinks in isoquants have important implications for producer behavior. (Chapter 6 treats this issue.)

Isoquants Can Intersect

A fundamental principle of consumer theory is that *indifference curves cannot intersect*. As the production analogues of indifference curves, it might seem that isoquants, too, cannot intersect. FDO ensures that this is true *in the single-output case*. That happens because y is then measured by a real number and not a vector of real numbers. Hence, as we pointed out earlier, two real numbers, y^o and y^* can always be ranked using $\geq$ or $\leq$. Thus, for the single-output case, FDO requires that either $X(y^o) \subset X(y^*)$ or $X(y^*) \subset X(y^o)$. It is possible that the isoquants can coincide, $\bar{X}(y^o) = \bar{X}(y^*)$, but they cannot cut one another. More generally, however, because pairs of output bundles exist for which neither $y^o \geq y^*$ nor $y^* \geq y^o$, their isoquants can intersect under FDO.

4.4 Output Sets

Definition 10. *The* output set *for x, Y(x), gives the collection of output bundles that can be produced by input bundle x.*

Written in mathematical terms, that definition becomes

$$\begin{aligned} Y(x) &\equiv \{y : x \text{ can produce } y\} \\ &= \{y : (x, y) \in T\} \\ &= \{y : x \in X(y)\}. \end{aligned}$$

Under free disposability of outputs,

$$Y(x) = \{y : f(x) \geq y\},$$

for a single-output technology so that the production function is the upper bound of $Y(x)$. Thus, $Y(x)$ resembles the production function in that it takes

[6] The set of real numbers falling between the slope of $x'x^o$ and 0 has infinitely many members.

x as the independent variable and defines a range of producible output but different because it isolates *sets of output vectors* rather than a single output.

The following equivalence relations are immediate consequences of the definitions:

$$x \in X(y) \Leftrightarrow (x, y) \in T \Leftrightarrow y \in Y(x).$$

These relations reveal that in each case we study the same object, the technology, but from different perspectives. The equivalence relation $(x, y) \in T \Leftrightarrow y \in Y(x)$ is crucial in establishing the properties of $Y(x)$.

T not empty

If $T \neq \emptyset$, a feasible (x, y) bundle must exist. Take that x and note that by definition $y \in Y(x)$. That gives:

- $T \neq \emptyset \Rightarrow \exists\, x : Y(x) \neq \emptyset.$

T not empty ensures that at least one input bundle, x, has a nonempty output set, $Y(x)$. It does not imply that $Y(x) \neq \emptyset$ for all x.

Free Disposability of Outputs

FDO requires that if x can produce y, it can produce any output bundle y' whose elements are all smaller than the corresponding element in y. Figure 4.9 illustrates free disposability of output visually by choosing a point y that belongs to the output set for x. The output bundles y' that satisfy $y \geq y'$ are those to the southwest of y. FDO requires that all belong to $Y(x)$. Applying the equivalence relationship, $(x, y) \in T \Leftrightarrow y \in Y(x)$, to

- $FDO \Rightarrow (x, y) \in T$ then $(x, y') \in T$ for $y \geq y'$

gives

- $FDO \Rightarrow y \in Y(x)$ then $y' \in Y(x)$ for $y \geq y'$.

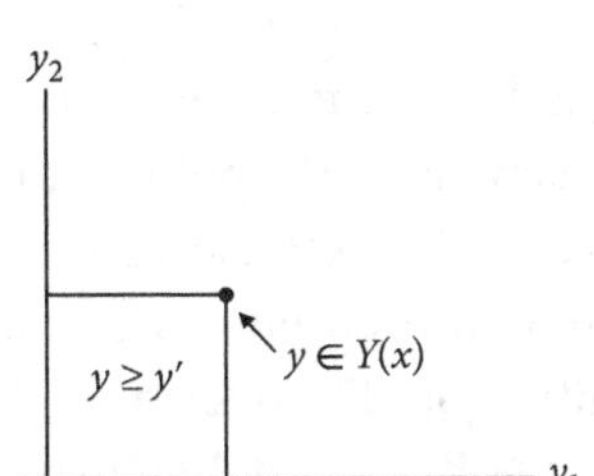

Figure 4.9 FDO and $Y(x)$

Convexity

We have already learned that convexity requires T to be a convex set in (x, y) space and $X(y)$ to be a convex set in x space. It's reasonable to conjecture that convexity requires $Y(x)$ to be a convex set in y space. Showing that the conjecture is true is an easy consequence of the definition of convexity and the equivalence relation, $(x, y) \in T \Leftrightarrow y \in Y(x)$. The definition of convexity requires

$$(x^o, y^o) \in T \text{ and } (x', y') \in T \Rightarrow \lambda (x^o, y^o) + (1 - \lambda)(x', y') \in T$$

for $\lambda \in (0, 1)$. Now take $x^o = x' = x$ so that we keep the input constant. Then using the equivalence relation gives:

- *Convexity* $\Rightarrow y^o \in Y(x)$ and $y' \in Y(x) \Rightarrow \lambda y^o + (1 - \lambda) y' \in Y(x)$

for $\lambda \in (0, 1)$. All weighted averages of y^o and y' belonging to $Y(x)$ also belong to $Y(x)$. $Y(x)$ is a *convex* set in output space.

You can visualize the impact of imposing convexity by plotting two points y^o and y' in the (y_1, y_2) plane. (The actual artwork is left to you as part of Exercise 10.) Convexity implies that $Y(x)$ contains all of the points on a line segment connecting the two points.

Free Disposability of Inputs

Recall from Chapter 3 that FDI implies that $f(x)$ is nondecreasing in x (nonnegative marginal product). Intuition, therefore, suggests that a similar property applies here. And it does.

The argument is as follows. Isolate $Y(x)$ for x. Now consider what happens when the input bundle is increased in any of its N dimensions to x'. FDI requires that any output bundle that could be produced using x can still be produced. That means that every point in $Y(x)$ must also belong to $Y(x')$ for $x' \geq x$. $Y(x)$ is a subset of $Y(x')$, that is

- *FDO* $\Rightarrow \; Y(x) \subset Y(x')$ for $x' \geq x$

Output sets do not get smaller as the input bundle grows. Or more output bundles can be produced using larger input bundles than smaller ones. (You are asked to illustrate the result in Exercise 11.)

There are three points to consider. First, you can arrive at this conclusion by using the original definition of FDI in terms of T, applying the equivalence relationship, $(x, y) \in T \Leftrightarrow y \in Y(x)$, and then using the definition of a subset. Second, FDI is a statement about x' and x that can be ranked using $\geq$. Not all input bundles can be ranked according to $\geq$ when there are multiple inputs. FDI imposes no restrictions over input bundles that cannot be ranked using $\geq$. Third, we speak in terms of not getting smaller to ensure precision. But the intuition is that increasing input bundles expands output sets.

No Free Lunch and No Fixed Cost

Deriving the consequences of NFL and NFC for $Y(x)$ is a simple matter of applying the equivalence relationship, $(x, y) \in T \Leftrightarrow y \in Y(x)$, to

- $NFL \Rightarrow (0, y) \notin T$ if $y \geq 0$ and $y \neq 0$ and $NFC \Rightarrow (0, 0) \in T$,

to obtain

- $NFL \Rightarrow y \notin Y(0)$ if $y \geq 0$ and $y \neq 0$ and $NFC \Rightarrow 0 \in Y(0)$.

In words, zero input cannot produce a positive input, and zero input can produce zero output.

4.5 Transformation Curve and the Marginal Rate of Transformation

Figure 4.10 depicts the output set for x as everything on or below the curve labeled $\bar{Y}(x)$. As drawn, $Y(x)$ is consistent with a two-output, multiple-input canonical technology. You can verify for yourself that it satisfies FDO and convexity. FDI will require that $Y(x)$ gets no smaller as x expands, and NFL is satisfied so long as $x \neq 0$.

We have isolated a point A, through which we have drawn the ray μA. That ray consists of all *radial* (that is, along a ray) expansions or contractions of output bundle A. Comparing A with the point where μA intersects the curve

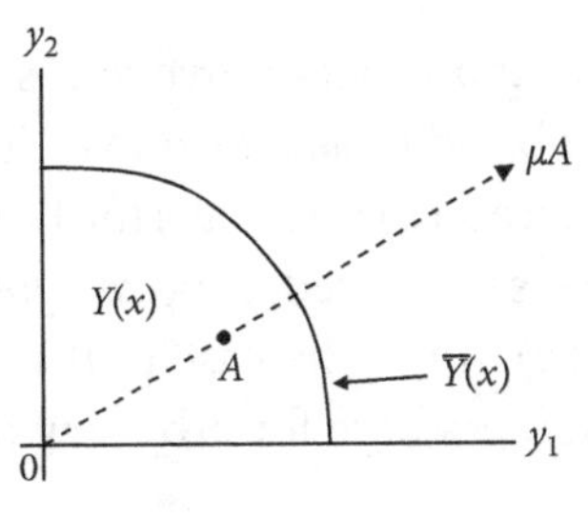

Figure 4.10 The Transformation Curve

$\bar{Y}(x)$ shows that the latter has more of both y_1 and y_2 than the former. Therefore, a self-interested individual who owned the rights to selling the output bundles produced using x would prefer the point on $\bar{Y}(x)$ to A.

The curve $\bar{Y}(x)$ has several aliases in economics. We call it the *transformation curve for x*.[7] But other writers refer to it as, among others, the *production possibilities curve*, the *production possibilities frontier*, or the *transformation frontier*. Regardless of semantics, the set of output bundles it portrays is of special interest to economists. It gives the set of output bundles in $Y(x)$ from which self-interested individuals make their production choices. The analogy with the isoquant is exact.

Definition 11. *An output vector, y, belongs to the* transformation curve *for x, $\bar{Y}(x)$, if and only if y belongs to the output set for x, but any proportional expansion of y outward from the origin does not belong to the output set for x*

The corresponding mathematical statement is

$$\bar{Y}(x) \equiv \{y \in Y(x) : \lambda y \notin Y(x) \quad \text{for } \lambda > 1\}.$$

Thus, $\bar{Y}(x)$ provides an *outer boundary* for $Y(x)$. Any radial movement from it to the northeast carries the output bundle out of the output set.

Just as we are interested in how inputs can be substituted for one another as economic circumstances change, we are also interested in how producers, using a fixed input bundle, respond to changing economic circumstances. Because self-interested producers will locate on the transformation curve, economists have developed a notion of adjustments along that curve that parallels the idea of a marginal rate of substitution. We have:

Definition 12. *The* marginal rate of transformation *(MRT) of output y_1 for output y_2 is the rate at which marginal changes in y_1 in $\bar{Y}(x)$ are transformed into marginal changes in output y_2 while holding input x and all other outputs constant.*

The notion of *transformation* that is invoked is that of producers changing the mix of their output bundles as they move along the boundary of $\bar{Y}(x)$. Starting from the point where $\bar{Y}(x)$ intersects the horizontal axis so that a positive amount of y_1 but no y_2 is produced, y_1 is *transformed* into y_2 as one moves to the northwest along $\bar{Y}(x)$. As in the case of the marginal rate of substitution, y_1 and y_2 are placeholders here for arbitrary outputs. It makes sense to

[7] Given our definition, the term *transformation set* would be more precise, but that clashes with more familiar economic jargon.

speak of a marginal rate of transformation between any two outputs holding the other outputs and inputs constant. Our geometric definition is:

Definition 13. *Marginal rate of transformation (MRT) at* $y \in \bar{Y}(x)$ *equals the slope of transformation curve at y.*

Referring to Figure 4.10, you will see that the MRT is nonpositive for all points on $\bar{Y}(x)$.[8] It can approach zero, but it will never become positive. This is a consequence of FDO. If FDO is violated, we cannot argue that the slope remains nonpositive. Moreover, as you move from the point of intersection between $\bar{Y}(x)$ and the vertical axis to the southeast along the transformation curve, its slope becomes steeper (more nearly vertical). That is a consequence of convexity and is referred to as an *increasing marginal rate of transformation.*

This phenomenon is the flip-side of the decreasing rate of marginal substitution and is illustrated using a parallel thought experiment. Imagine that you are a producer with a fixed bundle of inputs. You can choose how to allocate those inputs to different activities, but you cannot vary their absolute amount. Now starting at a point where all of your x is devoted to producing y_2 (where $\bar{Y}(x)$ intersects the vertical axis), imagine trying to increase the production of y_1 successively by the same amount. As we showed in the single-output case with $e(y)$, this requires larger and larger reallocations of that fixed-input bundle toward producing y_1. But diverting resources from y_2, by the principle of diminishing marginal returns, evokes ever larger decreases in y_2. The visual manifestation is a steeper slope for $\bar{Y}(x)$.

4.6 A Closing Word about Convexity*

Imposing convexity upon T ensures that the graphs of $f(x)$, $e(y)$, $\bar{X}(y)$, and $\bar{Y}(x)$ possess a curvature that is consistent with the generalized principle of diminishing returns. From our presentation, it's natural to construe that a diminishing marginal productivity, a diminishing marginal rate of substitution, and an increasing marginal rate of transformation all manifest the same phenomenon.

While intuitive, it's not correct. Our discussion shows that imposing convexity on T implies a diminishing marginal product, a diminishing rate of substitution, and an increasing marginal rate of transformation. But it is not

[8] Many authors define the marginal rate of transformation in absolute value terms. Just as we avoided defining the marginal rate of substitution in absolute value terms, we avoid the similar convention for MRT.

true that if $X(y)$ is a convex set, which is the basis for the diminishing marginal rate of substitution, that T must be a convex set. Nor is it true that if $Y(x)$ is a convex set then T must be convex. Thus, while a diminishing marginal rate of substitution and an increasing rate of transformation manifest phenomena similar to a diminishing marginal product, they are different.

To illustrate, we use the equivalence relationships

$$x \in X(y) \Leftrightarrow (x, y) \in T \Leftrightarrow y \in Y(x).$$

For $X(y)$ to be a convex set, all weighted averages (convex combinations) of all its elements must belong to $X(y)$. We write this as

$$x^o \in X(y) \text{ and } x' \in X(y) \Rightarrow \lambda x^o + (1 - \lambda) x' \in X(y) \text{ for } \lambda \in (0, 1).$$

Using the equivalence relationship shows that this requires that

$$y \in Y(x^o) \text{ and } y \in Y(x') \Rightarrow y \in Y(\lambda x^o + (1 - \lambda) x') \text{ for } \lambda \in (0, 1). \quad (4.1)$$

Expression (4.1) requires that if y belongs to both $Y(x^o)$ and $Y(x')$, it must belong to the output sets for all weighted averages of x^o and x'. But y belonging to $Y(x^o)$ and $Y(x')$ means that it belongs to their intersection, $y \in Y(x^o) \cap Y(x')$. Thus, expression (4.1) becomes

$$y \in Y(x^o) \cap Y(x') \Rightarrow y \in Y(\lambda x^o + (1 - \lambda) x') \text{ for } \lambda \in (0, 1). \quad (4.2)$$

Expression (4.2) does not require that $Y(x)$ is convex as a set, which is required by convexity of T.[9] Therefore, convexity of $X(y)$ and T as sets have different consequences for $Y(x)$. They are different properties. And because convexity of T implies convexity of $X(y)$, but not the other way around, convexity of T is the *stronger* restriction.

4.7 Exercises

Exercise 7. *Explain why nonemptiness of T ($T \neq \emptyset$) does not imply that $X(y) \neq \emptyset$ for all y.*

Exercise 8. *Suppose that you know that $x' \in X(y)$ and $x^o \in X(y)$. Impose free disposability of inputs (FDI) and illustrate the result. Impose convexity on the resulting set and illustrate the result. Compare and contrast it with Figure 4.4.*

[9] For the single-output, multiple-input technology, this condition requires that $f(x)$ is *quasi-concave*.

Exercise 9. *Explain why nonemptiness of T ($T \neq \emptyset$) does not imply that $Y(x) \neq \emptyset$ for all x.*

Exercise 10. *Let $y' \in Y(x)$ and $y^o \in Y(x)$. Impose convexity on T and illustrate the consequences for $X(y)$. Illustrate the consequences of free disposability of output on the result.*

Exercise 11. *Illustrate and discuss the consequence of imposing FDI upon $Y(x)$.*

Exercise 12. **Illustrate the property described in expression (4.2) geometrically.*

Exercise 13. **Derive and illustrate geometrically the consequences of requiring $Y(x)$ to be a convex set (without imposing convexity on T) for $X(y)$.*

5
A Primer on Rational Producers

5.1 Introduction

So far, our focus has been on the technology, T. In this chapter, we start our economic analysis by introducing the concepts of *profit*, *cost*, *revenue*, and their geometric illustrations. We then use a simple single-input, single-output model to study the basic principles of profit maximization. We close by showing that profit-maximizing producers always minimize cost and maximize revenue. That demonstration identifies the relationships between three important economic objects—the *profit function*, the *cost function*, and the *revenue function*—that provide the primary focus of Chapters 6 through 9.

5.2 Profit, Cost, and Revenue: Definitions and a Geometric Overview

As explained in Chapter 2, we study producers who operate in competitive markets and face fixed prices that they cannot manipulate. The prices for inputs are strictly positive, and we denote them by the N-dimensional real vector $w = (w_1, w_2, \ldots, w_N)$. Here, for example, w_n represents the price of the nth input. The prices at which producers sell their outputs are strictly positive and are denoted by the M-dimensional real vector $p = (p_1, p_2, \ldots, p_M)$.

A self-interested, price-taking producer seeks the largest possible *profit*. *Profit* is the difference between the producer's *revenue* and the producer's *cost*. We denote it by π (the Greek letter 'pi'), so that

$$\pi \equiv r - c,$$

where

$$r \equiv py \equiv \sum_m p_m y_m = p_1 y_1 + p_2 y_2 + \cdots + p_M y_M,$$

the sum taken over all outputs of each output price times the amount sold, is *revenue*, and

Lectures on Neoclassical Production Economics. Robert G. Chambers, Oxford University Press.
 DOI: 10.1093/9780197817759.003.0006

$$c \equiv wx \equiv \sum_n w_n x_n = w_1 x_1 + w_2 x_2 + \cdots + w_N x_N,$$

the sum taken over all inputs of the input price times the amount purchased, is *cost.*

The assumption that prices are positive ($p > 0$ and $w > 0$) means that markets evaluate inputs and outputs as "goods" rather than as "bads." We saw in Chapter 2 that inputs and outputs can be undesirable, but our basic producer model abstracts from such issues to narrow the focus on the economic principles guiding producer behavior.[1] Because we treat profit maximizers, we assume that the producer has the exclusive right to revenue from output sales and the sole responsibility for production costs.

Prices, profit, cost, and revenue are expressed in currency units. Economists call prices, profit, cost, or revenue denominated in currency units (be they dollars, euros, renminbi, etc.) *nominal.* In contrast, the *real* or *relative* price of commodity A in units of commodity B is derived by dividing A's nominal price by B's nominal price to obtain p_A/p_B.[2] When B's price is used as the divisor in creating a real price, B is called the *numeraire.* The real price of the numeraire is thus 1. Real profit, cost, and revenue are derived in a similar fashion.

Economists often distinguish nominal changes from real changes by representing a nominal change as multiplying the nominal value of each variable by a common positive real number, $\mu > 0$. Such changes are also called *proportional* because the percentage changes are common across the variables. For example, by moving from p to $3p$ (so that $\mu = 3$), the proportional change in the mth price is

$$\frac{3p_m - p_m}{p_m} = 2$$

which is common for all m. Such changes are nominal because they leave relative prices unchanged. For example, if output 1 is the numeraire, then before and after multiplication of nominal prices by a common positive real number the real prices satisfy

$$\left(1, \frac{p_2}{p_1}, \ldots, \frac{p_M}{p_1}\right) = \left(1, \frac{\mu p_2}{\mu p_1}, \ldots, \frac{\mu p_M}{\mu p_1}\right).$$

[1] The appropriate modeling of good and bad inputs and outputs remains controversial, especially in certain areas of economics, such as environmental economics, that often ignore technical production issues in their models. We revisit such problems in Chapter 12.

[2] The terms *real* and *relative* are used interchangeably throughout the chapters.

Visual illustrations of profit, revenue, and cost are key to explaining our ideas. Take profit, and assume that T has a single input and a single output. Profit is now a linear function of the input and the output (x, y),

$$\pi = py - wx.$$

We rewrite this expression with output, y, treated as the dependent variable of a function of input, x, and real profit, π/p. Divide both sides of the profit definition by the output price, p, and add $\frac{w}{p}x$ to both sides to obtain

$$y = \frac{\pi}{p} + \frac{w}{p}x.$$

Figure 5.1 depicts this linear function as the straight line that intersects the vertical axis (measuring y) at π/p (real profit in units of output) that has slope in x of w/p (real price of the input in units of the output).[3] This line traces out the set of points in the (x, y) plane that give a real profit of π/p when prices are (w, p). We call it the *isoprofit line (hyperplane)* for (π, p, w), and we represent it in symbols as $\bar{P}(\pi, p, w)$. (A hyperplane is a higher dimensional version of a line.)

As its name suggests, the isoprofit line is similar to the isoquant (and the transformation curve) because it isolates a collection (set) of quantities that give the same outcome. It differs, however, because it arises from producer interaction with competitive markets and not from the technology, T.

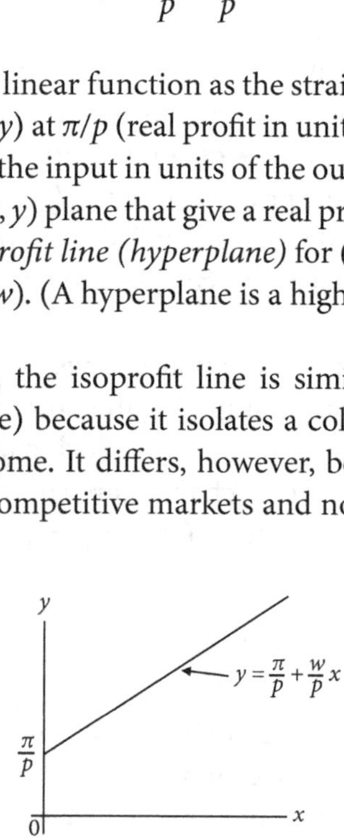

Figure 5.1 Isoprofit Line

[3] The choice of the dependent variable and the independent variable in Figure 5.1 is arbitrary. We use y because our convention is to represent T, with outputs depicted on the vertical axis and inputs on the horizontal axis. But if you choose x to be the dependent variable, you obtain

$$x = \frac{p}{w}y - \frac{\pi}{w},$$

as the formula for the isoprofit line. If you graph this version in (x, y) space you obtain Figure 5.1.

Its formal definition (which applies regardless of the dimension of x and y) is as follows:

Definition 14. *An* isoprofit line *(hyperplane) for* (π, p, w), $\bar{\mathcal{P}}(\pi, p, w)$, *is the set of input–output bundles that give a profit of* π *at prices* (p, w).

We write this verbal definition in mathematical symbols as:

$$\bar{\mathcal{P}}(\pi, p, w) \equiv \{(x, y) : \ \pi = py - wx\}.$$

Exercise 14 asks you to show that if (π, p, w) vary proportionately so that $(\pi/p, w/p)$ remain unchanged, $\bar{\mathcal{P}}(\pi, p, w)$ remains unchanged (the isoprofit line is *homogeneous of degree zero* in (π, p, w)); if π increases holding (p, w) constant, the vertical intercept of the isoprofit line shifts up, and the slope remains unchanged, resulting in a parallel upwards shift; if w increases while holding (π, p) constant, so that inputs become more expensive, the slope of the isoprofit line becomes steeper without changing the vertical intercept; and if p increases while holding (π, w) constant, the vertical intercept shifts downward and the slope becomes flatter. (You, of course, are encouraged to also consider what happens when these increases are replaced by decreases.)

The areas in (x, y) space on or above an isoprofit line (hyperplane)

$$\mathcal{P}^{+}(\pi, p, w) \equiv \{(x, y) : py - wx \geq \pi\}$$

or on or below it

$$\mathcal{P}^{-}(\pi, p, w) \equiv \{(x, y) : py - wx \leq \pi\}$$

are called closed *half spaces.* Because they are defined as everything on or to one side of a line (hyperplane), half spaces form convex sets in (x, y) space. You can verify this by inspecting Figure 5.2. For example, take any two points

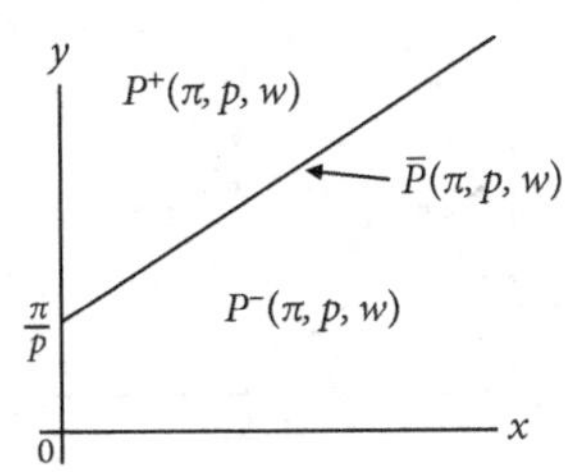

Figure 5.2 Profit Half Spaces

falling on or below the isoprofit line $\bar{\mathcal{P}}(\pi, p, w)$ in the area labeled $\mathcal{P}^{-}(\pi, p, w)$. If you connect them with a straight line segment, all the resulting weighted averages fall on or below the isoprofit line.

Turning to cost, let $N = 2$ so that cost, c, is a linear function of x_1 and x_2

$$c = w_1 x_1 + w_2 x_2.$$

To represent this in the (x_1, x_2) plane, we rewrite it as

$$x_2 = \frac{c}{w_2} - \frac{w_1}{w_2} x_1$$

and depict it in Figure 5.3 by the line with negative slope $-\frac{w_1}{w_2}$, vertical intercept $\frac{c}{w_2}$, and horizontal intercept $\frac{c}{w_1}$. It gives all the points in the (x_1, x_2) plane that incur a cost of c when input prices are (w_1, w_2). We call this line the *isocost line* (hyperplane) and denote it by $\bar{C}(c, w)$. Its definition (which applies regardless of the dimension of x) is as follows.

Definition 15. *An* isocost line *(hyperplane) for* (c, w), $\bar{C}(c, w)$, *is the set of input bundles that give a cost of c at input prices w.*

The mathematical version is:

$$\bar{C}(c, w) \equiv \{x : c = wx\}$$

Exercise 15 asks you to show that if (c, w_1, w_2) vary proportionately keeping $(c/w_2, w_1/w_2)$ constant, $\bar{C}(c, w)$ is unchanged ($\bar{C}(c, w)$ is *homogeneous of degree zero* in (c, w)); decreasing c while leaving (w_1, w_2) unchanged causes a *parallel shift* in the isocost line toward the origin; increasing w_1 holding c and w_2 constant causes the horizontal intercept of $\bar{C}(c, w)$ to shift toward the

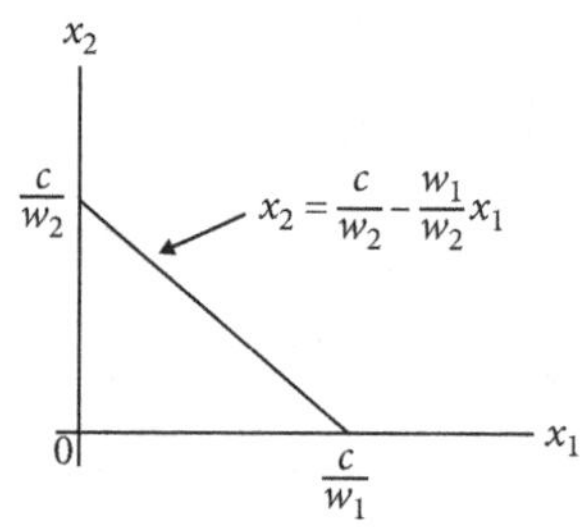

Figure 5.3 Isocost Line

origin and the slope of the isocost line to become steeper (when viewed from the perspective of x_2); increasing w_2 while holding c and w_1 constant causes the horizontal intercept to shift toward the origin and the slope of the isocost cost line to become flatter.

The half spaces in (x_1, x_2) space associated with $\bar{C}(c, w)$ are:

$$C^+(c, w) \equiv \{x : wx \geq c\}$$

and

$$C^-(c, w) \equiv \{x : wx \leq c\}.$$

That brings us to revenue. Let $M = 2$ (two outputs) so that

$$r = p_1 y_1 + p_2 y_2.$$

Mimicking arguments made for π and c, we transform this expression into a function of real revenue ($\frac{r}{p_2}$) and real revenue from sales of good 1 ($\frac{p_1}{p_2} y_1$) with y_2 as the dependent variable

$$y_2 = \frac{r}{p_2} - \frac{p_1}{p_2} y_1$$

that we illustrate in Figure 5.4 by the line segment with vertical intercept $\frac{r}{p_2}$, slope $-\frac{p_1}{p_2}$, and horizontal intercept $\frac{r}{p_1}$. We call that line the *isorevenue line*, denote it by $\bar{\mathcal{R}}(r, p)$, and define it as

Definition 16. *An* isorevenue line *(hyperplane) for* (r, p), $\bar{\mathcal{R}}(r, p)$, *is the set of output bundles that give a revenue of* r *at output prices* p.

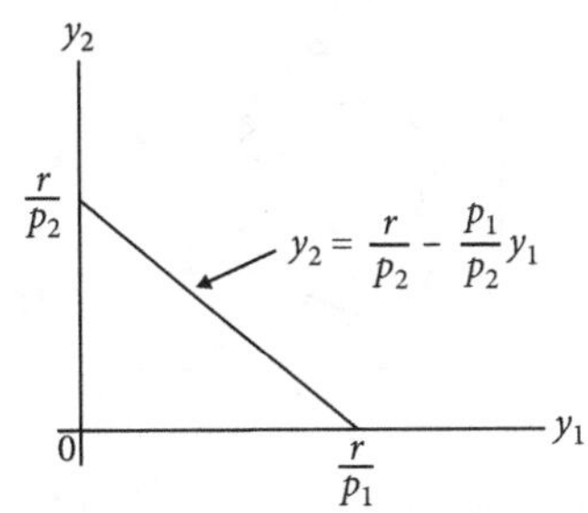

Figure 5.4 Isorevenue Line

The mathematical definition of $\bar{\mathcal{R}}(r,p)$ is

$$\bar{\mathcal{R}}(r,p) \equiv \{y : r = py\}.$$

You should experiment with Figure 5.4 to determine how various permutations of changes in (r,p) change the visual representation of $\bar{\mathcal{R}}(r,p)$.

5.3 Profit-maximizing (Rational) Producers

We now have the tools to examine the behavior of self-interested, price-taking producers. That behavior captures how producers respond to *market signals* in the form of prices (p,w) in the presence of feasibility constraints imposed by T. The producer's problem is to choose a technically feasible input–output bundle, $(x,y) \in T$, that makes profit, $py - wx$, as large as possible. In mathematical terms, the producer's profit-maximization problem is written:

$$\pi(p,w) \equiv \max_{x,y}\{py - wx : (x,y) \in T\}.$$

Here $\pi(p,w)$ is the real-valued function of output and input prices that gives the maximum feasible profit for prices (p,w). As before, $\max_{x,y}\{\cdot\}$ is an instruction to search over x and y to find the largest element in the set $\{\cdot\}$ that contains profits, $py - wx$, conditional on $(x,y) \in T$. That means the producer seeks an $(x^*,y^*) \in T$ such that

$$py^* - wx^* \geq py - wx,$$

for all $(x,y) \in T$. We call $\pi(\cdot)$ the *profit function*.

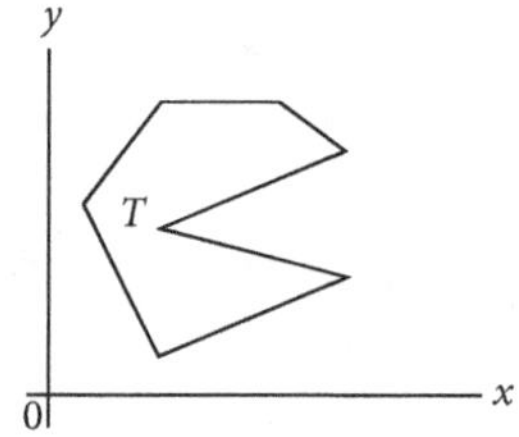

Figure 5.5 A Technology Set

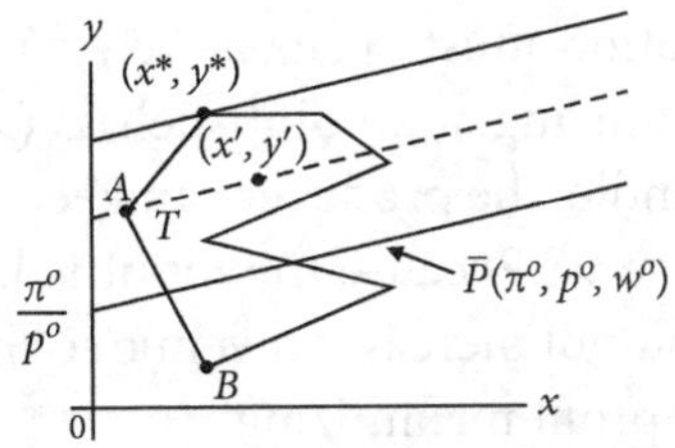

Figure 5.6 Maximizing Profit

We take a geometric approach and first treat the simple, single-input, single-output case. Figure 5.5 depicts the technology set, T, as an irregular heptagon. This shape may appear bizarre, but it was chosen purposely to ensure that T does not satisfy FDI, FDO, and convexity. That's done to emphasize that those properties are not essential to the argument.

Figure 5.6 augments Figure 5.5 by introducing the isoprofit line for (π^o, p^o, w^o), $\bar{P}(\pi^o, p^o, w^o)$. The producer, as a price taker, cannot manipulate p^o or w^o. But in the case illustrated, the producer can make a higher profit than π^o because a feasible input–output bundle, (x', y'), exists that lies on a higher isoprofit line. You can verify this by noting that (x', y') lies on the dotted line segment having the same slope as $\bar{P}(\pi^o, p^o, w^o)$ that intersects the vertical axis above $\frac{\pi^o}{p^o}$ so that $p^o y' - w^o x' > \pi^o$. Therefore, π^o is not the largest profit available from T.

Instead, the producer maximizes profit for prices (p^o, w^o) at the point (x^*, y^*). The isoprofit line through (x^*, y^*), $\bar{P}(p^o y^* - w^o x^*, p^o, w^o)$, shares a point in common with (intersects) T and defines the closed half space below it, $P^-(p^o y^* - w^o x^*, p^o, w^o)$, that contains T as a subset. We write these conditions, respectively, in symbols as

$$(x^*, y^*) \in \bar{P}(p^o y^* - w^o x^*, p^o, w^o) \cap T,$$

and

$$T \subset P^-(p^o y^* - w^o x^*, p^o, w^o).$$

Together, they require that $(x^*, y^*) \in T$ and

$$p^o y^* - w^o x^* \geq p^o y - w^o x,$$

for all $(x, y) \in T$.

Let's see why the solution must occur at (x^*, y^*). Consider, for example, the consequences of producing at a point such as (x', y') that falls inside T. At that input–output bundle, the producer can keep the input fixed at x' and increase the output above y'. Because the input is held fixed, cost does not change. But increasing output increases revenue so that profit increases. That means (x', y') cannot be profit maximizing.

Another way to reach the same conclusion is to keep the output fixed at y', but to decrease x below x'. That leaves revenue unchanged but decreases cost. Again profit increases. Points such as (x', y') cannot be profit maximizing.

The general principle is as follows: *Any input–output choice that falls on an isoprofit line that passes* ***inside*** *of the technology set cannot be profit maximizing.* To illustrate, take point A in Figure 5.6. Because it's on the boundary of T, it's technically feasible. But it falls on an isoprofit line that passes inside the heptagon defining T. That isoprofit line, however, contains points such as (x', y') that admit profit-increasing moves within T. Point A and (x', y') share a common profit. Thus, A cannot be profit maximizing because feasible points exist that are more profitable than it and (x', y').

The producer maximizes profit by finding an input–output bundle whose isoprofit line touches T without going inside it. Because the isoprofit line just "touches," or more euphemistically "kisses," T's boundary, it is *tangent* to T's boundary. A tangency is needed. But it is not enough. In addition, T cannot contain points lying on a higher isoprofit line than the profit maximizer. T, therefore, has to fall in the half space on or below the isoprofit line through (x^*, y^*).

Thus, the isoprofit line (hyperplane) for the solution, $\bar{P}(p^o y^* - w^o x^*, p^o, w^o)$, bounds T from above while sharing a point with it. The hyperplane is said to *support T from above.* Perhaps, you've seen optimal solutions described elsewhere by *tangencies.* That's not wrong, but more is required. You can experiment with Figure 5.6 to find isoprofit lines with the same slope as the one through (x^*, y^*) that "kiss" T, but involve a lower profit. (See Exercise 18.)

In characterizing the profit-maximizing solution, we used $\in$ rather than $=$ in the statement

$$(x^*, y^*) \in \bar{P}(p^o y^* - w^o x^*, p^o, w^o) \cap T.$$

That was intentional. Depending upon the shape of T and the structure of real prices, situations can arise where multiple elements of T solve the profit-maximizing problem. Figure 5.7 illustrates a case where a continuum (an infinity) of points belonging to T are profit maximizing.

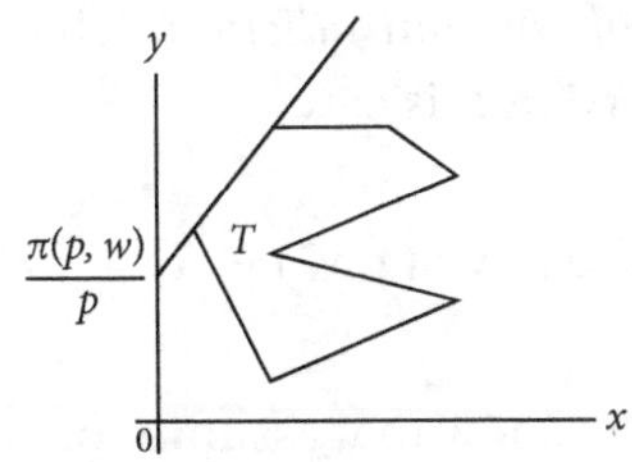

Figure 5.7 Multiple Profit-Maximizing Solutions

5.4 Profit Maximizers Are Cost Minimizers and Revenue Maximizers

You can confirm in Figure 5.6 that $y^* = f(x^*)$ and $x^* = e(y^*)$. In the single-input, single-output setting that implies that y^* solves

$$R(p, x^*) \equiv \max_y \{py : (x^*, y) \in T\}$$

and that x^* solves

$$c(w, y^*) \equiv \min_x \{wx : (x, y^*) \in T\}.$$

That is, y^* maximizes the revenue that can be generated using x^*, and x^* is the cheapest feasible way to produce y^*. This result manifests the following general principle that applies regardless of the dimension of x and y.

Proposition 1. *Profit-maximizing producers always produce their optimal output at minimal cost and maximize the revenue received from their optimal input.*

To demonstrate Proposition 1, let (x^*, y^*) be a profit-maximizing choice of inputs and outputs for (p, w), so that

$$\begin{aligned}\pi(p, w) &= \max_{x,y} \{py - wx : (x, y) \in T\} \\ &= py^* - wx^*\end{aligned}$$

The first statement in Proposition 1 claims that x^* is the cheapest way to produce y^*. Stated in mathematical terms, that requires

$$\min_x \{wx : (x, y^*) \in T\} = wx^*.$$

To verify, we use a *proof by contradiction.* That is, we assume that the statement we want to verify, in this case,

$$\min_{x} \{wx : (x, y^*) \in T\} = wx^*$$

is *false*, and then we want to show that assumption leads to a contradiction of known facts.

So, assume that the first part of Proposition 1 is false and that x^* is not the cheapest way to produce y^*. That means that another input bundle, call it x^o, must exist that can produce y^*, $(x^o, y^*) \in T$, and that is strictly cheaper than x^*,

$$wx^o < wx^*.$$

But this inequality implies that

$$py^* - wx^o > py^* - wx^* = \pi(p, w),$$

which says that $(x^o, y^*) \in T$ gives *more than the maximal feasible profit* $\pi(p, w)$. We have arrived at a contradiction, and we conclude that profit maximizing x^* is cost minimizing for y^*.

A parallel argument, which we leave to you as Exercise 19, verifies the second part of Proposition 1. This proposition has important analytic consequences. It shows that we can recast the profit-maximization problem as

$$\begin{aligned} \pi(p, w) &= \max_{x,y} \{py - wx : (x, y) \in T\} \\ &= \max_{y} \{py - c(w, y)\}, \end{aligned}$$

or as

$$\begin{aligned} \pi(p, w) &= \max_{x,y} \{py - wx : (x, y) \in T\} \\ &= \max_{x} \{R(p, x) - wx\}. \end{aligned}$$

Thus, three distinct, but equivalent, versions of the profit-maximization problem exist.

The first version is the one illustrated using Figure 5.6. The second version is a two-stage approach. In the first stage (*cost minimization*), the producer chooses inputs to minimize the cost of producing a given output bundle, y. That is, the producer solves

$$c(w,y) \equiv \min_x \{wx : (x,y) \in T\}$$

to obtain the *cost function*, $c(w,y)$. In the second stage, the producer solves the profit-maximization problem by choosing the profit-maximizing output bundle.

The third version offers a different two-stage approach. In it, the first-stage *revenue-maximization* problem is to choose output to maximize the revenue attainable from a fixed input bundle, x. The producer solves

$$R(p,x) \equiv \max_y \{py : (x,y) \in T\}$$

to obtain the *revenue function*, $R(p,x)$, that gives the maximum revenue that can be generated from the input bundle x. In the second stage, the producer chooses the profit-maximizing input bundle.

These two-stage versions of the profit-maximization problem facilitate more focused economic analyses. The cost-minimization case focuses on input interaction, and the revenue-maximization case focuses on output interaction. Both are examples of thought experiments. In the cost instance, output variation is "controlled" by holding y fixed, permitting inputs to vary. In the revenue instance, the roles are switched. This analytic device follows a familiar strategy for solving complex decisions. Break them into more tractable "sub-problems." (These decompositions are special cases of a more general principle on maximization known as *Bellman's Principle*, after the twentieth-century mathematician Richard E. Bellman.)

This decomposition approach to solving the profit maximization is an *analytic tactic* that offers a tractable way for production economists to analyze producer behavior. The argument isn't that real-world producers are automatons who follow these two-stage algorithms. Instead, it's that solutions to the original problem and the two-stage problems are the same. The latter thus may offer insights that might be otherwise overlooked.

5.5 Exercises

Exercise 14. *Show that if (π, p, w) vary proportionately so that $(\pi/p, w/p)$ remain unchanged, $\bar{P}(\pi, p, w)$ remains unchanged (the isoprofit line is* homogeneous of degree zero *in (π, p, w)); if π increases holding (p, w) constant, the vertical intercept* *of the isoprofit line shifts up, and the slope remains unchanged, resulting in a parallel upward shift; if w increases while holding (π, p) constant, so that inputs become more expensive, the slope of the isoprofit line becomes steeper without changing the vertical intercept; and if p increases while holding (π, w) constant, the vertical intercept shifts downward and the slope becomes flatter.*

Exercise 15. *Show that if (c, w_1, w_2) vary proportionately so that $(c/w_2, w_1/w_2)$ remain unchanged, $\bar{C}(c, w)$ remains unchanged ($\bar{C}(c, w)$ is homogeneous of degree zero in (c, w)); decreasing c while leaving (w_1, w_2) unchanged causes a* parallel shift *in the isocost line toward the origin; increasing w_1 holding c and w_2 constant causes the horizontal intercept of $\bar{C}(c, w)$ to shift back toward the origin and slope of the isocost line to become steeper (when viewed from the perspective of x_2); increasing w_2 while holding c and w_1 constant causes the horizontal intercept to shift toward the origin and slope of the isocost cost line to become flatter.*

Exercise 16. *Illustrate $C^+(c, w)$ and $C^-(c, w)$.*

Exercise 17. *Illustrate $\mathcal{R}^+(r, p)$ and $\mathcal{R}^-(r, p)$.*

Exercise 18. *An isoprofit line (not drawn) for prices (p^o, w^o) through B in Figure 5.6 is tangent to the boundary of T. Explain why B is not profit maximizing.*

Exercise 19. *Let (x^*, y^*) be profit maximizing. Prove that*

$$\max_y \{py : (x^*, y) \in T\} = py^*,$$

6
The Cost Function

6.1 Introduction

This chapter studies producers who minimize the cost of producing their output. The core notion is the *cost function*, $c(w, y)$, introduced in Chapter 5. As Chapter 5 shows (see Figure 5.6), when the technology has a single input, $c(w, y) = we(y)$. So, one natural interpretation of $c(w, y)$ is as the *money-metric* generalization of the input-requirement function. The natural roadblock to generalizing $e(y)$ to multiple inputs is our inability to add different inputs in a meaningful manner. The cost function removes that obstacle by converting inputs to monetary values and then adding.

We first illustrate the solution to the cost-minimization problem using the style of argument introduced in Chapter 5. Then we characterize $c(w, y)$'s *behavior as a function of the input prices*, w. We emphasize that this characterization *only* requires one restriction on T, which is that $X(y) \neq \emptyset$. We close the chapter by examining the consequences for $c(w, y)$, as a function of outputs, y, of imposing restrictions upon T.

6.2 A Visual Perspective on Cost Minimization

Figure 6.1 depicts two objects in the (x_1, x_2) plane. The first is a nonempty input set with isoquant, $\bar{X}(y)$. It's drawn to be smooth, consistent with convexity, and to satisfy the free disposability of inputs (FDI). (These are not essential to the argument.) The second object is the isocost line for a cost of c^o dollars and input prices w, $\bar{C}(c^o, w)$. The isocost line and the input set intersect, $\bar{C}(c^o, w) \cap X(y) \neq \emptyset$. So, points on the isocost line fall in the input set, and the producer can spend c^o dollars and afford to produce y.

There are input bundles that fall below $\bar{C}(c^o, w)$ but above $\bar{X}(y)$. Such input bundles can produce y but fall inside $C^-(c^o, w)$, and so they cost less than c^o. c^o is not the minimal cost to produce y. Following the arguments used in Chapter 5, a cost-minimizing solution cannot occur inside of $X(y)$ or at a point on $\bar{X}(y)$ that is on an isocost line that passes inside of $X(y)$. The cost-minimizing

Lectures on Neoclassical Production Economics. Robert G. Chambers, Oxford University Press.
 DOI: 10.1093/9780197817759.003.0007

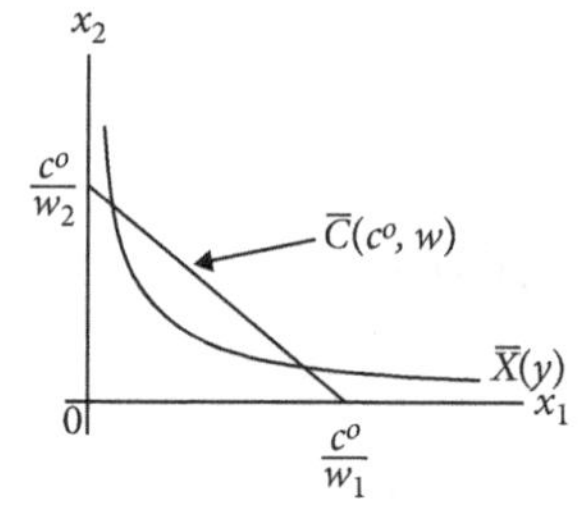

Figure 6.1 The Minimal Cost Problem

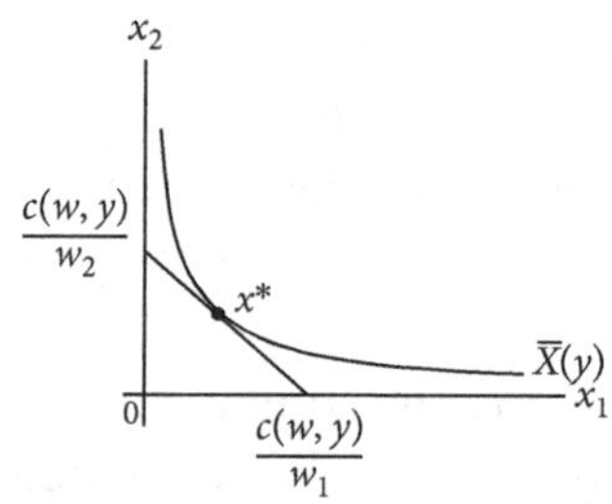

Figure 6.2 A Minimal-Cost Solution

solution, call it x^*, occurs where its isocost line, $\bar{C}(wx^*, w)$, touches $\bar{X}(y)$ and $X(y)$ is contained in the half space above it, $C^+(wx^*, w)$. That is, x^* is cost minimizing for y if and only if

$$\begin{aligned} x^* &\in X(y) \cap \bar{C}(wx^*, w) \text{ and} \\ X(y) &\subset C^+(wx^*, w) \end{aligned}$$

so that $\bar{C}(wx^*, w)$ *supports* $X(y)$ *from below.*[1] The input set is tangent to and "sits" on the isocost line. The implied tangency between $\bar{X}(y)$ and $\bar{C}(c, w)$ gives the rule-of-thumb for cost minimization: *the marginal rate of substitution equals (minus) the input-price ratio.* See Figure 6.2.

6.3 The Cost Function and Its Properties in Input Prices

Definition 17. *The* cost function, $c(w, y)$, *for input prices, w, and output bundle, y, gives the minimal cost of producing y.*

[1] Recall from Chapter 5 that the requirement for profit maximization is that the isoprofit line support T from above. We seek to minimize cost so that the logic and intuition are reversed and support must be from below.

The mathematical version of this definition reiterates the one offered in Chapter 5:[2]

$$\begin{aligned} c(w,y) &\equiv \min_x \{wx : (x,y) \in T\} \\ &= \min_x \{wx : x \in X(y)\}. \end{aligned}$$

Provided that y can be produced, that is, $X(y) \neq \emptyset$, $c(w,y)$ is well defined. We state its properties as a function of input prices, w. Then we explain and discuss them.

Cost Function Properties in Input Prices

- $c(w,y) \geq 0$ ($c(w,y)$ nonnegative)
- $w' \geq w \Rightarrow c(w',y) \geq c(w,y)$ (nondecreasing in w)
- $c(\mu w,y) = \mu c(w,y) \quad \mu > 0$ (positively homogeneous in w)
- $c(\lambda w^o + (1-\lambda) w', y) \geq \lambda c(w^o,y) + (1-\lambda) c(w',y) \quad \lambda \in (0,1)$ (concave in w)

$c(w,y)$ nonnegative

This property follows from measuring inputs and input prices as nonnegative real numbers. Cost, as the sum of input prices times input use, must be nonnegative.

$c(w,y)$ is nondecreasing in w

Let x' be the cheapest way to produce y for w', so that

$$w'x' = c(w',y).$$

Now let input prices fall to w from w' so that $w' \geq w$. Because $X(y)$ does not depend upon input prices, x' can still produce y. Thus, "doing nothing" is a feasible response to the input price change. The cost of the "do-nothing" response is

$$wx' \leq w'x'.$$

The best producer response to input prices falling cannot cost more than the "do-nothing" response, so that

$$c(w,y) = \min\{wx : x \in X(y)\} \leq wx'.$$

[2] In mathematical terms, the cost function, $c(w,y)$, is the (lower) *support function* for the input set $X(y)$.

Combining these arguments gives

$$c(w', y) \geq wx' \geq c(w, y)$$

for $w' \geq w$, as required.

If inputs become more expensive, the minimal cost of producing an output cannot decrease. When depicted in (w, c) space, the graph of $c(w, y)$ can have a positive or zero slope, but never negative.

Positive Homogeneity in w (only real prices matter)

The aphorism "only real prices matter" summarizes this property. *Producers do not respond to nominal input price changes that leave real input prices unchanged.*

Look at Figure 6.1 and consider multiplying all input prices, w, by a common positive number, $\mu > 0$. That causes the vertical and horizontal intercepts of the isocost line to shift toward the origin if $\mu > 1$ and toward ∞ if $\mu < 1$. But its slope is unchanged because

$$-\frac{\mu w_1}{\mu w_2} = -\frac{w_1}{w_2}.$$

As Figure 6.2 illustrates, the key to where the producer locates on $\bar{X}(y)$ is where its slope equals the isocost's slope $-\frac{w_1}{w_2}$. Call the solution x^*. Because $-\frac{w_1}{w_2}$ is constant for nominal price changes, x^* stays a solution when all input prices are multiplied by a common multiple. Nominal costs change to $\mu w x^* = \mu c(w, y)$, however, as nominal input prices move to μw from w.

The formal version of this argument invokes the definition of $c(w, y)$ at $\mu > 0$:

$$\begin{aligned} c(\mu w, y) &= \min\{\mu w x : x \in X(y)\} \\ &= \mu \min\{w x : x \in X(y)\} \\ &= \mu c(w, y) \end{aligned}$$

The second equality is the key. It recognizes that making $\mu w x$ as small as possible by varying x, with μ a fixed positive number, requires making wx as small as possible. And so, if x^* makes wx as small as possible, it does the same for $\mu w x$.

One way to think about why "only real prices matter" is to think of restating prices denominated in U.S. dollars ($) in terms of cents. Moving from dollars to cents multiplies nominal prices by 100, a special case of $\mu > 0$. But in terms of real buying power, nothing changes.

$c(w, y)$ Is Concave in w

Before showing that $c(w, y)$ is concave in w, let's see its economic meaning. We know that the graph of $c(w, y)$ in (w, c) space does not have a negative slope. So, our intuition is that $c(w, y)$ rises as input prices rise. From our discussion of concave production functions in Chapter 3, we know that concavity in w means that $c(w, y)$'s *slope* is nonincreasing in w. Figure 6.3 illustrates the case where it is decreasing.

Pick an arbitrary input price, w^*, and mark off its cost on the vertical axis in Figure 6.3,

$$c(w^*, y) = w^* x^*,$$

where x^* now represents the cost-minimizing input bundle when input prices are w^*. When input prices change, the producer must decide how to adjust the input bundle. Because input price changes do not affect $X(y)$, the only technical requirement is that the adjustment keeps the input bundle in $X(y)$. "Doing nothing" is a feasible response. So, let prices change to w^o and assume that the producer does nothing. The producer's cost is now $w^o x^*$, and the cost change is $(w^o - w^*) x^*$. We illustrate the "do-nothing" response in Figure 6.4 by moving along the line segment connecting $(w^*, w^* x^*)$ and $(w^o, w^o x^*)$, whose slope is x^*. (Exercise 21 asks you to verify that similar reasoning applies for price rises.)

Because "doing nothing" is a feasible reaction, it places an *upper bound* on the producer's best response to the price change. Therefore, the minimal cost at the new prices w^o cannot be larger than $w^o x^*$; that is.

$$c(w^o, y) \leq w^o x^*.$$

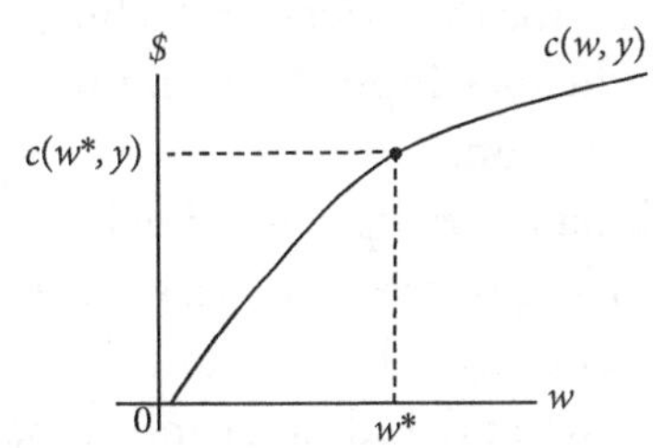

Figure 6.3 Cost Concave in w

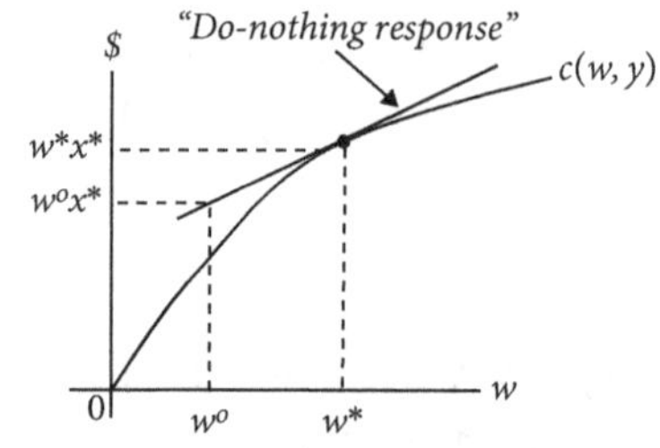

Figure 6.4 Shephard's Lemma

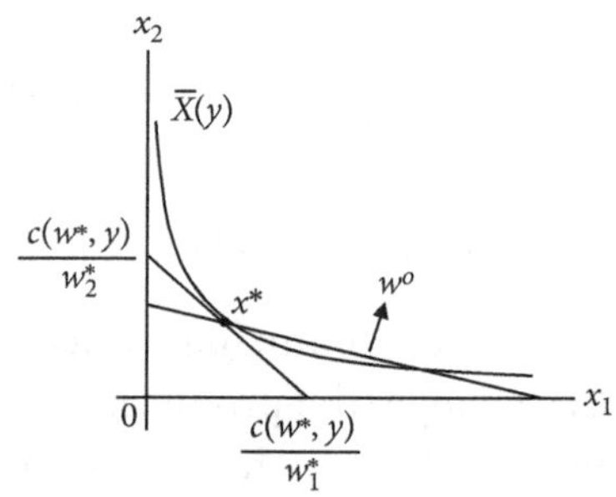

Figure 6.5 Price Change Causes Substitution

But that's what a cost function concave in w predicts, as Figure 6.4 shows.

Why is this true? In Figure 6.4, we assume that the producer does not respond to the input-price change. This is possible, but is it expected? Let's return to Figure 6.2 and consider how that solution changes if prices change. If both prices change proportionately, no adjustment is made. But if the price of input 1 falls by 50 percent, the slope of the isocost line becomes flatter (from the perspective of the x_2 axis). The isocost line through the "do-nothing" option now passes inside $X(y)$. As Figure 6.5 illustrates, cheaper alternatives are available. (In Figure 6.5, the line segment labeled with a perpendicular arrow w^o is the isocost line for the prices w^o.) Thus, if the producer can substitute more of the now cheaper input 1 for input 2, costs can be decreased beyond the "do-nothing" option.

Concavity of the cost function in input prices manifests the producer's ability to substitute between inputs in response to price changes.

Verifying these arguments in arbitrary dimensions is easy but requires some algebra (multiplication and addition) and reasoning. We want to compare three values: $c(\lambda w^o + (1-\lambda) w', y)$, $c(w^o, y)$, and $c(w', y)$. Let x^* represent the input bundle that solves the cost-minimizing problem for a weighted average of w^o and w', $\lambda w^o + (1-\lambda) w'$ for some $\lambda \in (0,1)$. That is,

$$\left(\lambda w^o + (1-\lambda)\, w'\right) x^* = c\left(\lambda w^o + (1-\lambda)\, w', y\right).$$

Because x^* is the solution to the cost-minimizing problem for this weighted average price, $\lambda w^o + (1-\lambda)\, w'$, it must belong to $X(y)$. But that means

$$\begin{aligned} w^o x^* &\geq c(w^o, y) \text{ and} \\ w' x^* &\geq c\left(w', y\right). \end{aligned}$$

x^* must be at least as expensive at input prices w^o and w^* as the respective cost-minimizing bundles. Multiplying both sides of the first inequality by $\lambda > 0$, both sides of the second by $1 - \lambda > 0$, and adding the results gives

$$\left(\lambda w^o + (1-\lambda)\, w'\right) x^* \geq \lambda c(w^o, y) + (1-\lambda)\, c\left(w', y\right).$$

The left-hand side of this inequality equals $c(\lambda w^o + (1-\lambda)\, w', y)$. Making that substitution, we have

$$c\left(\lambda w^o + (1-\lambda)\, w', y\right) \geq \lambda c(w^o, y) + (1-\lambda)\, c\left(w', y\right)$$

for $\lambda \in (0, 1)$, which is what we wanted to show. This concludes the argument.

Cost-Minimizing Input Demands Just as we are interested in how costs behave as input prices change, so too are we interested in how *cost - minimizing demands* respond to price changes.

Definition 18. *A cost-minimizing demand vector,* $x(w, y)$, *for input prices w and output y is any solution to the cost- minimization problem for w and y.*

The mathematical version of the definition is

$$x(w, y) \in \underset{x}{\operatorname{argmin}} \{wx : x \in X(y)\}.$$

Here the expression "$\operatorname{argmin}_x \{\cdot\}$" can be written in words as "any x that gives the minimal value in the set $\{\cdot\}$." We intentionally use $\in$ rather than $=$ because there can be multiple input bundles that provide the same minimal cost (see Exercise 22).

Our focus is on $x(w, y)$ as a function of w *holding y constant.* We start by repeating a basic observation. Because $x(w, y)$ is cost minimizing for y, it must belong to $X(y)$. Therefore, if we choose an arbitrary w^*

$$w^o x(w^*, y) \geq c(w^o, y)$$

for all possible w^o, and

$$w^* x(w^*, y) = c(w^*, y).$$

In words, $w^o x(w^*, y)$ is always greater than or equal to the minimal cost for input prices w^o, $c(w^o, y)$, and equals it when $w^o = w^*$. Subtracting the second expression from the first gives expression (6.1)

$$(w^o - w^*) x(w^*, y) \geq c(w^o, y) - c(w^*, y) \tag{6.1}$$

for all w^o as a condition that cost-minimizing demands must satisfy.[3] The intuition is that the cost change associated with doing nothing as input prices change is always larger than the change in minimal cost.

The expression

$$w^o x(w^*, y) \equiv \sum_{n=1}^{N} w_n^o x_n(w^*, y),$$

where $x_n(w^*, y)$ represents the cost-minimizing demand for the *nth* input, is a *linear function* of the input prices w^o whose slopes equal the respective cost-minimizing demands, $(x_1(w^*, y), x_2(w^*, y), \ldots, x_N(w^*, y))$. We have just shown that the cost function, $c(w^o, y)$, is a concave function of the input prices w^o. So, we can rephrase

$$w^o x(w^*, y) \geq c(w^o, y),$$

and

$$w^* x(w^*, y) = c(w^*, y)$$

for all w^o as requiring that the linear function $w^o x(w^*, y)$ provides an upper bound to the concave function $c(w^o, y)$ that equals it when $w^o = w^*$. In geometric terms, the graph of the linear function, $w^o x(w^*, y)$, always lies above the graph of the concave function, $c(w^o, y)$, in (w^o, c) space and coincides with it at $(w^*, c(w^*, y))$.

[3] In mathematical jargon, expression (6.1) says that the input demand, $x(w^*, y)$, is a *supergradient for* $c(w, y)$ *at* w^*.

To visualize, consider Figure 6.4 and let $x(w^*, y) \equiv x^*$ in the figure. The graph of the linear function, $w^o x^*$ in the (w^o, c) plane is illustrated by the "do-nothing" line segment passing through $(w^*, c(w^*, y))$ and $(w^o, w^o x^*)$. The "do-nothing" line segment lies everywhere above the graph of the cost function and just touches (is tangent to) it at $(w^*, c(w^*, y))$. We conclude that the cost-minimizing demand for the input at input prices w^* is given by the slope of the "do-nothing" line tangent to the graph of $c(w, y)$ at $(w^*, c(w^*, y))$.

Our argument works regardless of the number of inputs. When a linear function has more than one argument, its graph is not referred to as a line but as a *hyperplane* (plane works for two dimensions; the hyper is for three dimensions and above), and the N-dimensional analogue of the slope is a vector referred to as its *normal*. Thus, for the linear function of w^o,

$$w^o x(w^*, y) \equiv \sum_{n=1}^{N} w_n^0 x_n(w^*, y),$$

its *normal* is the vector

$$(x_1(w^*, y), x_2(w^*, y), \ldots, x_N(w^*, y)) \equiv x(w^*, y)$$

of cost-minimizing demands at w^*.

These arguments yield a famous result in economics:[4]

Shephard's Lemma. *For all w^* and y, any solution to the cost-minimization problem, $x(w^*, y)$ must be the normal for a hyperplane tangent to the graph of $c(w, y)$ at $(w^*, c(w^*, y))$.*

Overstating the importance of Shephard's Lemma is hard. It offers a way to recapture cost-minimizing demands. And *because those input demands can be captured from $c(w, y)$, they inherit their properties in w from $c(w, y)$* as we now show.

Positive homogeneity of the cost function in input prices, $c(\mu w, y) = \mu c(w, y)$, implies that cost-minimizing demands don't respond to nominal price changes that leave real prices unchanged. Let's look at this using Shephard's Lemma. For input prices w^* the cost-minimizing input demand vector, $x(w^*, y)$, satisfies expression (6.1). Now suppose that we hold $x(w^*, y)$

[4] You may encounter another version of this result elsewhere, which runs: The vector of cost-minimizing demands at w^* equals the gradient of the cost function at w^*. That isn't wrong, but it requires additional structure upon T. Thus, it is less general. The more precise version that applies generally is that the vector of cost-minimizing demands is a *supergradient* of the cost function at w^*, which is what our statement requires. See also footnote 3.

constant but let input prices w^* and w^o in (6.1) move to μw^* and μw^o. Will $x(w^*, y)$ still satisfy (6.1)? The answer is yes because positive homogeneity of cost ensures that

$$c(\mu w^o, y) - c(\mu w^*, y) = \mu(c(w^o, y) - c(w^*, y)).$$

Thus,

$$\begin{aligned} (w^o - w^*)x(w^*, y) &\geq c(w^o, y) - c(w^*, y) \\ &\Updownarrow \\ \mu(w^o - w^*)x(w^*, y) &\geq \mu[c(w^o, y) - c(w^*, y)] \\ &\Updownarrow \\ (\mu w^o - \mu w^*)x(w^*, y) &\geq c(\mu w^o, y) - c(\mu w^*, y) \end{aligned}$$

for $\mu > 0$. Therefore, $x(w^*, y)$ remains cost-minimizing for μw^*, whence

$$x(\mu w, y) = \mu c(w, y) \quad \mu > 0.$$

Cost-minimizing input demands *are homogeneous of degree zero in input prices*, *w*, which is the mathematical version of "only real price matters."

Figure 6.4 illustrates the consequences of *real* price changes for cost-minimizing input demands. The graph of $c(w, y)$ is steeper at w^o than at w^*. Applying Shephard's Lemma gives $x(w^o, y) \geq x(w^*, y)$ or

$$(x(w^o, y) - x(w^*, y))(w^o - w^*) \leq 0. \qquad (6.2)$$

The input price and the cost-minimizing demand vary inversely. Graphing $x(w, y)$ in the (x, w) plane gives a cost-minimizing *input demand curve* with a negative slope (see Figure 6.6).

Here we note a technical peculiarity associated with illustrating demand and supply curves. The mathematical convention is that the "independent" variable is represented along the horizontal axis and the "dependent" variable on the vertical axis. Because we represent demand for *x* as a function of *w*, *w* is the independent variable and *x* the dependent. Nevertheless, the tradition in economics is to plot demand and supply curves with price on the vertical axis and quantity on the horizontal axis. At the risk of confusing readers with more mathematical backgrounds, we adhere to the economics convention.

We confirm the visual story with a simple but rigorous argument. (It holds regardless of the dimension of *x* and *w*.) Take two cost-minimizing demand

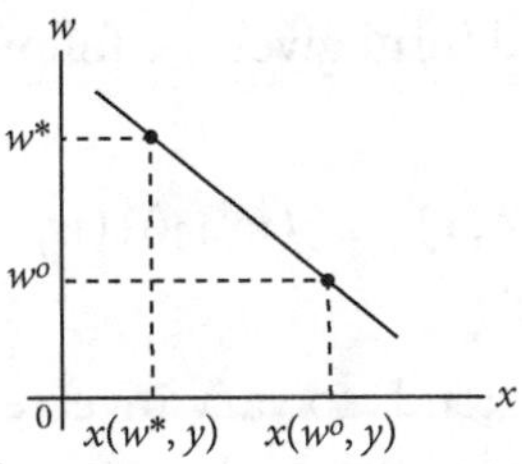

Figure 6.6 Cost-Minimizing Input Demand Curve

bundles, $x(w^*, y)$ and $x(w^o, y)$, for the same output y but for different price vectors, w^* and w^o. Because they are cost-minimizing demands for y, both must belong to $X(y)$. And although each is cost minimizing for its respective input prices, they are not cost minimizing for the others. That is,

$$w^* x(w^o, y) \geq w^* x(w^*, y)$$
$$w^o x(w^*, y) \geq w^o x(w^o, y)$$

Adding these inequalities together gives

$$w^* x(w^o, y) + w^o x(w^*, y) \geq w^o x(w^o, y) + w^* x(w^*, y),$$

and collecting terms gives

$$(x(w^o, y) - x(w^*, y))(w^o - w^*) \leq 0,$$

which repeats (6.2) that we obtained from Figure 6.4.[5]

[5] Expression (6.2) is an important special case of a more general result. Consider three input-price vectors, w^1, w^2, and w^3 and their respective input demands. By the definition of a cost-minimizing demand, it must be true that

$$w^1 x(w^1, y) \leq w^1 x(w^2, y)$$
$$w^2 x(w^2, y) \leq w^2 x(w^3, y)$$
$$w^3 x(w^3, y) \leq w^3 x(w^1, y).$$

Adding gives

$$w^1 (x(w^1, y) - x(w^2, y)) + w^2 (x(w^2, y) - x(w^3, y)) + w^3 (x(w^3, y) - x(w^1, y)) \leq 0.$$

And repeating the same argument for $w^1, w^2, w^3, \ldots, w^K$, with K arbitrary gives

$$w^1 (x(w^1, y) - x(w^2, y)) + w^2 (x(w^2, y) - x(w^3, y)) + \ldots + w^K (x(w^K, y) - x(w^1, y)) \leq 0.$$

Writing (6.2) in expanded form gives the following expression

$$\sum_{n=1}^{N} (x_n(w^o, y) - x_n(w^*, y))(w_n^o - w_n^*) \leq 0. \tag{6.3}$$

Cost-minimizing input use tends to vary inversely with input prices. If only the price for input k changes so that $(w_n^o - w_n^*) = 0$ for $n \neq k$, expression (6.3) becomes

$$(x_k(w^o, y) - x_k(w^*, y))(w_k^o - w_k^*) \leq 0.$$

The kth cost-minimizing demand is nonincreasing in the kth input price. The choice of k was arbitrary, so the result must hold for all cost-minimizing demands. Cost-minimizing demands must be nonincreasing functions of their *own price*, where the *own price* for input k is w_k. As elsewhere, we use the term *nonincreasing* to be precise. But the intuition is that cost-minimizing demands are decreasing in their own prices and cannot slope upward. There are no "Giffen" input demands.

How do we expect cost-minimizing input demands to respond to changes in the prices of *other* inputs? Answering this question carries us beyond what our theory predicts. We can say some things about what happens, but questions remain.

For example, we observed in Figure 6.5 that halving the price of input 1 led to an increase in the use of input 1 and a decrease in the use of input 2. The demand for input 2 fell as the price of input 1 fell. We referred to that as input 1 substituting for input 2. When there are only two inputs (which is unrealistic in most instances), this pattern must apply under FDI. As the real price between them changes, one input's use must decrease while the others must increase. So, if we look at Figure 6.6 and assume that the input and input price depicted in the graph are x_2 and w_2, respectively, halving w_1 leads to the demand curve for x_2 to shift inward. Less of x_2 is demanded at every w_2 when the two inputs are substitutes after w_1 falls.

From the perspective of input 2, economists call the price of input 1 a *cross price* and the induced adjustment of input 2 a *cross-price demand adjustment.* In general, for input k, a change in any input price, w_j, with $j \neq k$ is a *cross-price change.* When inputs k and j have *positive* cross-price adjustments, they are called *input substitutes.* When inputs k and j have *negative* cross-price adjustments, they are *input complements.*

as a consequence of cost minimization. This property of cost- minimizing demands is called *cyclical monotonicity in w*, and it, along with homogeneity of degree zero, exhaustively characterizes the behavior of cost-minimizing demands in w.

The intuitive story is that input demands vary inversely with their own prices. Thus, if its own price falls, more of the input is used. Under FDI, that suggests that to keep output, y, constant, some other input's use must fall as the producer moves along the isoquant, $\bar{X}(y)$. Those whose use falls are the *substitutes*. But FDI does not require that all other inputs decrease.

A concrete example illustrates. Think of a farmer who grows and harvests corn using different kinds of capital equipment (tractors, sprayers, combines), labor, land, fertilizers, pesticides, and other inputs. Now suppose that the price of land falls. How would you expect the farmer to adjust input use to keep output constant? Without empirical work, we can't know for sure, but it's easy to imagine instances where the farmer would use more labor. Land and labor would then be complements.

We close this discussion with a brief look at a canonical technology for which an input price change causes no change in input use (also see Exercise 22). In Figure 6.7, the piecewise linear curve $\bar{X}(y)x^*\bar{X}(y)$ depicts an isoquant. If the input set for y, $X(y)$, is everything on or above this piecewise linear object, it satisfies nonemptiness, FDI, and convexity. But we have drawn in two separate isocost lines, one, w^*, with a higher real price of input 1, $\frac{w_1}{w_2}$, than the other w^o that generate the same x^* as the cost- minimizing choice.

Is Figure 6.7 realistic? Judging from observed behavior, *maybe* is a good answer. If you compare Figures 6.5 and 6.7, you will note that Figure 6.5 suggests that producers respond to even tiny price changes by altering their input usage. That often doesn't happen. Producers often make no input adjustments even for relatively large price changes. Figure 6.7 explains such behavior. Some who have been seduced by drawing smooth isoquants might believe such behavior contradicts the theory. Figure 6.7 shows that's wrong. (This is one area where economists' predilection for calculus-based arguments has caused needless confusion.)

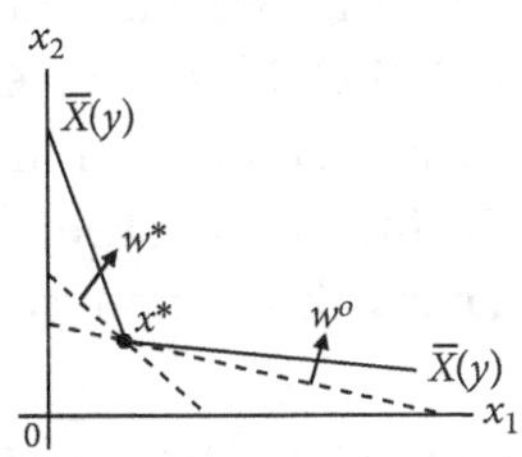

Figure 6.7 Input Price Change Causes No Demand Change

6.4 Properties of the Cost Function in y

The properties of the cost function in input prices, including Shephard's Lemma, follow from the type of decisionmakers we study and the environment in which they operate, and not from specific restrictions upon T (for example, FDI or convexity). Assuming that producers are price-takers means that they treat costs incurred by purchasing inputs as a *linear function* of inputs. That, in turn, means that the set of input bundles costing the same amount, what we call $\bar{C}(c, w)$, is a line (hyperplane). The profit-maximization assumption implies that producers minimize cost and seek to operate on the lowest isocost line (hyperplane) consistent with producing y. Their optimal choice must be separated from other feasible alternatives by a linear inequality from which the properties of $c(w, y)$ flow.

The assumptions about the setting, however, do not determine how minimal costs vary with output. To make those kinds of predictions, we need more. We now examine how imposing assumptions on $X(y)$ affects the cost function's behavior as a function of y.

Cost Function Properties in Outputs

- $FDO \Rightarrow c(w, y') \geq c(w, y),\ \ y' \geq y$ (nondecreasing in y)
- Convexity of $T \Rightarrow c(w, \lambda y^o + (1 - \lambda) y') \leq \lambda c(w, y^o) + (1 - \lambda) c(w, y')$ *for* $\lambda \in (0, 1)$ (convex in output)
- $NFL \Rightarrow c(w, y) > 0$ *for* $y \geq 0, y \neq 0$. $NFC \Rightarrow c(w, 0) = 0$.

FDO Implies Costs Are Nondecreasing in Output

Recall that FDO requires that input sets get smaller as outputs expand, or said another way, that they get larger as outputs decrease. We wrote this as

$$FDO \Rightarrow X(y') \subset X(y)$$

for $y' \geq y$. Assume, therefore, that we have identified a cost-minimizing input bundle for y', $x(w, y')$. By FDO, $x(w, y') \in X(y)$ for $y' \geq y$, the cost-minimizing input demand for y' ("Doing nothing") is a feasible response to output moving from y' to y. Doing nothing keeps cost constant. Therefore, a cost-minimizing producer, having this option, cannot respond by increasing cost.

Figure 6.8 illustrates the argument. There $\bar{X}(y)$ and $\bar{X}(y')$ depict the isoquants for y and y'. The cost-minimizing solution for y' is at $x(w, y')$. The isoquants have been drawn so that $X(y')$ is contained in $X(y)$, and $x(w, y')$

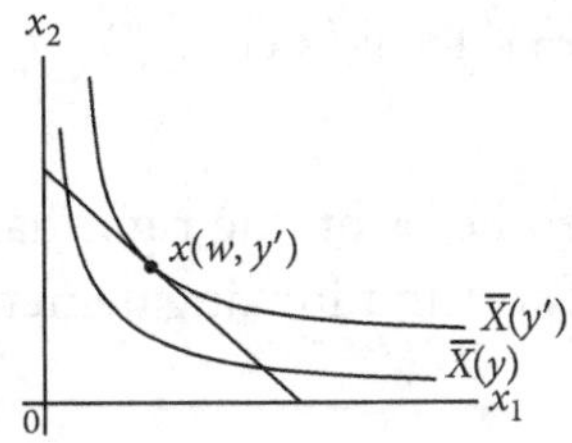

Figure 6.8 FDO and Minimal Cost

can produce y but is not cost minimizing. Therefore, *marginal cost* is nonnegative, where *marginal cost* is the cost-analogue of *marginal product*. In the single-output case, it's the change in cost divided by a change in output. So for "tiny" output changes, marginal cost is $c(w, y)$'s slope in the (y, c) plane. In the multiple-output case, the marginal costs of the different outputs at, for example, y^* are given by the elements of the normal to the hyperplane tangent to the graph of $c(w, y)$ at $(y^*, c(w, y^*))$.

Convexity Implies the Cost Function Is Convex in Output

You will recall from Chapter 3 that a convex T ensures that the input-requirement function, $e(y)$, is convex as a function of y. (See Figure 3.2 in Chapter 3.) The cost function is the money-metric generalization of the input-requirement function, and it, too, is convex as a function of y for convex T.

Marginal cost curves graphed in $(y, \$)$ space for a cost function convex in y have a positive slope that rises as output rises. (Exercise 24 asks you to explain why this is true and to draw the appropriate pictures.) This is viewed as the normal state of affairs, and many (but not all) visual depictions of marginal cost are drawn this way.[6]

We use a familiar strategy to show this result. Take minimizing input bundles for two arbitrary output bundles, y^o and y', and denote them as $x(w, y^o)$ and $x(w, y')$. Because T is a convex set, any weighted average of these bundles,

$$\lambda x(w, y^o) + (1 - \lambda) x(w, y'),$$

can produce the corresponding weighted average of y^o and y', $\lambda y^o + (1 - \lambda) y'$. But that means its associated cost is at least as large as minimal cost,

[6] Some graphical illustrations will have negatively sloped marginal costs for low-output levels, but they eventually turn upward.

$$c\left(w, \lambda y^o + (1 - \lambda) y'\right) \leq w\left(\lambda x\left(w, y^o\right) + (1 - \lambda) x\left(w, y'\right)\right).$$

Bringing w inside the parentheses on the right-hand side of this expression and using the definition of cost-minimizing demands gives

$$c\left(w, \lambda y^o + (1 - \lambda) y'\right) \leq \lambda c\left(w, y^o\right) + (1 - \lambda) c\left(w, y'\right) \ for \ \lambda \in (0, 1),$$

as desired.

No Free Lunch and No Fixed Costs

The names of these properties evoke their consequences for $c(w, y)$. NFL means what it says: you can't get something for nothing. To produce a positive output, you must incur a positive cost. It is a direct consequence of requiring a positive input to produce a positive output. NFC, on the other hand, means that the producer need not incur a cost to produce nothing because inaction is possible.

A brief comment on the notion of *fixed cost* is appropriate. The cost function, $c(w, y)$, treats y as fixed. Thus, it is a short-run concept. But all inputs, x, remain variable. No fixed costs (NFC) signals that when all inputs are variable, the producer can use a zero input vector to produce nothing. This contrasts with situations where the producer is obligated, either by contractual or other means, to purchase a fixed input bundle regardless of the amount produced. In that case, fixed costs are present, NFC does not apply, and we cannot show that $c(w, 0) = 0$.

Figure 6.9 depicts the cost function for a canonical technology in the two-output case. It emanates from the origin and is nondecreasing and convex in y.

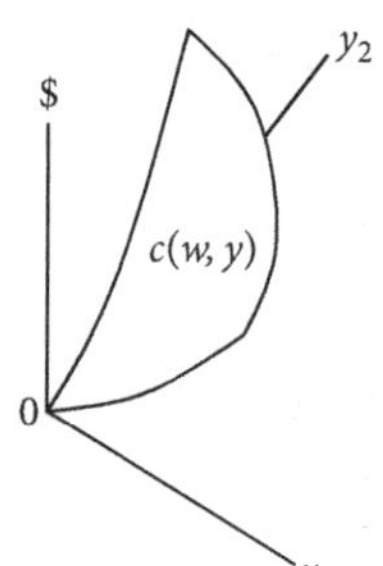

Figure 6.9 Cost Function for a Canonical Technology

Cost-Minimizing Input Demand and Outputs

We close the chapter by examining the response of cost-minimizing demand to changes in output, y. General results are scarce. Input demands can respond in different ways to output changes. Sometimes increasing the production of an output means increasing the use of an input while decreasing the use of others. Or it can mean increasing all inputs. Much depends on the setting and the applied circumstances.

Faced with such analytic ambiguity, economists settle for a taxonomy of input behavior. If input k is an increasing function of output m, input k is *progressive* in output m. If input k is a decreasing function of output m, input k is *regressive* in output m. In Figure 6.6, if the input depicted is progressive in output m, an increase in output m leads that demand curve to shift to the right. Conversely, if it is regressive, it shifts to the left.

6.5 Exercises

Exercise 20. *Figure 6.10 depicts an isoquant for a noncanonical technology. Isolate all the points that could be cost minimizing for some combination of strictly positive input prices. Explain your answer.*

Exercise 21. *Using Figure 6.4, explain why the producer's best response to price rising from w^* to $\hat{w}$ must involve a minimal cost that satisfies $\hat{w}x^* \geq c(\hat{w}, y)$.*

Exercise 22. *Figure 6.11, which is borrowed from Chapter 4, depicts an isoquant for a canonical technology. Describe how the cost-minimizing demands for both inputs change as the real price of input 1, $\frac{w_1}{w_2}$, varies over the interval $0 < \frac{w_1}{w_2} < \infty$. Illustrate in the (x_1, w_1) plane the demand curve for input 1 that results when $w_2 = 1$.*

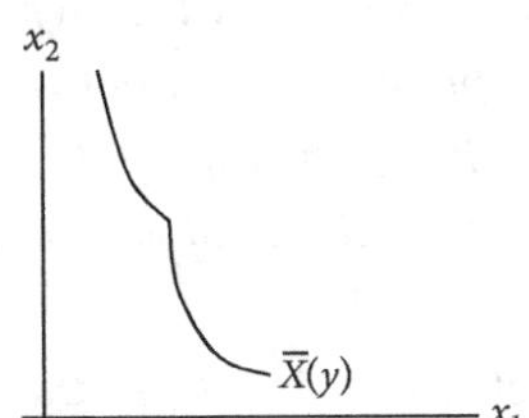

Figure 6.10 Noncanonical Isoquant

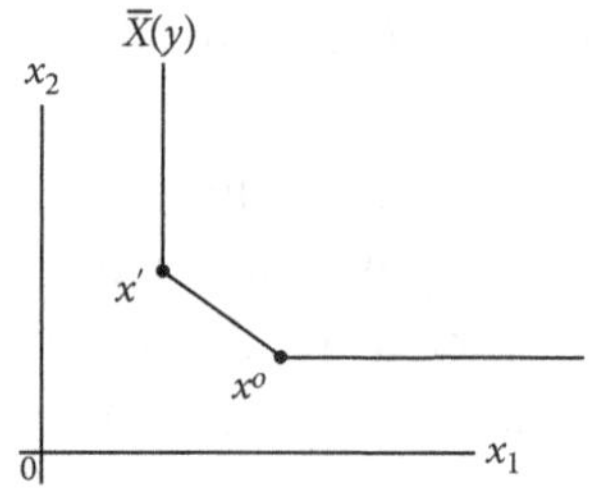

Figure 6.11 Deriving Input Demands

Exercise 23. * *Show that cyclical monotonicity of* $c(w, y)$ *in* w *(see footnote 5).*

$$w^1 \left(x\left(w^1, y\right) - x\left(w^2, y\right)\right) + w^2 \left(x\left(w^2, y\right) - x\left(w^3, y\right)\right) + \cdots +$$
$$w^K \left(x\left(w^K, y\right) - x\left(w^1, y\right)\right) \leq 0$$

implies that

$$\left(w_k^o - w_k'\right)\left(x_k\left(w^o, y\right) - x_k\left(w', y\right)\right) \leq 0$$

if $w_j^o = w_j'$ *for* $j \neq k$.

Exercise 24. *Explain why convexity of T ensures that marginal cost is a nondecreasing function of output and illustrate it with a picture.*

Exercise 25. *Two chicken farmers use the same production process that employs chicken feed and hired labor to produce chickens. The farmers live in different states (Arkansas and Maryland) and therefore face different input and output prices, but it turns out for contractual reasons that they both want to produce the same number of chickens. The price of chicken feed in Arkansas is \$2.00 a pound, while the price of hired labor is \$5.00 an hour. In Maryland, the high-cost state, the price of chicken feed is \$4.00 a pound, while the price of hired labor is \$10.00 per hour. Decide which region has the higher cost, which region employs the most labor, and which region employs the most chicken feed. Explain all of your answers.*

Exercise 26. * *The* isocost set *(as distinct from the isocost line) is defined as the set of outputs that give a level of cost no greater than c for input prices w. Its mathematical definition is*

$$Y^{*}(c, w) \equiv \{y : c(w, y) \leq c\}$$

Draw a picture in (y_1, y_2) *space illustrating* $Y^{*}(c, w)$ *for a two-output canonical technology.*

Exercise 27. * *Prove that if T is a convex set,* $Y^{*}(c, w)$ *is a convex set.*

Exercise 28. * *Prove that* $Y^{*}(c, w)$ *being a convex set* does not imply *that T is convex.*

7
The Revenue Function

7.1 Introduction

The subject of this chapter is the revenue function defined in Chapter 5. It is the money-metric generalization of the single-output production function that solves the problem of adding unlike output quantities by converting them into value terms. The analytic approach echoes the approach used in Chapters 5 and 6. Now, however, we seek the highest isorevenue line (hyperplane), $\bar{\mathcal{R}}(r,p)$, consistent with a given output set, $Y(x)$. As Figure 7.1 illustrates, the revenue-maximizing solution, denoted by $y(p,x)$, occurs where an isorevenue line (hyperplane) supports the output set from above, so that

$$\bar{\mathcal{R}}(py(p,x),p) \cap Y(x) \neq \emptyset \text{ and} \tag{7.1}$$

$$Y(x) \subset \mathcal{R}^{-}(py(p,x),x) \tag{7.2}$$

characterizes the solution.

Chapter 6 showed that the behavior of the cost function as a function of input prices depends only upon a mild restriction on the technology. Moreover, the properties of $c(w,y)$ in w characterize the behavior of cost-minimizing behavior input demands in w. The parallel result for the revenue function is that its behavior as a function of output prices only requires a mild (but slightly stronger) restriction upon the technology and that it characterizes the behavior of revenue-maximizing supplies in output prices.

We proceed as follows. First, we examine the properties of the revenue function in output prices. Then we examine the consequences of FDI, convexity, NFC, and NFL for $R(p,x)$. Because the argument parallels those presented in Chapters 5 and 6, we adopt a terser style to avoid repeating basic principles. Those readers who are just "dropping in" to this chapter will benefit from reviewing Chapters 5 and 6.

Lectures on Neoclassical Production Economics. Robert G. Chambers, Oxford University Press.
 DOI: 10.1093/9780197817759.003.0008

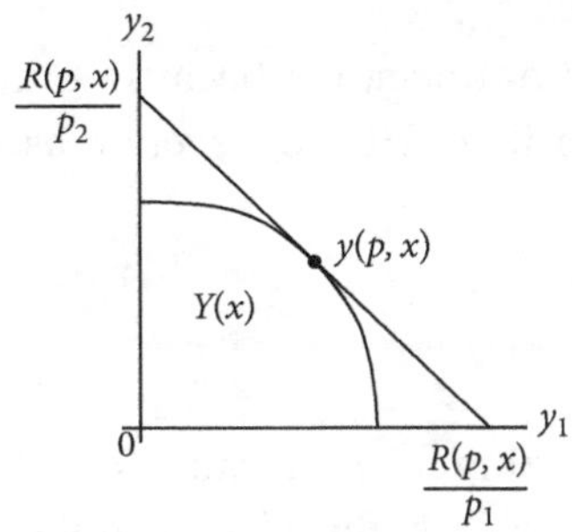

Figure 7.1 Revenue Maximization

7.2 The Revenue Function Defined and Its Properties in Output Prices

Definition 19. *The revenue function, $R(p,x)$, for output prices p and input bundle x is the maximal revenue that can be realized from the output set for x, $Y(x)$.*

We recall Chapter 5's mathematical definition of $R(p,x)$.[1]

$$\begin{aligned} R(p,x) &\equiv \max_y \{py : (x,y) \in T\} \\ &= \max_y \{px : y \in Y(x)\}. \end{aligned}$$

The revenue function is well defined if the output set is nonempty, $Y(x) \neq \emptyset$, and "bounded."[2] We first state mathematical versions of $R(p,x)$'s properties and follow with a discussion of each.

The Revenue Function as a Function of Output Prices

- $R(p,x) \geq 0$ (nonnegative)
- $R(p',x) \geq R(p,x)$ for $p' \geq p$ (nondecreasing in p)
- $R(\mu p,x) = \mu R(p,x)$ for $\mu > 0$ (positively homogeneous in p)
- $R(\lambda p^o + (1-\lambda)p^*,x) \leq \lambda R(p^o,x) + (1-\lambda)R(p^*,x)$ $\lambda \in (0,1)$ (convex in p)

[1] The mathematical name of the revenue function is the (upper) *support function* for $Y(x)$.

[2] Boundedness is a technical requirement that ensures that there are no infinitely large feasible output bundles.

Nonnegative

The revenue function is nonnegative because outputs, y, are nonnegative and output prices are positive. Hence, revenue as their product cannot be negative.

Nondecreasing in p

Let y^* be revenue maximizing for p. Because $Y(x)$ does not depend upon p, y^* remains producible for $p' \geq p$. But $p' \geq p$ implies that the revenue for the "do-nothing" response satisfies

$$p'y^* \geq py^* = R(p,x),$$

so that $R(p',x) \geq R(p,x)$. When depicted in $(p, \$)$ space, the graph of $R(p,x)$ has a nonnegative slope.

Positively Homogeneous in p

Inspecting Figure 7.1 while recalling that the isorevenue line's slope only depends upon real prices implies that a nominal price change leaves that solution unchanged. Once again, "only real prices matter" is the core principle. Producers respond to real but not nominal price changes. The mathematical argument follows the same method used to demonstrate the positive homogeneity of $c(w,y)$ in w.

$$\begin{aligned} R(\mu p,x) &= \max_y \{\mu py : y \in Y(x)\} \\ &= \mu \max_y \{py : y \in Y(x)\} \\ &= \mu R(p,x) \end{aligned}$$

for $\mu > 0$. Here the key idea is that making μpy as large as possible reduces to making py as large as possible if we hold μ fixed. Thus, if y^*, for example, solves

$$\max_y \{py : y \in Y(x)\},$$

it must also solve

$$\max_y \{\mu py : y \in Y(x)\}.$$

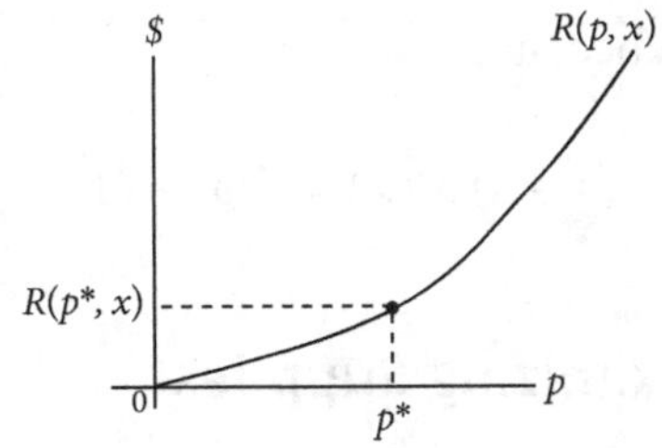

Figure 7.2 Convex Revenue Function

Convex in p

A nondecreasing, convex function is visualized as one that has a positive and increasing slope (see Figure 7.2 for an illustration).

To show the reasoning: pick an arbitrary output-price vector, p^*, in Figure 7.2 and label its revenue-maximizing output bundle y^*, so that $R(p^*, x) = p^* y^*$. Let the output price rise to $p^o > p^*$. (Exercise 30 asks you to develop the associated geometric argument.[3]) How do you illustrate the associated change in revenue if the producer keeps production at y^*? Is that a feasible response? How does it compare to an optimal response? Answering these questions confirms that the convex shape in Figure 7.2 is not only possible, but expected, if producers can adjust (transform) their output production in response to changes in p.

For a more formal argument, let

$$\hat{p} \equiv \lambda p^o + (1 - \lambda) p^*$$

for $\lambda \in (0, 1)$, and let $\hat{y} \in Y(x)$ denote a revenue-maximizing solution for $\hat{p}$. By definition

$$\begin{aligned} p^o \hat{y} &\leq R(p^o, x) \\ p^* \hat{y} &\leq R(p^*, x). \end{aligned}$$

Multiplying the first by λ, the second by $1 - \lambda$, adding, and rearranging gives

$$R(\lambda p^o + (1 - \lambda) p^*, x) \leq \lambda R(p^o, x) + (1 - \lambda) R(p^*, x),$$

[3] You may wish to consult Figures 6.3 and 6.4 and the surrounding discussion in Chapter 6 in fleshing out the elaboration.

for $\lambda \in (0, 1)$ as desired because

$$R(\lambda p^o + (1 - \lambda) p^*, x) = (\lambda p^o + (1 - \lambda) p^*) \hat{y}.$$

7.2.1 Revenue-Maximizing Supplies

Definition 20. *A revenue-maximizing supply vector, $y(p,x)$, for prices p and input bundle x is any solution to the revenue- maximization problem for p and x.*

In mathematical form, that definition becomes

$$y(p,x) \in \underset{y}{\operatorname{argmax}} \{py : y \in Y(x)\}.$$

Our investigation of $y(p,x)$'s behavior starts with noting that each such supply vector, $y(p^*,x)$, defines a linear function of output prices p, $py(p^*,x) \equiv \sum_{m=1}^{M} p_m y_m(p^*,x)$, that satisfies

$$p^o y(p^*,x) \leq R(p^o,x)$$

and

$$p^* y(p^*,x) = R(p^*,x),$$

for all p^* and p^o. Rephrased in geometric terms: the linear function of p^o, $p^o y(p^*,x)$, with normal $y(p^*,x)$ defines a *lower bound* for the revenue function, $R(p^o,x)$, that equals it when $p^o = p^*$. Subtracting the equality from the inequality gives

$$(p^o - p^*) y(p^*,x) \leq R(p^o,x) - R(p^*,x), \tag{7.3}$$

for all p^o as a requirement for $y(p,x)$ to be revenue-maximizing (illustrated in Figure 7.3).[4] The graph of the linear function, $py(p^*,x)$, is illustrated by the line segment passing through $(p^*, p^* y^*)$ and $(p^o, p^o y^*)$, where now $y^* = y(p^*,x)$.

The economic implication is that the "do-nothing" response of keeping output at $y^* = y(p^*,x)$ as output price changes from p^* to p^o never generates more revenue than the optimal response. Expression (7.3) is the analogue of Shephard's Lemma for the revenue function.

[4] Expression (7.3) says that the revenue-maximizing supply vector is a *subgradient* of $R(p,x)$ at p^*.

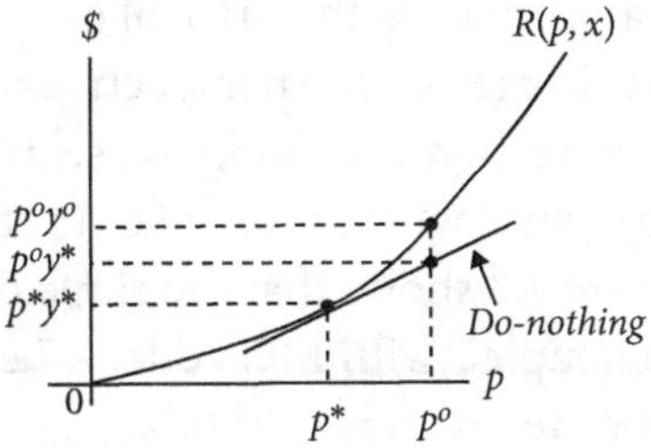

Figure 7.3 McFadden's Lemma

McFadden's Lemma *For all* p^* *and* x*, any solution to the revenue-maximization problem,* $y(p^*, x)$ *must be the normal for a hyperplane tangent to the graph of* $R(p, x)$ *at* $(p^*, R(p^*, x))$*.*[5]

McFadden's Lemma links revenue-maximizing supplies, $y(p, x)$, to the slope of the revenue function in p. That implies that the behavior of $R(p, x)$ in p will characterize the behavior of $y(p, x)$. For example, we have argued that the revenue function is positively homogeneous in p, or that "only real price matters" in determining revenue-maximizing supplies. Let's confirm that argument using McFadden's Lemma and the properties of $R(p, x)$.

Following an argument developed in Chapter 6, we note that if $y(p^*, x)$ satisfies expression (7.3), positive homogeneity of $R(p, x)$ in p ensures that it also satisfies

$$(\mu p^o - \mu p^*)\, y(p^*, x) \leq R(\mu p^o, x) - R(\mu p^*, x) \qquad (7.4)$$

for all μp^o and μp^* because positive homogeneity allows expression (7.4) to be rewritten as

$$\mu (p^o - p^*)\, y(p^*, x) \leq \mu (R(p^o, x) - R(p^*, x)).$$

And dividing both sides by $\mu > 0$ gives expression (7.3). Thus, expressions (7.3) and (7.4) are equivalent. Applying McFadden's Lemma, we conclude, therefore, that

$$y(\mu p, x) = y(p, x) \quad \text{for} \quad \mu > 0.$$

Revenue-maximizing supplies are *homogeneous of degree zero* in p, and nominal price changes do not affect them.

[5] Alternatively: Any solution to the revenue-maximization problem at (p^*, x) must be a subgradient for $R(p, x)$ at $R(p^*, x)$.

Figure 7.1 suggests that increasing the price of output 1, p_1, makes the slope of the isorevenue line steeper (from the perspective of the vertical axis). That suggests that the producer responds to an increase in p_1 by moving along the transformation curve to a point where more of output 1 and less of output 2 is produced. Similarly, Figure 7.3 shows that the slope of $R(p,x)$ is steeper at p^o than at p^*, which when coupled with McFadden's Lemma also suggests that output responds positively to an increased price.

We confirm these intuitive arguments by using the two inequalities

$$\begin{aligned} p^o y(p^*,x) &\leq p^o y(p^o,x) \\ p^* y(p^o,x) &\leq p^* y(p^*,x) \end{aligned}$$

that are a necessary consequence of revenue maximization for all p^o and p^*. (These two inequalities say that revenue-maximizing supplies generate more revenue at the prices for which they are revenue maximizing than revenue-maximizing supplies for other prices.) Adding them together and rearranging gives[6]

$$(p^o - p^*)(y(p^o,x) - y(p^*,x)) \geq 0, \tag{7.5}$$

or in expanded form

$$\sum_{m=1}^{M} (p^o_m - p^*_m)(y_m(p^o,x) - y_m(p^*,x)) \geq 0.$$

Revenue-maximizing supplies and output prices tend to vary together. Taking $p^o_k = p^*_k$ for all $k \neq j$ gives

$$\left(p^o_j - p^*_j\right)(y_j(p^o,x) - y_j(p^*,x)) \geq 0,$$

which confirms that all revenue-maximizing supplies are upward sloping (more precisely not downward sloping) in their own prices. See Figure 7.4 for an illustration.

From the discussion of Figure 7.1, we anticipate that an increase in the price of one output tends to suppress production of other commodities. Using a

[6] Following the line of argument in footnote 5 of Chapter 6, we can show that expression (7.5) is a special case of revenue-maximizing supplies satisfying the following *cyclical monotonicity* property in p:

$$p^1(y(p^1,x) - y(p^2,x)) + p^2(y(p^2,x) - y(p^3,x)) + \ldots + p^K(y(p^K,x) - y(p^1,x)) \geq 0.$$

Together with zero homogeneity, cyclical monotonicity exhaustively characterizes the behavior of revenue-maximizing supplies in p.

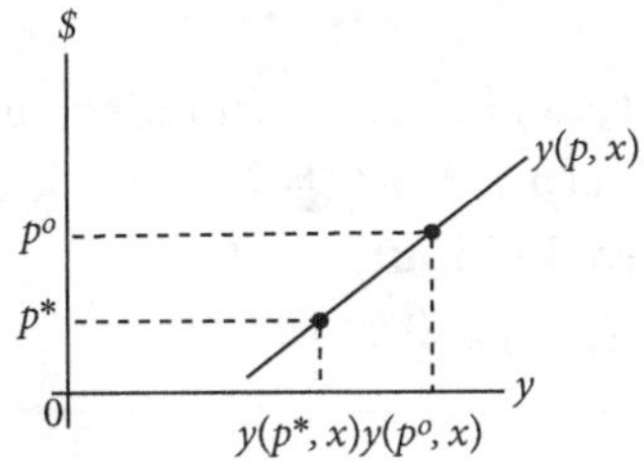

Figure 7.4 Revenue-Maximizing Supply

bit more jargon, we might therefore conclude that *cross price adjustments* of revenue-maximizing supplies tend to be negative (more precisely nonpositive). If FDO applies, and there are only two outputs, this is indeed true. More generally, however, it's not.

Consider, for example, a farmer who produces wheat and beef for the local market. Because a necessary by-product of beef production is hide production (which can be used in leather production), one expects that an increase in the price of beef would lead to an increase in hide production even if the price of hides remained constant. In fact, one would not be surprised if an increase in the price of beef led to an increase in hide production *even if the price of hides fell.* Such things can and do happen.

Outputs whose supply increases as cross price p_k increases are *complements* for output k. *Substitutes* for k are outputs whose supply decreases as p_k falls. Referring to Figure 7.4, let the supply illustrated there be for output $m \neq k$ so that the price illustrated on the vertical axis will be p_m. If output m is a substitute for output k, an increase in p_k will cause the demand curve to shift to the left so that less of output m is supplied at all levels of p_m. On the other hand, if output m is a complement for output k, an increase in p_k will cause the supply curve for output m to shift to the right as the production of m increases with the production of k.

7.3 Revenue Function as a Function of Inputs, x

How $R(p, x)$ responds to changes in x depends upon $Y(x)$. Because $R(p, x)$ is the money-metric generalization of the production function, $f(x)$, that accommodates multiple outputs (for the single-output case $R(p, x) = pf(x)$), its behavior in x has natural parallels in the behavior of $f(x)$. We first list the implications for $R(p, x)$ of restrictions imposed on $Y(x)$, and then we discuss them.

Properties of $R(p, x)$ in x

- *FDI* $\Rightarrow R(p, x') \geq R(p, x)$ for $x' \geq x$ (nondecreasing in x)
- Convexity of $T \Rightarrow R(p, \lambda x^o + (1-\lambda)x^*) \geq \lambda R(p, x^o) + (1-\lambda)R(p, x^*)$ for $\lambda \in (0,1)$ (concave in input)
- *NFL and NFC* $\Rightarrow R(p, 0) = 0$.

Nondecreasing in x

Free disposability of inputs ensures that maximal revenue cannot decrease as a result of an increase in the input bundle, x. The demonstration follows the "do-nothing" principle. Because $y(p, x) \in Y(x)$, FDI ensures that it also belongs to $Y(x')$ for $x' \geq x$. Therefore, the producer can respond to an input increase by producing the same output bundle. And because that choice results in no revenue change, the best response cannot decrease revenue.

When $R(p, x)$ is graphed as a function of x, nondecreasing in x rules out a negatively sloped curve. The parallel property for the production function was called a positive (nonnegative) marginal productivity. Here the parallel concept is *marginal revenue.* If there is only a single input, *marginal revenue* is defined as the change in revenue divided by the change in the input, $\frac{\Delta R(p, x)}{\Delta x}$, or as the slope of the line segment tangent to the graph of $R(p, x)$ at $(x, R(p, x))$. In the multiple-input case, the marginal revenues form the normal to the hyperplane tangent to $R(p, x)$ at $(x, R(p, x))$. They are all nonnegative under FDI.

Concave as a Function of x

Concavity of $R(p, x)$ as a function of x echoes the concavity of the production function. It manifests the principle of diminishing returns and implies that successive marginal input increases evoke decreasing (more precisely nonincreasing) marginal revenue increases. In more casual terms, convexity of T implies decreasing marginal revenue for each input. This evokes a revenue function with the same basic shape as the production function presented in Figure 3.1. The only change is that the vertical axis is denominated in nominal value (dollar) terms rather than in terms of output.

The more formal demonstration follows a now well-trod path. For x^o and x^* find $y(p, x^o)$ and $y(p, x^*)$. Convexity of T ensures that $\lambda y(p, x^o) + (1-\lambda)y(p, x^*) \in Y(\lambda x^o + (1-\lambda)x^*)$ for $\lambda \in (0,1)$. But that requires that

$$R(p, \lambda x^o + (1-\lambda)x^*) \geq p(\lambda y(p, x^o) + (1-\lambda)y(p, x^*)),$$

and the desired conclusion follows immediately from the definition of $y(p, x)$ as revenue maximizing.

NFL and NFC

No free lunch ensures that a positive amount of any output cannot be produced by a zero input bundle. No fixed cost, on the other hand, means that 0 is a feasible output choice for a 0 input. Together, they imply that $R(p, 0) = 0$.

Revenue-Maximizing Supply and Input Use

As a general principle, we expect an increase in the application of inputs to lead producers to increase their outputs. But it is also easy to imagine instances where increasing some inputs will cause certain revenue-maximizing outputs to increase and others to decrease. Let's consider a farmer producing a livestock output and a crop output from a bundle of inputs that consists of land, fertilizer, livestock feed, and labor. If livestock feed increases, one might envision the farmer diverting some labor from crop production to increased feed handling and distribution. The result would be increased livestock production but decreased crop production. Similarly, an increase in fertilizer availability might prompt the farmer to divert labor from livestock to crop-production activities.

If increasing input k is associated with an increase in the revenue-maximizing amount of output m, output m is *normal* or *progressive* in input k. If increasing input k is associated with a decrease in the revenue-maximizing amount of output m, output m is *regressive* in input k. If output m is normal in input k, an increase in input k causes the supply curve for output m to shift to the right, leading to more output supplied for all levels of p_m. If output m is regressive in input k, the same change in x_k causes the supply curve to shift to the left.

7.4 Exercises

Exercise 29. *Figure 7.5 depicts an output set for a technology. As $\frac{p_1}{p_2}$ varies over the interval $0 < \frac{p_1}{p_2} < \infty$, identify the revenue-maximizing supplies for both outputs. Graph the resulting revenue-maximizing supply for output 2 in (y_2, p_2) space.*

Exercise 30. *Develop a geometric illustration of the demonstration that $R(p, x)$ is convex in* p.

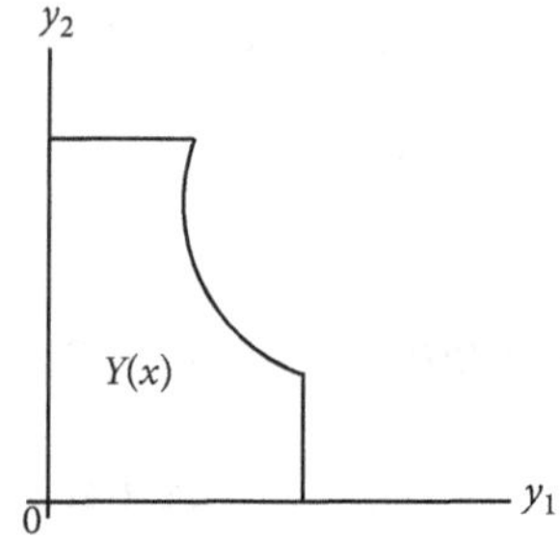

Figure 7.5 Solving the revenue-maximization problem

Exercise 31. *Develop a geometric illustration of a revenue function in (x, \$) space for a canonical technology with two outputs and one input.*

Exercise 32. *Consider a farmer who is producing both corn and wheat using two inputs, fertilizer and land. Also assume that the farmer has a given amount of fertilizer and land and is trying to make as much profit from them as possible. The price of corn is initially \$4/bushel, and the price of wheat is initially \$7/bushel. Explain how the farmer decides how much wheat to produce and how much corn to produce. What happens to the supply of wheat, the supply of corn, and your revenue if the price of wheat falls from \$7 to \$5?*

Exercise 33. * *Consider three output-price vectors, p^1, p^2, and p^3 and their respective revenue-maximizing supplies. By the definitions of the revenue function and revenue-maximizing supplies:*

$$\begin{aligned} p^1 y(p^1, x) &\geq p^1 y(p^2, x) \\ p^2 y(p^2, x) &\geq p^2 y(p^3, x) \\ p^3 y(p^3, x) &\geq p^3 y(p^1, x). \end{aligned}$$

Adding these three expressions together and rearranging gives

$$p^1 \left(y(p^1, x) - y(p^2, x)\right) + p^2 \left(y(p^2, x) - y(p^3, x)\right) + p^3 \left(y(p^3, x) - y(p^1, x)\right) \geq 0.$$

Show that this last expression implies

$$(p^1 - p^3)\left(y(p^1, x) - y(p^3, x)\right) \geq 0,$$

and explain its economic meaning intuitively.

8
The Profit Function

8.1 Introduction

We introduced the profit function, $\pi(p, w)$, in Chapter 5 and discussed it for the single-input, single-output technology. This chapter examines it and its associated profit-maximizing supplies and input demands for general technologies. The analytic principles remain unchanged, and the producer seeks a point where an isoprofit line (hyperplane) supports T from above. Thus, the intuitive arguments and visual illustrations often parallel those used in discussing $c(w, y)$ and $R(p, x)$. That often makes for a terser argument than those adopted in Chapters 5–7.

We start the chapter by discussing some easily overlooked nuances associated with using a maximal value function to characterize producer behavior. Then we turn to an examination of the properties of the profit function defined in terms of the technology, T:

$$\pi(p, w) \equiv \max_{x,y}\{py : (x, y) \in T\},$$

and we close by discussing the two-stage versions of the profit-maximization problem:

$$\pi(p, w) \equiv \max_{x}\{R(p, x) - wx\}$$

and

$$\pi(p, w) \equiv \max_{y}\{py - c(w, y)\}.$$

8.2 Maxima and Behavior

Figure 8.1 depicts T as everything on or below the ray from the origin labeled $0Y$. You should verify that this representation corresponds to a canonical

Lectures on Neoclassical Production Economics. Robert G. Chambers, Oxford University Press.
 DOI: 10.1093/9780197817759.003.0009

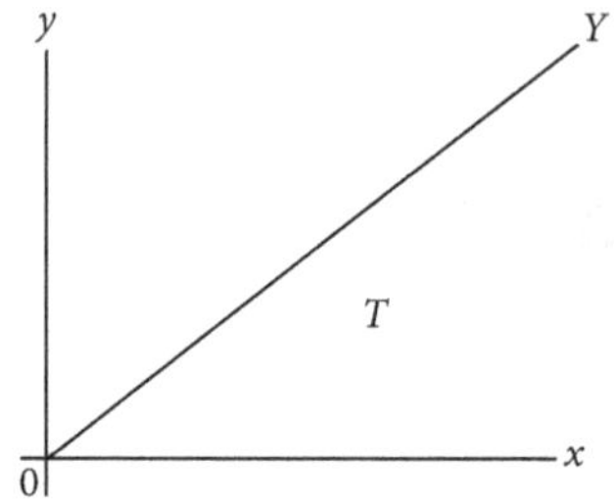

Figure 8.1 Constant Returns Technology

technology. But it's important to note that the linear nature of T's upper bound also ensures that T satisfies:[1]

- **Constant Returns Technology** $(x, y) \in T \Rightarrow (\mu x, \mu y) \quad \mu > 0$.

Suppose that a producer finds a profitable (x, y) bundle. Can the producer produce $2(x, y)$ and double profits, $3(x, y)$ and triple profits, and so on? The answer is yes for a constant-returns T.

Interpreting the profit function and the profit-maximizing solution for a constant-returns technology is subtle.[2] Figure 8.2 superimposes an isoprofit line, $\bar{\mathcal{P}}(\pi, p, w)$, on the technology in Figure 8.1. Any point on $\bar{\mathcal{P}}(\pi, p, w)$ that lies inside T is technically feasible and yields a profit of $\pi > 0$. (Note that the vertical intercept of the isoprofit line is positive.) For example, take the point labeled (x^*, y^*). Because the technology satisfies constant returns, $(\mu x^*, \mu y^*) \in T$, even as μ becomes infinitely large. But if $\pi = py^* - wx^* > 0$, $\mu\pi = p\mu y^* - w\mu x^*$ goes to infinity as μ is made arbitrarily large. Therefore, if $\pi > 0$ is available for a constant-returns technology, so too is an infinite profit and $\pi(p, w) = \infty$.[3]

On the other hand, if input and output prices are such that the isocost line, $\bar{\mathcal{P}}(\pi, p, w)$, is more steeply sloped (not drawn) than $0Y$, maximal profit occurs at the origin (see Exercise 1). In this case, firms do not operate, and profit is zero. Zero profit also occurs, regardless of how much is produced, in the knife-edge case where relative prices define isoprofit lines having the same slope as the boundary of the constant-returns T. Thus, for the constant returns

[1] A constant-returns technology set, T is a special case of a mathematical object called a *cone*. For that reason, some writers refer to constant-returns technologies as being *conical*. By definition, $K \subset \mathbb{R}^J$ is a *cone* if $k \in K \Rightarrow \lambda k \in K$ for all $\lambda > 0$.

[2] See Chapter 12 for further discussion of *economies of size* and *economies of scale*.

[3] Infinity is not a real number, so what this means is that profit has an infinite limit in such cases. In any case, the intuition is apparent. Constant returns allow producers to make unbounded profits.

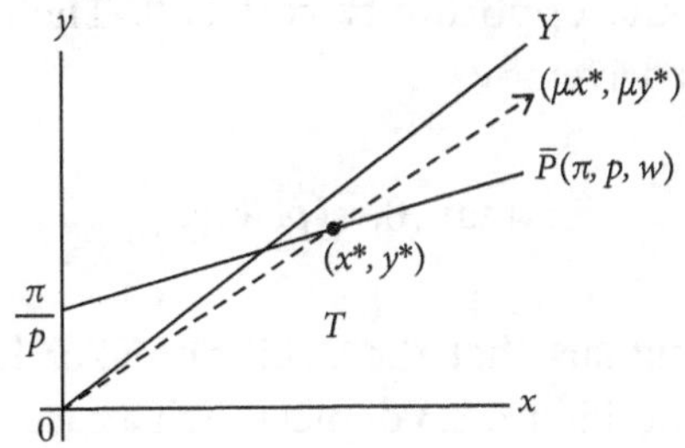

Figure 8.2 Infinite Profit and Constant Returns

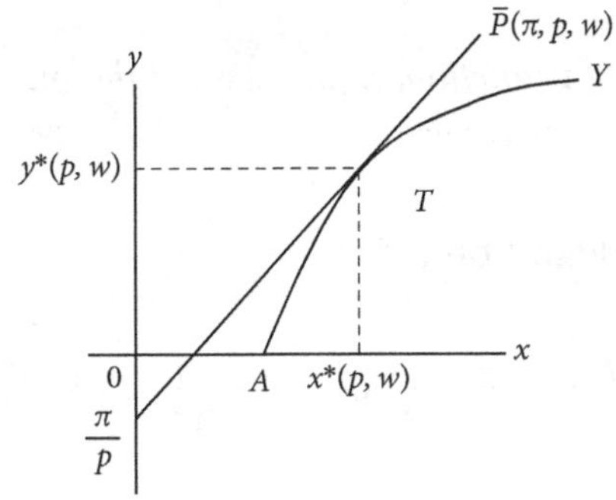

Figure 8.3 Should the Producer Produce?

technology, $\pi(p, w)$ always assumes one of two bounding values either 0 or ∞.[4]

In Figure 8.3, the technology set is depicted as everything on or below the curve *AY*. This *T* violates no fixed cost, *NFC*. Nevertheless, profit is maximized where an isoprofit line, $\bar{P}(\pi, p, w)$, supports *T* from above. As drawn, however, $\frac{\pi}{p} < 0$, maximal profit is negative for the relative price that defines the slope of $\bar{P}(\pi, p, w)$.

Is it plausible to believe that a producer would tolerate a negative profit? We introduced the technology, *T*, as a constraint on *production choices*. But we have not discussed *what causes a decisionmaker to be a producer*. Is the decisionmaker free to pursue alternative employment? In a free-market setting, the answer is presumably yes. And decisionmakers are free to choose between acting as producers and earning $\pi(p, w)$ or pursuing alternative employment. Economists call the *best-possible remuneration from alternative employment* the decisionmaker's *opportunity cost* of being a producer. To keep things

[4] Why market prices should fall in any of these regions is the "stuff" of competitive market analysis and lies beyond the scope of our discussion.

simple, suppose that the opportunity cost is 0. Then the decisionmaker's employment choice is driven by

$$\max\{0, \pi(p, w)\},$$

where $0 > \pi(p, w)$ signals that the decisionmaker is better off pursuing alternative employment. Figure 8.3 depicts such a case.

8.3 Properties of the Profit Function

Definition 21. *The profit function, $\pi(p, w)$, gives the maximal feasible profit at output prices p and input prices w.*

The mathematical definition is:[5]

$$\pi(p, w) \equiv \max_{x,y}\{py - wx : (x, y) \in T\}.$$

We state $\pi(p, w)$'s properties and then discuss them.

Properties of the Profit Function

- $p' \geq p \Rightarrow \pi(p', w) \geq \pi(p, w)$ and $w' \geq w \Rightarrow \pi(p, w') \leq \pi(p, w)$ (nondecreasing in p and nonincreasing in w)
- $\pi(\mu p, \mu w) = \mu\pi(p, w) \quad \mu > 0$ (positively homogeneous)
- $\pi(\lambda p^o + (1-\lambda)p^*, \lambda w^o + (1-\lambda)w^*) \leq \lambda\pi(p^o, w^o) + (1-\lambda)\pi(p^*, w^*)$ $\lambda \in (0, 1)$ (convex)

Nondecreasing in p and Nonincreasing in w

Let (x^*, y^*) be profit maximizing for (p, w). By responding to a price rise of p to p' by "doing nothing," the producer realizes a profit of

$$p'y^* - wx^* \geq py^* - wx^* = \pi(p, w).$$

The producer's "best response" to the price change necessarily dominates the "do-nothing response." Hence, $\pi(p', w) \geq \pi(p, w)$ for $p' \geq p$. By responding to

[5] The math literature refers to $\pi(p, w)$ as a *support function* for the set T in terms of $(p, -w)$.

an input price decrease from w' to w by "doing nothing," the producer realizes a profit of

$$py^* - wx^* \geq py^* - w'x^* = \pi(p, w').$$

The producer's "best response" necessarily dominates the "do-nothing" response, whence $\pi(p, w') \leq \pi(p, w)$ for $w' \geq w$.

When graphed in the (p, π) plane, $\pi(p, w)$ has a nonnegative slope, and when graphed in the (w, π) plane it has a nonpositive slope.

Positively Homogeneous in Prices

The underlying principle is that "only real prices matter." Visually, the principle is captured by remembering that nominal price changes do not affect an isoprofit line's slope, $\bar{P}(\pi, p, w)$. (See Chapter 5, Figure 5.3.) Hence, where an isoprofit line (hyperplane) supports T is not affected by nominal price changes.

The formal demonstration follows the same line of argument used in discussing $c(w, y)$ and $R(p, x)$:

$$\begin{aligned} \pi(\mu p, \mu w) &= \max_{x,y}\{\mu py - \mu wx : (x, y) \in T\} \\ &= \max_{x,y}\{\mu(py - wx) : (x, y) \in T\} \\ &= \mu \max_{x,y}\{py - wx : (x, y) \in T\} \\ &= \mu\pi(p, w) \quad \mu > 0. \end{aligned}$$

Convex in Prices

Let (x^*, y^*) be profit maximizing for (p, w). If prices change to (p^o, w^o), the "do-nothing" profit change is

$$(p^o - p)y^* - (w^o - w)x^*,$$

which defines a linear function of the price changes $(p^o - p)$ and $(w^o - w)$. By definition, the producer's best response must at least weakly dominate this "do-nothing" response. Thus, the best-response profit change must be better for the producer than the do-nothing response.

Figure 8.4 depicts a "better than linear" response for an input-price increase. (Exercise 35 asks you to develop the analogous figures for an output price change.) If the input price rises to w^o from w, and the producer stays at (x^*, y^*), profit falls as costs increase from wx^* to $w^o x^*$.

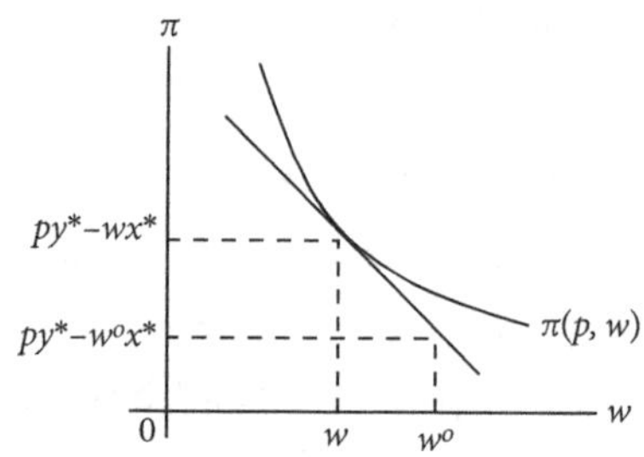

Figure 8.4 Profit Function Convex in Prices

This is illustrated in the negatively sloped line segment connecting $(w, py^* - wx^*)$ and $(w^o, py^* - w^o x^*)$. (The slope of the line segment is $-x^*$.) The producer's best response must at least weakly dominate the "do-nothing" response, suggesting that $\pi(p, w)$ falls less than $(w^o - w)\,x^*$.

The formal demonstration that $\pi(p, w)$ is convex in prices also follows a familiar path. We need to compare $\pi(p^o, w^o)$, $\pi(p^*, w^*)$, and $\pi(\lambda p^o + (1-\lambda)\,p^*, \lambda w^o + (1-\lambda)\,w^*)$. Let $(\hat{x}, \hat{y}) \in T$ solve the profit-maximization problem for $\lambda p^o + (1-\lambda)\,p^*$ and $\lambda w^o + (1-\lambda)\,w^*$, so that

$$\pi(\lambda p^o + (1-\lambda)\,p^*, \lambda w^o + (1-\lambda)\,w^*) = (\lambda p^o + (1-\lambda)\,p^*)\,\hat{y} - (\lambda w^o + (1-\lambda)\,w^*)\,\hat{x}. \tag{8.1}$$

The definition of $\pi(p, w)$ ensures that

$$\begin{aligned} p^o\hat{y} - w^o\hat{x} &\leq \pi(p^o, w^o) \\ p^*\hat{y} - w^*\hat{x} &\leq \pi(p^*, w^*). \end{aligned}$$

That is, the profit from producing $(\hat{x}, \hat{y})$ when prices are (p^o, w^o) and (p^*, w^*), respectively, cannot exceed maximal profit at those prices. Multiplying the first inequality by $\lambda > 0$, the second inequality by $1 - \lambda > 0$, and adding gives

$$(\lambda p^o + (1-\lambda)\,p^*)\,\hat{y} - (\lambda w^o + (1-\lambda)\,w^*)\,\hat{x} \leq \lambda\pi(p^o, w^o) + (1-\lambda)\,\pi(p^*, w^*).$$

We can now rely on expression (8.1) to replace the left-hand side of this expression to get

$$\pi(\lambda p^o + (1-\lambda)\,p^*, \lambda w^o + (1-\lambda)\,w^*) \leq \lambda\pi(p^o, w^o) + (1-\lambda)\,\pi(p^*, w^*) \quad \lambda \in (0, 1),$$

which establishes the desired convexity property.

8.4 Profit-Maximizing Output Supply and Input Demand

We now study the role that the properties of $\pi(p, w)$ play in determining optimal producer behavior. Our starting point is a verbal definition of profit-maximizing input demands and output supply.

Definition 22. *Any solution, $(x^*(p, w), y^*(p, w))$, to the profit-maximization problem is a profit-maximizing input demand and output supply bundle.*

In mathematical terms,

$$(x^*(p, w), y^*(p, w)) \in \underset{x,y}{\operatorname{argmax}} \{py - wx : (x, y) \in T\}.$$

Here $\operatorname{argmax}_{x,y} \{\cdot\}$ selects the input and output bundles that give the maximal value in the set $\{\cdot\}$.[6] In Chapters 6 and 7, we learned that optimal solutions to the cost-minimization and revenue-maximization problems are normals for hyperplanes tangent to the graphs of $c(w, y)$ and $R(p, x)$, respectively. A bit more informally, cost-minimizing demands are given by the slopes of $c(w, y)$ in w and revenue-maximizing supplies by the slopes of $R(p, x)$ in p. Figure 8.4, which shows that a line segment with slope $-x^*(p, w)$ supports the graph of $\pi(p, w)$ from below in (w, π) space, suggests that a similar phenomenon applies to the profit function, $\pi(p, w)$. (Exercise 36 asks you to develop and illustrate the analogous property in the output price.) The general result is:[7]

Hotelling's Lemma *For all p^* and w^*, $(-x^*(p^*, w^*), y^*(p^*, w^*))$ is the normal for a hyperplane tangent to the graph of $\pi(p, w)$ at $(w^*, p^*, \pi(p^*, w^*))$.*

We establish Hotelling's Lemma using arguments that parallel those used for Shephard's Lemma and McFadden's Lemma. Because $(x^*(p^*, w^*), y^*(p^*, w^*)) \in T$, the definition of $\pi(p, w)$ requires that

$$py^*(p^*, w^*) - wx^*(p^*, w^*) \leq \pi(p, w)$$

for all (p, w) and (p^*, w^*), and

[6] We intentionally say bundles rather than bundle here because in appropriate circumstances, more than one input–output configuration can achieve the same maximal profit for given (p, w).

[7] Hotelling's Lemma is often phrased in terms of gradients of the profit function. As with Shephard's Lemma, the gradient version requires imposing further structure upon T. Our statement applies for the general case.

$$p^* y^* (p^*, w^*) - w^* x^* (p^*, w^*) = \pi (p^*, w^*).$$

That is, maximal profit for (p, w) is always greater than or equal to profit available from $(x^* (p^*, w^*), y^* (p^*, w^*))$ at (p, w) and equal to it when $(p, w) = (p^*, w^*)$. Subtracting the equality from the inequality gives

$$(p - p^*) y^* (p^*, w^*) - (w - w^*) x^* (p^*, w^*) \leq \pi (p, w) - \pi (p^*, w^*), \qquad (8.2)$$

for all (p, w) as a condition that must hold at the profit-maximizing solution.[8] Expression (8.2) reiterates that doing nothing is dominated profit-wise by the optimal response. Its geometric manifestation is that a hyperplane with normal $(-x^* (p^*, w^*), y^* (p^*, w^*))$ must support the graph of $\pi (p, w)$ from below at $(w^*, p^*, \pi (p^*, w^*))$.

"Only real prices matter" in determining cost-minimizing demands and revenue-maximizing supplies. A parallel result applies for profit-maximizing input demands and output supplies. To show this property, we use the positive homogeneity property of the profit function. Multiplying both sides of expression (8.2) by $\mu > 0$ gives

$$(\mu p - \mu p^*) y^* (p^*, w^*) - (\mu w - \mu w^*) x^* (p^*, w^*) \leq \mu (\pi (p, w) - \pi (p^*, w^*)).$$

By invoking positive homogeneity of $\pi (p, w)$, we can rewrite the right-hand side of this expression as $\pi (\mu p, \mu w) - \pi (\mu p^*, \mu w^*)$. Making that substitution, we conclude that

$$(\mu p - \mu p^*) y^* (p^*, w^*) - (\mu w - \mu w^*) x^* (p^*, w^*) \leq \pi (\mu p, \mu w) - \pi (\mu p^*, \mu w^*)$$

for all (p, w, p^*, w^*) and $\mu > 0$. So, if (8.2) is satisfied by $(x^* (p^*, w^*), y^* (p^*, w^*))$, it will remain satisfied for all nominal changes of (p, w) and (p^*, w^*). "Only real prices matter" to profit maximizers and

- $(x^* (\mu p, \mu w), y^* (\mu p, \mu w)) = (x^* (p, w), y^* (p, w))$ for $\mu > 0$,

optimal supply and input demand bundles are *homogeneous of degree zero* in (p, w).

Having concluded that nominal price changes do not cause profit-maximizing producers to adjust their inputs and outputs, it's natural to wonder how they respond to real or relative price changes. Shephard's Lemma,

[8] An input–output bundle, $(-x^* (p^*, w^*), y^* (p^*, w^*))$, satisfying expression (8.2) is called a *subgradient* for the profit function at (w^*, p^*).

when coupled with concavity of $c(w,y)$ in w, taught us that cost-minimizing producers respond to an increase in the price of an input by decreasing use of that input. McFadden's Lemma and convexity of $R(p,x)$ in p taught us that revenue-maximizing producers react to an increase in p_m by increasing their supply of y_m. You are asked in Exercise 37 to draw similar lessons from the convexity of $\pi(p,w)$ and Hotelling's Lemma, while we restrict ourselves to an analysis that only requires a "do-nothing" argument, addition, and a tiny bit of algebra.

Because profit-maximizing input and output bundles belong to T,

$$\begin{aligned} p^o y^*(p^o,w^o) - w^o x^*(p^o,w^o) &\geq p^o y^*(\hat{p},\hat{w}) - w^o x^*(\hat{p},\hat{w}), \text{ and} \\ \hat{p} y^*(\hat{p},\hat{w}) - \hat{p} x^*(\hat{p},\hat{w}) &\geq \hat{p} y^*(p^o,w^o) - \hat{w} x^*(p^o,w^o), \end{aligned}$$

for all (p^o,w^o) and $(\hat{p},\hat{w})$. The left-hand side of these expressions is, by definition, maximal profit for, respectively, (p^o,w^o) and $(\hat{p},\hat{w})$. The right-hand side is profit realized from producing the profit-maximizing bundle for prices $(\hat{p},\hat{w})$ and (p^o,w^o), respectively, when (p^o,w^o) and $(\hat{p},\hat{w})$ prevail. Adding the inequalities and collecting terms gives:

$$\left(p^o - \hat{p}\right)\left(y^*(p^o,w^o) - y^*(\hat{p},\hat{w})\right) - \left(w^o - \hat{w}\right)\left(x^*(p^o,w^o) - x^*(\hat{p},\hat{w})\right) \geq 0. \tag{8.3}$$

Expression (8.3) generalizes results obtained for cost-minimizing demands and revenue-maximizing supplies.[9] If $\hat{p} = p^o$ expression (8.3) implies

$$\left(w^o - \hat{w}\right)\left(x^*(p^o,w^o) - x^*(p^o,\hat{w})\right) \leq 0.$$

Profit-maximizing input demands tend to vary inversely with input price changes. Allowing only one input price, say for input k, to change gives

$$\left(w_k^o - \hat{w}_k\right)\left(x_k^*(p^o,w^o) - x_k^*(p^o,\hat{w})\right) \leq 0.$$

Profit-maximizing input demands are nonincreasing functions of their own input prices. Input demand functions, when portrayed in the (x_k, w_k) plane,

[9] Following an argument established in footnote 5 of Lecture 6 and continued in footnote 5 of Lecture 7, we can show that (8.3) is a special case of the more general *cyclical monotonicity* result for profit-maximizing supplies and input demands:

$$\begin{aligned} p^1\left(y^*(p^1,w^1) - y^*(p^2,w^2)\right) \quad &+ \ldots + \quad p^K\left(y^*(p^K,w^K) - y^*(p^1,w^1)\right) \\ -w^1\left(x^*(p^1,w^1) - x^*(p^2,w^2)\right) \quad &- \ldots - \quad w^K\left(x^*(p^K,w^K) - x^*(p^1,w^1)\right) \geq 0, \end{aligned}$$

which together with zero homogeneity exhaustively characterizes profit-maximizing supply and input demand behavior.

have a nonpositive slope. There are no "Giffen" profit-maximizing input demands.

Exactly parallel arguments holding input prices constant establish that

$$(p^o - \hat{p})\left(y^*(p^o, w^o) - y^*(\hat{p}, w^o)\right) \geq 0,$$

and

$$(p_m^o - \hat{p}_m)\left(y_m^*(p^o, w^o) - y_m^*(\hat{p}, w^o)\right) \geq 0.$$

Profit-maximizing supply curves are nondecreasing functions of their own output prices; supply curves are upward sloping.

8.5 Two-stage Profit Maximization

Many introductory treatments of profit-maximizing behavior limit themselves to the single-output case and postulate the existence of a production function and a cost function. For the production function, $f(x)$, the profit-maximization problem is posed as maximizing the difference between the nonlinear function of inputs, $pf(x)$, and the linear function, wx. For the cost function, $c(w, y)$, the equivalent problem is to maximize the difference between the linear function of outputs, py, and the nonlinear cost function, $c(w, y)$. These different phrasings of the producer's problem are special cases of the different versions of the two-stage formulation of the profit-maximization problem developed in Chapter 5, to which we now turn.

First, we clarify terminology. A function, $g(x)$, is *linear* in x if

$$g(x) = \sum_{n=1}^{N} a_n x_n,$$

where $(a_1, a_2, \ldots, a_N)$ are constants. A function, $g(x)$, is *affine* in x if

$$g(x) = c + \sum_{n=1}^{N} a_n x_n, \tag{8.4}$$

where c and $(a_1, a_2, \ldots, a_N)$ are constants. Setting $c = 0$ shows that a linear function is a special case of an affine function. When depicted in the (x, y) plane, both a linear function and an affine function have graphs that are straight lines. The graphs of linear functions go through the origin; affine functions can have (positive or negative) intercepts on the vertical axis.

8.5.1 The Profit Function from the Revenue Function

The profit-maximization problem framed as

$$\pi(p, w) \equiv \max_{x} \{R(p, x) - wx\},$$

is illustrated in Figure 8.5. There the line wx depicts input cost as a linear function of x with a slope of $w > 0$, and $R(p, x)$ depicts maximal revenue as a function of x.[10] Both are denominated in money units, and profit for each input level is the vertical difference between the revenue curve and the cost line. The problem is to find where that vertical distance is the largest.

We can view the problem from a different perspective by performing the indicated subtraction for each x and then graphing the result in $(x, \$)$ space. Figure 8.6 illustrates. The optimal input demand is at $x^*(p, w)$ that is at the top of the hill-shaped figure. Figures 8.5 and 8.6 illustrate a "nice" case where the optimal solution is easily found. But regardless of how "nice" the case is, the principle is the same. One seeks a point where either increasing or decreasing input use reduces profit.

To show how we solve this problem, we note that $x^*(p, w)$ must satisfy

$$R(p, x^*(p, w)) - wx^*(p, w) \geq R(p, x) - wx$$

for all x. In words, if $x^*(p, w)$ is profit maximizing, it must generate more profit than any other x. This simply repeats the definition of profit maximizing. Adding wx to both sides of this inequality gives

$$R(p, x^*(p, w)) + w(x - x^*(p, w)) \geq R(p, x) \tag{8.5}$$

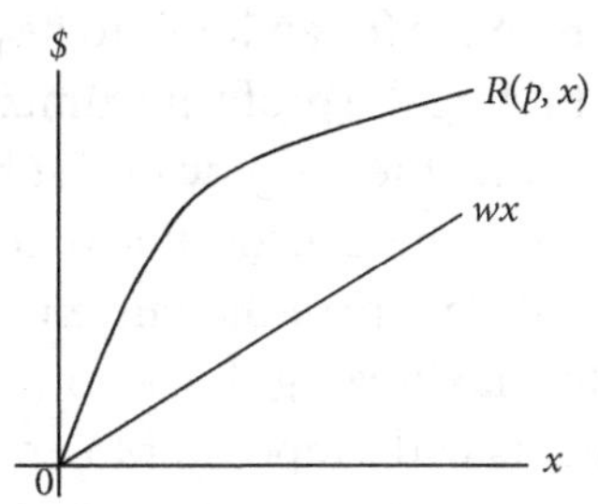

Figure 8.5 Profit and Revenue

[10] We depict $R(p, x)$ for a canonical technology. That is done for visual familiarity; it is not essential to the argument.

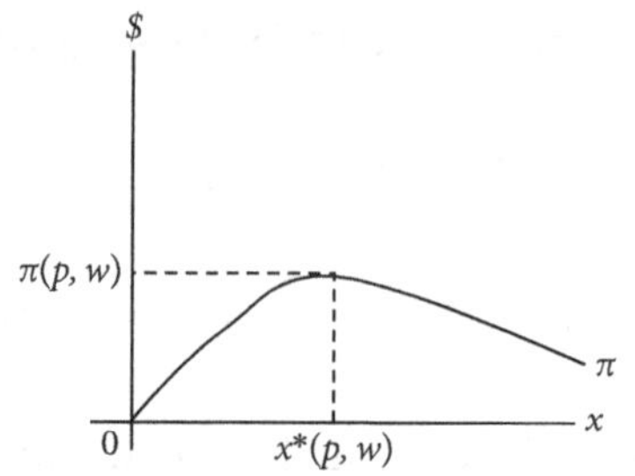

Figure 8.6 Profit as a Function of Input

for all x as the condition that the profit-maximizing choice of $x^*(p, w)$ must satisfy.

Expression (8.5) says that the *affine function* of x,

$$R(p, x^*(p, w)) + w(x - x^*(p, w)) = R(p, x^*(p, w)) - wx^*(p, w) + wx \quad (8.6)$$

is always greater than or equal to $R(p, x)$. (Here the analogue of c in expression (8.4) is $R(p, x^*(p, w)) - wx^*(p, w) \equiv \pi(p, w)$ that does not depend upon x.) Because the graph of an affine function in $(x, \$)$ space is a line (hyperplane), expression (8.5) requires that line (hyperplane) to be an upper bound for the graph of $R(p, x)$ for all x. That means that the graph of $R(p, x)$ must be contained in the half space below the line (hyperplane). By construction, however, the affine function and $R(p, x)$ share a common value at $x = x^*(p, w)$. Together these facts imply that the affine function must be *tangent to the graph of* $R(p, x)$ *from above at* $x^*(p, w)$.[11] Because the slope (normal) of the affine function is given by w, the tangency condition translates into economic terms as requiring that *the marginal revenue from x be equated to w* (see Figure 8.7).

Equating the marginal revenue for an input to its price is the standard economic rule-of-thumb for finding the profit-maximizing x. But it's only part of the story. The other part is that the tangency must be *from above* so that the graph of $R(p, x)$ must lie everywhere below that of the affine function in (8.6). Figure 8.8 illustrates a situation where the tangency condition is satisfied at three points. One is profit maximizing, but two (labeled A and B) are not. (See the dashed line segments with slope w.) Moreover, it's clear from inspection that there are input levels to the right and left of the input associated with

[11] If we rewrite (8.5) as

$$w(x - x^*(p, w)) \geq R(p, x) - R(p, x^*(p, w)),$$

and compare it to expression (1) in Chapter 6 (see also the associated footnote), we can recognize this condition as requiring that w be a *supergradient* for $R(p, x)$ at $x^*(p, w)$.

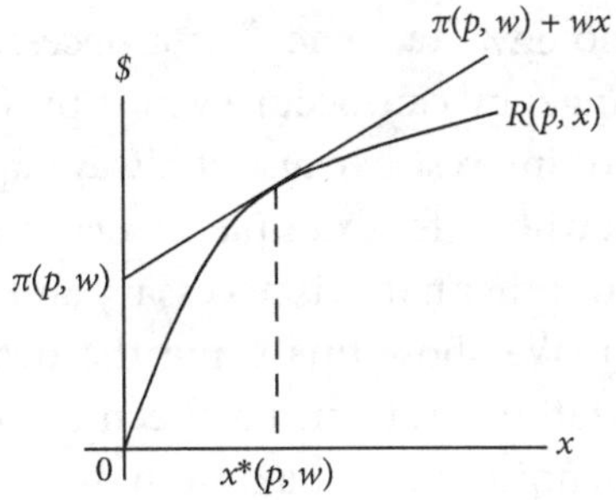

Figure 8.7 Profit-Maximizing Input Demand

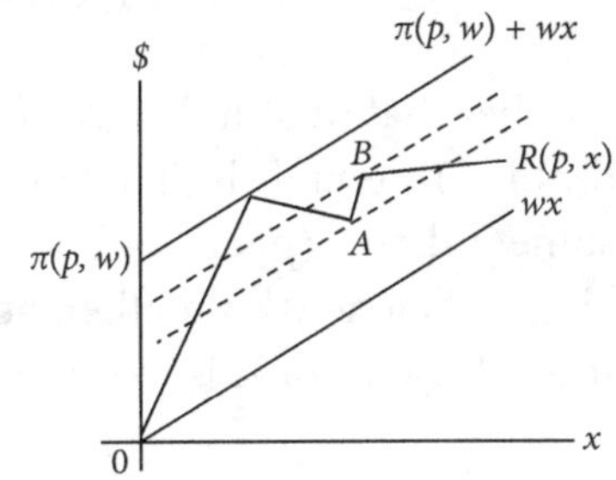

Figure 8.8 Tangency But Not Profit Maximizing

A that involve a higher profit than a producer would receive by operating at *A*. For small enough changes, the same is not true for *B*.

Point *A* is an example of what is referred to as a *local minimum* for the difference between revenue and cost. *It's what we're trying to avoid. Nevertheless, it satisfies the tangency condition. B* is an example of a *local maximum*. It's better than points close to it, but it's not the best. And the best is what we're looking for. Condition (8.5) characterizes it. Equating marginal revenue to *w* does not.[12]

Mathematicians use the concepts of "necessary" conditions and "sufficient" conditions in these types of discussions. Statement B is called a "necessary" condition for statement A to be true if it can be phrased as follows: If statement A holds, then B must be true. Thus, B being a necessary condition for A does not exclude it from holding when A is not true. Instead it only ensures that it must hold when A is true. Statement B is called a "sufficient" condition for A to hold if it can be phrased as follows: If statement B holds, then A must be true. In other words, B guarantees that A holds.

[12] For those with a calculus background, if you smoothed out the kinks, all three satisfy the first-order condition for a maximum. B also satisfies the second-order condition but remains nonoptimal.

So using this terminology, "tangency" is a necessary, but not sufficient, condition because a tangency can occur even if profit is not maximized. A tangency condition is of interest because it always applies at solutions. But because it can apply elsewhere (for example, at local minima), it's not enough.

Condition (8.5), on the other hand, is necessary and sufficient for the profit-maximization problem. We show this using the definitions. First, assume that the profit-maximization problem has been solved; we have identified $x^*(p,w)$. Then by the definition of a maximum

$$\begin{aligned} R(p, x^*(p,w)) - wx^*(p,w) &= \max_x \{R(p,x) - wx\} \\ &\geq R(p,x) - wx \end{aligned}$$

for all x. This, however, implies that (8.5) holds, verifying that it is necessary for $x^*(p,w)$ to be a maximum. To establish that condition (8.5) is sufficient, assume that it holds for some $\hat{x}$, then $R(p,\hat{x}) - w\hat{x} = \pi(p,w)$ by the definition of a maximum, establishing sufficiency.[13] A mathematical shorthand for saying that B is necessary and sufficient for A is to say that A occurs *if and only if* B is true, or $A \Leftrightarrow B$.

The solution to this version of the profit-maximization problem is the same as the solution to the profit-maximization problem posed in terms of T. But in this version, we only solve for $x^*(p,w)$. Optimal revenue is obtained by evaluating the revenue function at $x^*(p,w)$, $R(p, x^*(p,w))$. The profit-maximizing supplies, $y^*(p,w)$, therefore, equal the revenue-maximizing supplies derived in Chapter 7, $y(p,x)$, evaluated at $x = x^*(p,w)$. That is:

$$y^*(p,w) = y(p, x^*(p,w)). \tag{8.7}$$

Expression (8.7) opens the door to a deeper analysis of the supply response. To illustrate, we examine how supply responds to prices changing from (p^o, w^o) to (p', w'). By (8.7)

$$y^*(p',w') - y^*(p^o,w^o) = y(p', x^*(p',w')) - y(p^o, x^*(p^o,w^o)).$$

Now add zero in the form of $y(p', x^*(p^o,w^o)) - y(p', x^*(p^o,w^o))$ to get

$$\begin{aligned} y^*(p',w') - y^*(p^o,w^o) &= y(p', x^*(p^o,w^o)) - y(p^o, x^*(p^o,w^o)) \\ &+ y(p', x^*(p',w')) - y(p', x^*(p^o,w^o)) \end{aligned}$$

[13] As a technical matter, we must verify that a maximum actually exists, but this can always be ensured by making an appropriate assumption.

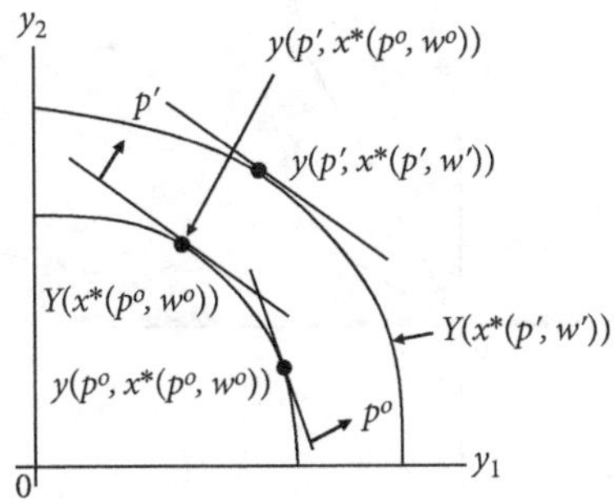

Figure 8.9 Output Substitution and Expansion

Supply adjustments to changing prices break into two components. One, $y(p', x^*(p^o, w^o)) - y(p^o, x^*(p^o, w^o))$, measures how the revenue-maximizing supply adjusts to changing output prices from p^o to p' holding input use at $x^*(p^o, w^o)$, the original profit-maximizing input demand. It is called the *substitution effect*. This is illustrated in Figure 8.9. (Exercise 41 asks you to analyze an alternative way of decomposing this adjustment.)

The second component, $y(p', x^*(p', w')) - y(p', x^*(p^o, w^o))$, measures the supply adjustment caused by the profit-maximizing change in input demand. The movement from $y(p', x^*(p^o, w^o))$ on $\bar{Y}(x^*(p^o, w^o))$ to $y(p', x^*(p', w'))$ on $\bar{Y}(x^*(p', w'))$ illustrates. It is called the *expansion effect* because it describes movement across output sets,

The ability to decompose supply adjustments into separate components enhances our ability to parse the causes of observed economic responses. For example, the substitution effect measures the revenue-maximizing supply response to output price changes. Its behavior is characterized by $R(p, x)$'s properties in p. Economists can predict that behavior. The expansion effect depends on $Y(x)$ and on how it adjusts to changes in x. Thus, it is less predictable. The transformation curves in Figure 8.9 are drawn for a canonical technology, but real-world technologies may not be so orderly.

8.5.2 The Profit Function from the Cost Function

This version of the profit-maximization problem is stated as

$$\pi(p, w) \equiv \max_y \{py - c(w, y)\}.$$

Figure 8.10 illustrates the problem as finding the output that gives the largest vertical difference between the ray py with slope p, which depicts revenue,

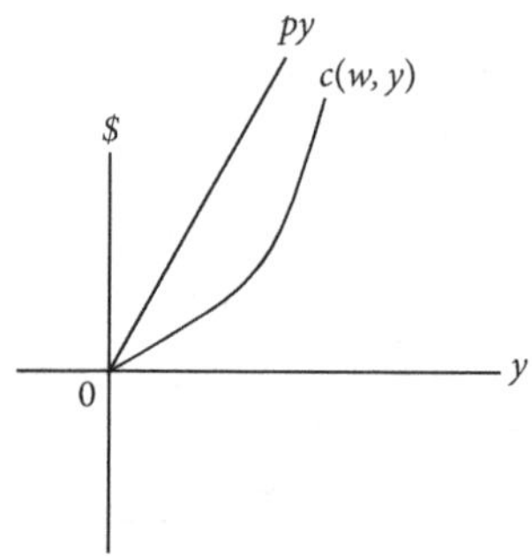

Figure 8.10 Profit Function from Cost Function

and the graph of the cost function, $c(w, y)$.[14] If one does the subtraction in $\{\cdot\}$ and graphs the result in the $(y, \$)$ plane, the result (not drawn) mirrors Figure 8.6. The difference is that the horizontal axis now measures y and not x.

Because $y^*(p, w)$ is profit maximizing for (p, w), it satisfies

$$py^*(p, w) - c(w, y^*(p, w)) \geq py - c(w, y),$$

for all y. Adding $c(w, y)$ to and subtracting $py^*(p, w) - c(w, y^*(p, w))$ from both sides gives

$$c(w, y) \geq py - [py^*(p, w) - c(w, y^*(p, w))] \tag{8.8}$$

for all y as the necessary and sufficient condition for profit maximization.

The minimal cost of producing the output, y, must be greater than or equal to the affine function of y,

$$py - [py^*(p, w) - c(w, y^*(p, w))], \tag{8.9}$$

for all y and equal it at $y = y^*(p, w)$. Here the constant of the affine function is

$$-[py^*(p, w) - c(w, y^*(p, w))] = -\pi(p, w).$$

Thus, the graph of the cost function in the $(y, \$)$ space must be contained in the half space above the graph of this affine function, and the two must touch at the profit-maximizing y, $y^*(p, w)$.[15] Figure 8.11 illustrates the tangency for a canonical technology.

[14] The cost function in Figure 8.10 is drawn for a canonical technology. This is not essential to the analysis.

[15] Alternatively, p must be a subgradient of $c(w, y)$ at $(y^*(p, w), c(w, y^*(p, w)))$.

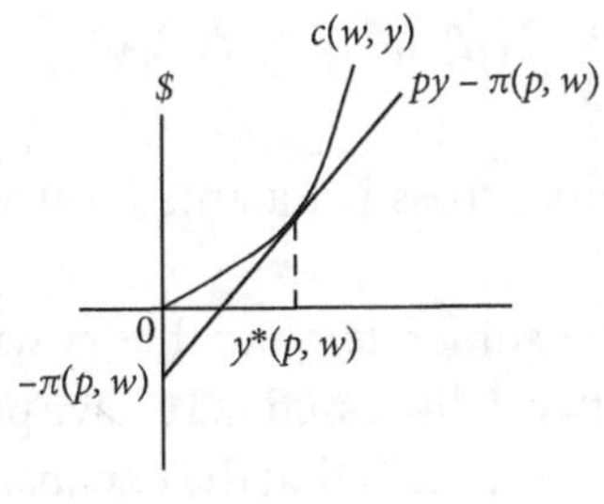

Figure 8.11 Profit-Maximizing Supply

The slope of the cost function is *marginal cost*, and the slope (normal) of the affine function in (8.9) is p. Thus, we have the familiar economic rule-of-thumb: *Profit-maximizing supply is determined by the producer equating price to marginal cost.* While that principle is true, more is required. This tangency must be from below, and the graph of $c(w, y)$ must lie everywhere above the affine function (8.9). (Exercise 40 asks you to illustrate a cost structure for which equating price to marginal cost does not ensure a profit-maximizing output choice.)

Because producers choose their profit-maximizing inputs to minimize the cost of producing their profit-maximizing output supplies:

$$x^*(p, w) = x(w, y^*(p, w)),$$

profit-maximizing input demands equal cost-minimizing demands evaluated at the profit-maximizing supply. Therefore,

$$x^*(p^o, w^o) - x^*(p, w) = x(w^o, y^*(p^o, w^o)) - x(w, y^*(p, w)).$$

Adding zero in the form of $x(w^o, y^*(p, w)) - x(w^o, y^*(p, w))$ gives

$$\begin{aligned} x^*(p^o, w^o) - x^*(p, w) &= x(w^o, y^*(p, w)) - x(w, y^*(p, w)) \\ &+ x(w^o, y^*(p^o, w^o)) - x(w^o, y^*(p, w)). \end{aligned}$$

Adjustments in input demand, therefore, break into two components. The first, the *substitution effect*,

$$x(w^o, y^*(p, w)) - x(w, y^*(p, w)),$$

captures movement along the isoquant for $y^*(p, w)$ made by a cost-minimizing producer in response to input prices changing from w to w^o. The second component, the *expansion effect*,

$$x(w^o, y^*(p^o, w^o)) - x(w^o, y^*(p, w)),$$

captures input adjustments across isoquants induced by supply responding to (p, w) change.

Readers familiar with consumer demand theory will recognize that the substitution and expansion effects discussed here have parallels in its substitution and income effects. One difference is that the expansion effect can never result in a profit-maximizing input demand curve sloping upward. There are no Giffen inputs.

8.6 Exercises

Exercise 34. *For the single-input, single-output case, the slope of an isoprofit line is determined by the input–output price ratio,* $\frac{w}{p}$. *For the single-input, single-output case with constant returns (as in Figure 8.1), draw a family of isoprofit lines for which maximal profit is zero.*

Exercise 35. *Figure 8.4 depicts the "do-nothing" and best-response case for a profit-maximizing producer facing an input-price change. Develop the analogous figure and discussion for an output-price change.*

Exercise 36. *Figure 8.4 illustrates Hotelling's Lemma for input prices. Develop the analogous representation in the output-price space.*

Exercise 37. *Using Hotelling's Lemma, construct a geometric explanation of why convexity of* $\pi(p, w)$ *implies that optimal supplies are upward sloping in their own prices and why input demands are downward sloping in their own prices.*

Exercise 38. *For the revenue function depicted in Figure 8.8, derive the profit-maximizing input demand as* w *varies over* $0 < w < \infty$. *Illustrate it in* (x, w) *space.*

Exercise 39. *Illustrate and explain the following decomposition of output response to a price change:*

$$\begin{aligned} y^*(p', w') - y^*(p^o, w^o) &= y(p^o, x^*(p', w')) - y(p^o, x^*(p^o, w^o)) \\ &+ y(p', x^*(p', w')) - y(p^o, x^*(p', w')) \end{aligned}$$

Exercise 40. *Illustrate a situation where equating price to marginal cost does not ensure a profit-maximizing output choice.*

Exercise 41. *Illustrate and explain the following decomposition of the input response to an input price change:*

$$\begin{aligned} x^*(p^o, w^o) - x^*(p, w) &= x\left(w, y^*(p^o, w^o)\right) - x\left(w, y^*(p, w)\right) \\ &+ x\left(w^o, y^*(p^o, w^o)\right) - x\left(w, y^*(p^o, w^o)\right). \end{aligned}$$

9
Duality

9.1 Introduction

We learned in Chapter 8 that the only technical restriction required to develop the properties of the profit function, $\pi(p, w)$, is that T be nonempty. Despite that, economists routinely model the technology as taking the canonical form. The reason is that *the existence of a positively homogeneous and convex profit function, $\pi(p, w)$, implies that a "dual technology," $\bar{T}$, that satisfies nonemptiness, free disposability of inputs, free disposability of outputs, and convexity must exist. Moreover,*

$$\pi(p, w) = \max_{x,y} \{py - wx : (x, y) \in \bar{T}\}.$$

If the decisionmaker's opportunity cost is zero and prices, (p, w), exist for which maximal profit is zero, $\bar{T}$ is a canonical technology.

Economists refer to this result as *the profit function, $\pi(p, w)$, being "dual" to a canonical technology, $\bar{T}$.* The result's origin is that expressions defined by multiplying prices times quantities define two distinct linear forms. For example, when we write[1]

$$\pi = \sum_{m=1}^{M} p_m y_m - \sum_{n=1}^{N} w_n x_n$$

profit, π, is the dependent variable, but both of the following statements are true:

- A: Profit is a linear function of the independent variables, *quantities* (y, x), with normal given by *prices* $(p, -w)$.
- B: Profit is a linear function of the independent variables, *prices* $(p, w,)$, with normal given by *quantities* $(y, -x)$.

[1] The expression $\sum_{m=1}^{M} p_m y_m - \sum_{n=1}^{N} w_n x_n$ is an example of what mathematicians also call a *bilinear* form.

Lectures on Neoclassical Production Economics. Robert G. Chambers, Oxford University Press.
 DOI: 10.1093/9780197817759.003.0010

Statement B is formed from statement A by switching the roles of quantities and prices in statement A. It is said to be *dual to A*. By the same token, A is *dual* to B. So profit can be interpreted either as a *linear function of quantities* with prices providing the relevant slopes or as a *linear function of prices* with quantities providing the relevant slopes. What's true for profit is also true for cost and revenue. Each is *bilinear* in the sense that it can be interpreted either as a linear function of quantities or as a linear function of prices.[2]

Duality is a principle in both mathematics and logic. Its exact definition varies. But a common one is that a *duality* translates one true statement into another true statement by exchanging two words or concepts. Statements A and B above illustrate. By convention, economists call relationships taking quantities as independent variables *primal relationships* and ones with *prices* as independent variables *dual relationships*.

The "duality" between $\pi(p, w)$ and $\bar{T}$ ensures that, regardless of T's true nature, economists studying price-taking profit maximizers lose no generality by modeling it "as if" it were canonical. This chapter proceeds as follows. We first give an overview of the intuition. Next, we develop the properties of the "dual technology" and examine its relationship to the "true" technology, T. Then we study different manifestations of this duality using optimization principles. The chapter concludes with some general remarks on dual structures.

9.2 The Dual Technology, $\bar{T}$, Defined

Profit-maximizing input demands and supplies, $(x^*(p, w), y^*(p, w))$, must be feasible,

$$(x^*(p, w), y^*(p, w)) \in T,$$

and generate more profit than any other feasible input-output bundle,

$$py^*(p, w) - wx^*(p, w) \geq py - wx$$

for all $(x, y) \in T$ and all prices (w, p). Substituting the definition of the profit function, $\pi(p, w)$, into the left-hand side of the inequality gives

$$\pi(p, w) \geq py - wx \tag{9.1}$$

[2] *The two-dimensional real coordinate plane and its N-dimensional extension are special cases of what mathematicians refer to as a *vector space*. For an arbitrary vector space, X, its *dual space*, denoted X^*, is the space of linear functions over X. For both, the two-dimensional real coordinate plane and its N-dimensional extension, its dual space is the space itself.

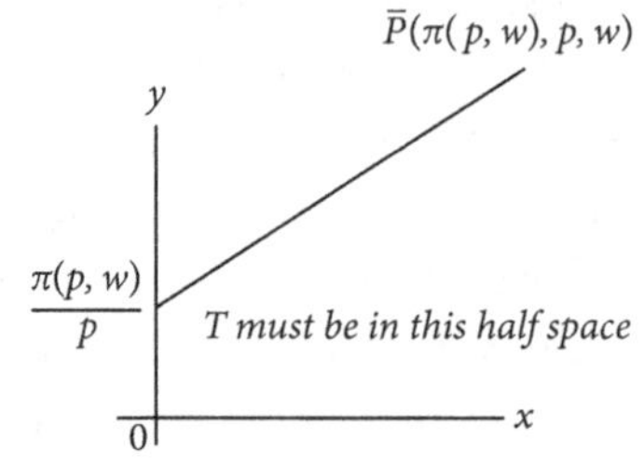

Figure 9.1 Isoprofit Line for $\pi(p, w)$

for all $(x, y) \in T$ as a restriction on feasible input-output bundles.

In the single-output case, expression (9.1) can be rewritten as

$$y \leq \frac{\pi(p, w)}{p} + \frac{w}{p}x$$

for all (p, w) and for all $(x, y) \in T$. This inequality requires that any (x, y) belonging to T must lie on or below the isoprofit line (hyperplane) defined by maximal profit, $\pi(p, w)$,

$$\bar{P}(\pi(p, w), p, w) = \{(x, y) : \pi(p, w) = py - wx\},$$

that Figure 9.1 illustrates as the line segment with vertical intercept $\frac{\pi(p, w)}{p}$. Because $\pi(p, w)$ represents the maximal profit available from T given (p, w), T cannot contain any input-output pairs lying above the line segment. Expression (9.1), however, holds for *all possible input and output prices*. Therefore, if we keep p constant (make it the numeraire), and vary the input price over, say, $w^2 > w^1 > w^0$, the same logic implies that T must fall below each of the resulting isoprofit lines. Because T must lie below each of these isoprofit lines, it must fall in the *intersection* of the half spaces below them. That is,

$$T \subset P^-(\pi(p, w^o), p, w^o) \cap P^-(\pi(p, w^1), p, w^1) \cap P^-(\pi(p, w^2), p, w^2).$$

Figure 9.2 depicts this intersection as the (x, y) pairs lying on or below the piecewise linear contour $\frac{\pi(p, w^2)}{p}ABC$.

Figure 9.2 is drawn for three input price levels. Letting w vary between $(0, \infty)$, however, partitions off all the half spaces in which T must fall. (Because only real prices matter, letting w vary over that range is the same as letting the real price $\frac{w}{p}$, which determines the slope of isoprofit lines, range over $(0, \infty)$). These arguments suggest the following theorem. (The theorem is true regardless of the dimension of x or y.)

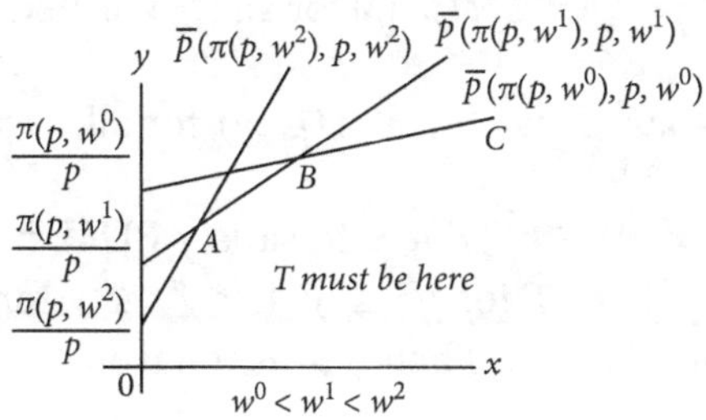

Figure 9.2 Constructing $\bar{T}$

Theorem 1. (Fundamental Duality Theorem) *$T \subset \bar{T}$ where*

$$\begin{aligned}\bar{T} &\equiv \{(x,y) : py \leq \pi(p,w) + wx \text{ for all } (p,w)\} \\ &= \cap_{p,w}\{(x,y) : py \leq \pi(p,w) + wx\}.\end{aligned}$$

Theorem 1 identifies the set of inputs and outputs, $\bar{T}$, that we call the "dual technology." We prove it by using a proof by contradiction: *Suppose that, contrary to Theorem 1, a technically feasible input-output bundle, $(x,y) \in T$, exists that does not belong to the dual technology, $(x,y) \notin \bar{T}$. Because it does not fall in $\bar{T}$, at least one (p,w) must exist for which $py - wx > \pi(p,w)$. This inequality requires that a technically feasible (x,y) exists that yields a higher profit than maximal available profit, $\pi(p,w)$, which gives the desired contradiction. Hence, Theorem 1 must be true.*

The intuition is that knowledge of the profit function can be used to "reverse-engineer" the profit-maximization problem to isolate a region of input-output space in which the technology must lie. The search for $\pi(p,w)$ assumes that the producer "knows" T and wants to find the highest possible isoprofit line (hyperplane) touching it. On the other hand, in constructing $\bar{T}$, we use knowledge of $\pi(p,w)$ and (p,w) to find the slopes and intercepts of the isoprofit lines (hyperplanes) under which T must fall.

9.3 Properties of the Dual Technology, $\bar{T}$

The area below the piece-wise linear $\frac{\pi(p,w^2)}{p}ABC$ in Figure 9.2 is nonempty, satisfies the free disposability of inputs and outputs (FDI and FDO), and is a convex set. We first show that these properties hold in general. Then we discuss conditions that ensure $\bar{T}$ satisfies NFL and NFC.

To verify that $\bar{T}$ satisfies FDI, we must show that

$$x' \geq x \text{ for } (x,y) \in \bar{T} \Rightarrow (x',y) \in \bar{T}.$$

Let $(x, y) \in \bar{T}$ so that $py - wx \leq \pi(p, w)$ for all (p, w). Taking $x' \geq x$ shows that

$$py - wx' \leq py - wx \leq \pi(p, w) \text{ for all } (p, w),$$

which ensures that $(x', y) \in \bar{T}$. For $\bar{T}$ to satisfy FDO, it must be true that if $(x, y) \in \bar{T}$, then $(x, y') \in \bar{T}$ for $y' \leq y$. Let $y' \leq y$ for $(x, y) \in \bar{T}$ so that $py - wx \leq \pi(p, w)$ for all (p, w). Then we must have

$$py' - wx \leq py - wx \leq \pi(p, w) \text{ for all } (p, w),$$

which ensures $(x, y') \in \bar{T}$.[3]

To show that $\bar{T}$ is convex, we must show that if $(x^o, y^o) \in \bar{T}$ and $(x^*, y^*) \in \bar{T}$, then any weighted average of (x^o, y^o) and (x^*, y^*) also belongs to $\bar{T}$. That is, we need to prove that

$$\begin{aligned} (x^o, y^o) \in \bar{T} \quad &\text{and} \quad (x^*, y^*) \in \bar{T} \\ &\Downarrow \\ p(\lambda y^o + (1 - \lambda) y^*) - w(\lambda x^o + (1 - \lambda) x^o) \quad &\leq \quad \pi(p, w) \text{ for all } (p, w), \end{aligned}$$

for $\lambda \in (0, 1)$. Because $(x^o, y^o) \in \bar{T}$ and $(x^*, y^*) \in \bar{T}$,

$$\begin{aligned} py^o - wx^o \quad &\leq \quad \pi(p, w) \text{ for all } (p, w) \\ py^* - wx^* \quad &\leq \quad \pi(p, w) \text{ for all } (p, w) \end{aligned}$$

Multiply both sides of the first inequality by $\lambda > 0$, the second by $(1 - \lambda) > 0$, and add the results to get

$$p(\lambda y^o + (1 - \lambda) y^*) - w(\lambda x^o + (1 - \lambda) x^o) \leq \pi(p, w) \text{ for all } (p, w),$$

which is what we needed to show.

That leaves no free lunch (NFL) and no fixed costs (NFC). Here, we assume that the decisionmaker's opportunity cost is 0 and that a set of prices exists for which $\pi(p, w) = 0$. If NFL is violated, there exists an $(0, y) \in T$ with $y \geq 0$ and $y \neq 0$. That input-output bundle generates a profit of $py - w0 > 0$, which cannot satisfy

$$py - wx \leq \pi(p, w) \text{ for all } (p, w)$$

if a (p, w) exists such that $\pi(p, w) = 0$.[4] Hence, $\bar{T}$ is consistent with NFL.

[3] For both FDI and FDO, recall that input and output prices are assumed positive.
[4] Again recall that all output prices are strictly positive.

If the decisionmaker's opportunity cost is zero, the decisionmaker will not produce at prices for which $\pi(p, w) < 0$. Thus, observed profit for those prices is zero but never negative, and

$$0 = p0 - w0 \leq \pi(p, w) \text{ for all } (p, w),$$

so that $(0, 0) \in \bar{T}$. $\bar{T}$ is thus consistent with NFC.

9.4 What Is the Dual Technology $\bar{T}$?

If the decisionmaker's opportunity cost is 0 and a set of prices exists for which $\pi(p, w) = 0$, the dual technology, $\bar{T}$, is canonical. We know, however, that a well-behaved profit function, $\pi(p, w)$, exists even if the technology, T, looks like Figure 5.5 in Chapter 5. Therefore, $\bar{T}$, in general, is not the same set as T. Nonetheless,

$$\bar{\pi}(p, w) \equiv \max_{x,y} \{py - wx : (x, y) \in \bar{T}\}$$

satisfies

$$\bar{\pi}(p, w) = \pi(p, w)$$

for all (p, w). Although $\bar{T}$ and T can differ, they have the same profit function.

To help explain, Figure 9.3 reproduces Figure 8.3 from Chapter 8. Recall that T in Chapter 8 consists of all (x, y) on or below the curve AY. It does not satisfy no fixed costs, and, therefore, it is not canonical. For the illustrated prices, maximal profit, $\pi(p, w)$, for T is negative, which is illustrated by its isoprofit line having a negative intercept. A decisionmaker facing this T and a zero opportunity cost foregoes production at these prices in favor of alternative employment (see Chapter 8). Because the decisionmaker does not act as a producer, the input-output bundle at these prices is zero and not $(x^*(p, w), y^*(p, w))$. By analogy, any real price $\frac{w}{p}$ for an isoprofit line that supports T from above but that has a negative intercept on the vertical axis leads the decisionmaker to forego production. Positive production is weakly preferred to the opportunity cost when the real price of the input falls to the level $\frac{\bar{w}}{p}$ depicted in Figure 9.4 as the slope of $\bar{P}(0, p, \bar{w})$. For that real input price, the profit-maximizing input-output bundle in T, labeled as point $\bar{A}$, produces a zero profit. The decisionmaker is indifferent between being a producer and alternative employment.

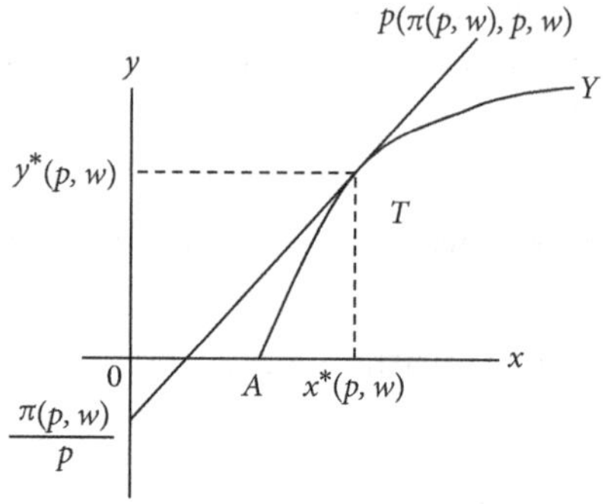

Figure 9.3 No Fixed Costs Violated

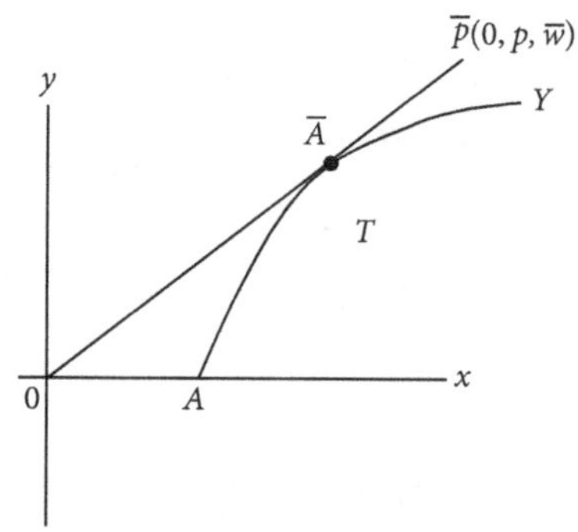

Figure 9.4 Observed Profit

Real input prices lower than $\frac{\bar{w}}{p}$, whose isoprofit lines are "flatter" than $\bar{P}(0, p, \bar{w})$, will support positive production of output with a positive profit. As the real price of the input falls, the producer moves along the boundary of T from $\bar{A}$ toward Y. Therefore, if the technology is the area on or below the curve AY in Figure 9.4, a decisionmaker with zero opportunity cost never produces along $A\bar{A}$ because that involves negative profit. The decisionmaker is better off not being a producer for those prices.

Now let's compare that behavior with that of a decisionmaker who faces a technology given by the area on or below $0\bar{A}Y$ in Figure 9.4. (That is, the graph of the production function for this technology would be the line segment $0\bar{A}$ and then $\bar{A}Y$ afterwards.) For real prices of the input higher than $\frac{\bar{w}}{p}$, whose isoprofit lines have "steeper" slope than $\bar{P}(0, p, \bar{w})$, profit maximization occurs at $(0, 0)$. For real input prices lower than $\frac{\bar{w}}{p}$, profit maximization occurs along the arc $\bar{A}Y$. The production pattern is the same as that for a profit maximizer who faces T in Figure 9.3 and has an opportunity cost of 0. The area on or

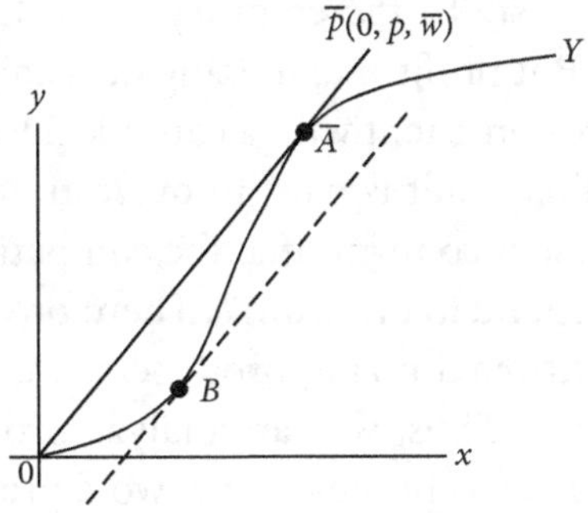

Figure 9.5 Nonconvex Technology

below $0\bar{A}Y$ is the $\bar{T}$ that would be constructed if the technology were that in Figure 9.3. It contains T as a subset and gives the same profit function.

Figure 9.5 offers another perspective. There T is everything on or below the curve $0Y$. This is the variable returns technology introduced in Figure 3.7 in Chapter 3. For real input prices higher than $\frac{\bar{w}}{p}$, which is depicted as the slope of the isoprofit line $\bar{P}(0, p, \bar{w})$, the profit-maximizing solution is $(0, 0)$.

If, however, you relied on the rule-of-thumb of finding a tangency between the isoprofit line and the boundary of T to determine the profit-maximizing point, you might think otherwise. Isoprofit lines can be tangent from above to the boundary of T for real prices higher than $\frac{\bar{w}}{p}$ in the region $B\bar{A}$. However, T is not fully contained in the half spaces below such isoprofit lines. Thus, these isoprofit lines fall below the one passing through $(0, 0)$. Tangencies can also occur along $0B$ for real input prices lower than $\frac{\bar{w}}{p}$. But these will occur from below. Drawing their isoprofit lines shows that higher isoprofit lines can be attained in the region $\bar{A}Y$, while staying in T.

If a decisionmaker faces the technology in Figure 9.5, profit-maximizing production occurs either at $(0, 0)$ or along its upper frontier in the region $\bar{A}Y$. If you compare the profit levels for a decisionmaker facing that technology with one facing a technology given by everything on or below $0\bar{A}Y$, you will find that they are same. In this case, $\bar{T}$ corresponds to everything below $0\bar{A}Y$. Again $T \subset \bar{T}$ and gives the same profit function.

The phenomena captured in Figures 9.3 through 9.5 are general. $\bar{T}$ does not give the technology. Instead it gives the smallest possible set in input-output space that satisfies—nonemptiness, FDI, FDO, convexity, NFC, NFL—*and that contains the true* T. Moreover, it has the same maximal profit as T for all prices (p, w). Figures 9.4 and 9.5 illustrate why. Profit-maximizing decisionmakers who have an opportunity cost of zero never operate in regions of T that are not consistent with a canonical technology. It's not that such regions can't or don't exist. To the contrary, since Chapter 2 we have recognized that they can. But profit-maximizing decisionmakers avoid them in favor of regions that are consistent with a canonical technology.[5]

The importance of this result is hard to overestimate. It carries immense analytic advantages. First, it confirms that the competitive profit-maximizing choices for $\bar{T}$ will correspond to those for T. Therefore, in studying the behavior of competitive profit-maximizing producers, we get the same answers, whether we study $\bar{T}$ or T. Thus, we can analyze producer behavior "as if" they respond to a canonical technology. The two representations are *observationally equivalent* for competitive profit maximizers. Second, it ensures that no generality is lost in studying profit-maximizing producer behavior by first specifying a well-behaved profit function. If the $\pi(p, w)$ is appropriately specified, there must exist a corresponding canonical $\bar{T}$ that encapsulates all the relevant economic information about the true technology, T, regardless of the underlying properties of T.

9.5 Other Manifestations of Duality

Because $\bar{T}$ satisfies the properties of a canonical technology, we can use it to develop both a cost function and a revenue function. That cost function would be nondecreasing and convex in outputs, and that revenue function would be nondecreasing and concave in inputs.

Instead of pursuing this approach, we investigate a cost function that is derived from the profit function as

$$\bar{c}(w, y) \equiv \max_{p} \{py - \pi(p, w)\} \tag{9.2}$$

and a revenue function derived from the profit function as

$$\bar{R}(p, x) \equiv \min_{w} \{wx + \pi(p, w)\} \tag{9.3}$$

that we refer to, respectively, as the *dual cost function* and the *dual revenue function*. Our focus in the dual cost function discussion is on it as a function of outputs, y, and the focus in the dual revenue discussion is on it as a function of inputs, x. Exercises 46 and 47 at the end of this chapter ask you to show that $\bar{c}(w, y)$ is positively homogeneous and concave as a function of w and

[5] $\bar{T}$ is called the *free-disposal convex hull of* T, meaning that it is the smallest set consistent with the properties of a canonical technology that contains T as a subset.

that $\bar{R}(p,x)$ is positively homogeneous and convex as a function of p. Thus, the "dual" structures satisfy the same properties in prices as the ones derived directly from T.

9.5.1 The Dual Cost Function, $\bar{c}(w,y)$

In this section, we first derive the dual cost function, and then we discuss its properties in output.

9.5.1.1 Solving the Dual Cost Problem

The definition of the profit function, $\pi(p,w)$, requires that

$$\pi(p,w) \geq py - c(w,y) \tag{9.4}$$

for all (p,y,w). A tiny bit of algebra applied to (9.4) gives

$$c(w,y) \geq py - \pi(p,w),$$

for all (p,y,w) as an immediate consequence. The difference between revenue from y and maximal profit, $\pi(p,w)$, is always less than or equal to the minimal cost of producing y. That is, *the difference between revenue from y and maximal profit, $\pi(p,w)$, provides a lower bound for the minimal cost of producing y.* This holds for all (p,y,w). In particular, because that is true, the inequality must continue to hold when we keep *y and w fixed, but choose p to maximize the difference between revenue from y and $\pi(p,w)$.* Thus,

$$\begin{aligned} c(w,y) &\geq \max_p \{py - \pi(p,w)\} \\ &\equiv \bar{c}(w,y) \end{aligned}$$

for all (w,y). The dual cost function, $\bar{c}(w,y)$, is a lower bound to $c(w,y)$. On the other hand, if y equals $y^*(p^o,w)$,

$$c(w,y^*(p^o,w)) = p^o y^*(p^o,w) - \pi(p^o,w).$$

But that means p^o must solve the version of (9.2) framed as

$$\bar{c}(w,y^*(p^o,w)) = \max_p \{py^*(p^o,w) - \pi(p,w)\},$$

which is the dual cost problem for the profit-maximizing supply $y^*(p^o,w)$.

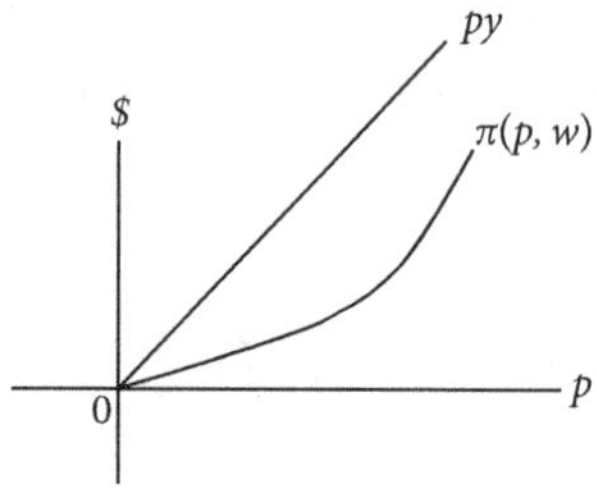

Figure 9.6 Deriving $\bar{c}(w, y)$

Therefore, the dual cost function, $\bar{c}(w,y)$, is a lower bound for the cost function, $c(w,y)$, that equals it whenever y is profit maximizing for (p,w). That leaves open the possibility that $\bar{c}(w,y) > c(w,y)$ when y is not a profit-maximizing vector of output supplies. This happens because $\bar{c}(w,y)$ is the minimal cost function for $\bar{T}$, not T. (We don't show this, but it is true.) The divergence between $\bar{c}(w,y)$ and $c(w,y)$ reflects the divergence between $\bar{T}$ and T.

Figure 9.6 illustrates the dual cost problem (9.2). We now seek a p that makes the vertical difference between the ray from the origin labeled py and the graph of the profit function $\pi(p,w)$ as large as possible. Note the similarity to Figure 10 of Chapter 8. The problem structures are the same even though the problems posed differ. The profit-maximization problem is posed in (primal) quantity space and maximizes profit given (dual) prices. The dual cost problem is posed in (dual) price space and maximizes the difference between revenue for given (primal) output and $\pi(p,w)$. The expression py is interpreted differently in the two problems. In Figure 10 of Chapter 8, it is a linear function of y with normal p. Those roles are reversed in Figure 6. But despite the *different intuitive interpretations*, the inherent mathematical structures of both problems are identical. Therefore, we use the same math techniques to solve problem (9.2) that we used to solve the profit maximization problem. The difference is that we now search over p instead of over y.

Denote price vectors that solve the dual cost minimization problem by

$$p(w,y) \in \underset{p}{\operatorname{argmax}} \{py - \pi(p,w)\}.$$

Here, $\operatorname{argmax}_p \{\cdot\}$ is an instruction to choose any price vector that gives the largest possible value in the set $\{\cdot\}$ and, thus, solves problem (9.2). Any solution[6] to the dual cost problem satisfies

[6] We say *any* solution because the problem can have multiple solutions. If that occurs, all the solutions give the same value of $py - \pi(p,w)$.

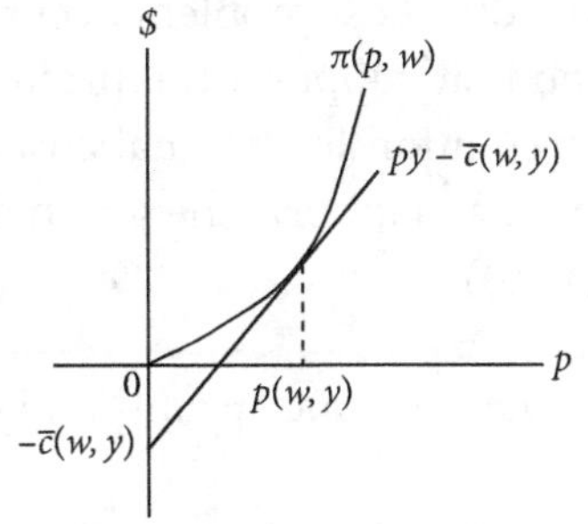

Figure 9.7 Solution to Dual Cost Problem (Hotelling's Lemma)

$$py - \pi(p, w) \leq p(w, y)\,y - \pi(p(w, y), w) \tag{9.5}$$

for all p with equality for $p = p(w, y)$. Thus, for $p(w, y)$ to solve the dual cost problem, y must be the normal for the affine function of p,

$$\pi(p(w, y), w) + y(p - p(w, y)) = py - \bar{c}(w, y),$$

whose graph supports the graph of $\pi(p, w)$ from below at $(p(w, y), \pi(p(w, y)))$. Figure 9.7 illustrates.[7]

The definition of the dual cost function, $\bar{c}(w, y)$, also requires that

$$\bar{c}(w, y^*) \geq p(w, y)\,y^* - \pi(p(w, y), w)$$

for all y^* and y and

$$\bar{c}(w, y) = p(w, y)\,y - \pi(p(w, y), w).$$

Subtracting the equality from the inequality gives

$$\bar{c}(w, y^*) \geq \bar{c}(w, y) + p(w, y)(y^* - y) \tag{9.6}$$

for all y^*. Any solution to the dual cost minimization problem, $p(w, y)$, must be the normal (slope) for an affine function of y^* whose graph supports (is tangent to) the graph of the dual cost function from below at $(y, \bar{c}(w, y))$.[8]

We summarize expressions (9.5) and (9.6), and the surrounding discussions in statement C, as follows.

[7] $p(w, y)$, thus, solves the dual cost problem if and only if y is a *subgradient* of $\pi(p, w)$ in p.
[8] The solution to the dual cost problem $p(w, y)$, therefore, is a *subgradient* of $\bar{c}(w, y)$.

- C: The solution to the dual cost problem occurs where y forms the normal for a hyperplane that supports the profit function from below at $(p, \pi(p, w))$, and any solution to the dual cost problem forms the normal for a hyperplane that supports the graph of the dual cost function from below at $(y, \bar{c}(w, y))$.

Switching the roles of "dual cost" and "profit" and y and p in C gives its dual

- D: The solution to the profit problem occurs where p forms the normal for a hyperplane that supports the dual cost function from below at $(y, \bar{c}(w, y))$, and any solution to the profit problem forms the normal for a hyperplane that supports the graph of the profit function from below at $(p, \pi(p, w))$.

The first (second) part of D (C) restates the condition developed in Chapter 8 (price equals marginal cost) that must be satisfied for y to solve

$$max_y \{py - \bar{c}(w, y)\},$$

and the second (first) part of D (C) restates part of Hotelling's Lemma. Both problem solutions give the same information.

9.5.1.2 Dual Cost as a Function of Output

We now show that $\bar{c}(w, y)$ is nondecreasing (nonnegative marginal cost) and convex in output (nondecreasing marginal cost), y. Because we obtain the dual cost function by solving a problem whose form is identical to that of the profit-maximization problem but involves different choice variables (p now instead of y), our method for demonstrating these properties mirrors the method used to establish that $\pi(p, w)$ is nondecreasing and convex in p.

We first show that $y' \geq y$ implies

$$\bar{c}(w, y') \geq \bar{c}(w, y).$$

To do so, we again deploy a "do-nothing" argument. If $y' \geq y$, it must be true that

$$p(w, y)y' - \pi(p(w, y), w) \geq p(w, y)y - \pi(p(w, y), w).$$

The left-hand side is the result of "doing nothing" to the solution of the dual cost problem in response to output increasing from y to y'. Because output prices, $p(w, y)$, are positive, increasing output while holding them constant forces revenue to increase. Because the dual cost problem is to maximize the difference between revenue and maximal profit, the best response must dominate the "do-nothing" response and cannot decrease dual cost.

For convexity, let

$$\hat{y} = \lambda y^0 + (1 - \lambda) y^1,$$

for $\lambda \in (0, 1)$ to denote a weighted average of two output bundles y^0 and y^1. To demonstrate that the dual cost structure is convex in output, we must show that the weighted average of $\bar{c}(w, y^0)$ and $\bar{c}(w, y^1)$ always is at least as large as the dual cost of $\hat{y}$, $\bar{c}(w, \hat{y})$. By the definition of the dual cost function:

$$\begin{aligned} \bar{c}(w, y^0) &\geq p(w, \hat{y}) y^0 - \pi(p(w, \hat{y}), w) \\ \bar{c}(w, y^1) &\geq p(w, \hat{y}) y^1 - \pi(p(w, \hat{y}), w) \end{aligned}$$

Multiply the first inequality by $\lambda > 0$ and the second by $(1 - \lambda) > 0$, and then add the result to obtain

$$\begin{aligned} \lambda \bar{c}(w, y^0) + (1 - \lambda) \bar{c}(w, y^1) &\geq p(w, \hat{y}) \left[\lambda y^0 + (1 - \lambda) y^1 \right] - \pi(p(w, \hat{y}), w) \\ &= \bar{c}(w, \hat{y}) \end{aligned}$$

for $\lambda \in (0, 1)$.

Figure 9.8 illustrates why $\bar{c}(w, y)$ and $c(w, y)$ do not coincide. As drawn, the illustrated cost function initially has decreasing marginal costs and then increasing marginal costs. If the price of the output is below $\bar{p}$, the graph of the ray from the origin that depicts revenue will always lie below the graph of the cost function. That means that profit is negative for all output levels except zero. The producer is best off, therefore, operating at the origin, producing nothing, and realizing a cost and profit of zero. For price $\bar{p}$, the producer makes zero profit by producing $y^* (\bar{p}, w)$ and is, therefore, indifferent between producing that amount and zero. For prices higher than $\bar{p}$, price can equal marginal cost in the region $0\bar{A}$ of the graph of the cost function. But such points fall on lower isoprofit lines than the parallel tangencies that occur in the region beyond $\bar{A}$. Thus, a profit maximizer never produces in the region $0\bar{A}$ of the cost function. And because $\bar{c}(w, y)$ is constructed from profit-maximizing solutions via $\pi(p, w)$, the closest approximation to $c(w, y)$ in that region is the shutdown solution that would occur if the slope of the cost curve coincided with $\bar{p}$ between 0 and $y^* (\bar{p}, w)$. The graph of $\bar{c}(w, y)$ in the $(y, \$)$ space thus follows the line segment $0\bar{A}$ until $y^* (\bar{p}, w)$ and the graph of $c(w, y)$ afterwards. And as required, $c(w, y) \geq \bar{c}(w, y)$, and both always involve the same profit.

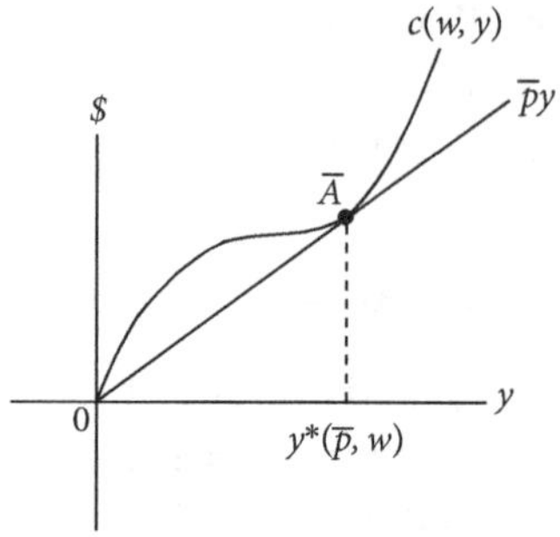

Figure 9.8 Nonconvex Cost and Profit Maximization

9.5.2 Dual Revenue from the Profit Function

9.5.2.1 Solving the Dual Revenue Problem

By the definition of the profit and revenue functions,

$$\pi(p, w) \geq R(p, x) - wx$$

for all (p, x, w). Some easy algebra gives

$$\pi(p, w) + wx \geq R(p, x)$$

for all (p, x, w). Because this inequality must hold for all possible values of $\pi(p, w) + wx$, it must hold when w makes it as small as possible. Therefore,

$$\min_{w} \{\pi(p, w) + wx\} \geq R(p, x),$$

for all (p, x). Hence,

$$\bar{R}(p, x) \geq R(p, x),$$

for all (p, x) and

$$\bar{R}(p, x^{*}(p, w)) = R(p, x^{*}(p, w)),$$

where

$$\bar{R}(p, x) \equiv \min_{w} \{\pi(p, w) + wx\}.$$

The *dual revenue function*, $\bar{R}(p, x)$, is an upper bound for the revenue function for T, and the two revenue functions coincide for profit-maximizing input vectors.

We use the same strategy to solve and analyze the dual revenue problem. As a result, the discussion is more terse. Denote input-price vectors that solve the dual revenue problem by:

$$w(p,x) \in \underset{w}{\operatorname{argmin}} \{\pi(p,w) + wx\}.$$

Here $\operatorname{argmin}_w \{\cdot\}$ is an instruction to choose the vector of input prices that gives the smallest possible value in the set $\{\cdot\}$. For given x, any such solution (there can be more than one) must satisfy:

$$\pi(p, w(p,x)) - x[w - w(p,x)] \leq \pi(p,w), \tag{9.7}$$

for all w. The interpretation of this condition is, by now, familiar. For an input-price vector $w(p,x)$ to solve the dual revenue problem, the graph of the affine function of w,

$$\pi(p, w(p,x)) + w(p,x)x - xw,$$

with normal $-x$ must support the graph of $\pi(p,w)$ from below at $(w(p,x), \pi(p, w(p,x)))$.[9] Expression (9.7) is illustrated by Figure 8.4 from Chapter 8, by taking x^* and w^* there to be, respectively, x and $w(p,x)$. Similarly, taking $p^* = p$, $w^* = w(p,x)$, and $x^*(p^*, w^*) = x$ in expression (8.2) in Chapter 8 gives expression (9.7), the second half of Hotelling's Lemma.

By the definition of the dual revenue function:

$$\begin{aligned} \bar{R}(p,x^*) &\leq \pi(p, w(p,x)) + w(p,x)x^*, \textit{ and} \\ \bar{R}(p,x) &= \pi(p, w(p,x)) + w(p,x)x, \end{aligned}$$

for all x^* and x. Hence,

$$\bar{R}(p,x^*) \leq \bar{R}(p,x) + w(p,x)(x^* - x) \tag{9.8}$$

for all x^*. Expression (9.8) requires that the graph of the affine function of x^*

$$\bar{R}(p,x) + w(p,x)(x^* - x)$$

with normal $w(p,x)$ must support the graph of $\bar{R}(p,x^*)$ from above at $(x, \bar{R}(p,x))$.

[9] In words, $-x$ must be a *subgradient* of $\pi(p,w)$ in w at the solution.

We summarize (9.7), expression (9.8), and the surrounding discussion in:

- E: The solution to the dual revenue problem occurs where $-x$ forms the normal for a hyperplane that supports the graph of the profit function from below at $(w, \pi(p, w))$, and any solution to the dual revenue problem forms the normal for a hyperplane that supports the graph of the dual revenue from above at $(x, \bar{R}(p, x))$.

Switching the roles of "dual revenue" and "profit" and $-x$ and w in E gives its dual

- F: The solution to the profit problem occurs where w forms the normal for a hyperplane that supports the graph of the dual revenue function from above at $(x, \bar{R}(p, x))$, and (minus) any solution to the profit problem forms the normal for a hyperplane that supports the graph of the profit function from below at $(w, \pi(p, w))$.

The first (second) part of F (E) restates the condition that must be satisfied for an input vector to be profit maximizing (input price equals marginal revenue from the input), and the second (first) part of F (E) restates part of Hotelling's Lemma.

9.5.2.2 Dual Revenue as a Function of Input

It remains to show that the dual revenue function, $\bar{R}(p, x)$, is nondecreasing and concave in the input vector x. The method used is analogous to that used to show that the cost function is nondecreasing and concave in w. That $\bar{R}(p, x)$ is nondecreasing in x follows from another "do nothing" argument. Suppose that in response to the input bundle falling from, say, x' to x, nothing is done to the solution of the dual revenue problem for x'. Then

$$\pi(p, w(p, x')) + w(p, x')x' \geq \pi(p, w(p, x')) + w(p, x')x$$

for $x' \geq x$. Because the best response to the change in x must be no worse than the "do nothing" response, $\bar{R}(p, x') \geq \bar{R}(p, x)$ as required.

To demonstrate concavity, let $\hat{x} = \lambda x^0 + (1 - \lambda) x^1$ for $\lambda \in (0, 1)$. By the definition of the dual revenue function, we must have

$$\begin{aligned}
\bar{R}(p, x^0) &\leq w(p, \hat{x}) x^0 + \pi(p, w(p, \hat{x})), \ \textit{and} \\
\bar{R}(p, x^1) &\leq w(p, \hat{x}) x^1 + \pi(p, w(p, \hat{x},)).
\end{aligned}$$

Multiply the first inequality by $\lambda > 0$, the second by $(1-\lambda) > 0$, and add the results to obtain

$$\begin{aligned}\lambda\bar{R}(p,x^0) + (1-\lambda)\bar{R}(p,x^1) &\leq w(p,\hat{x})(\lambda x^0 + (1-\lambda)x^1) + \pi(p, w(p,\hat{x})) \\ &= \bar{R}(p,\hat{x})\end{aligned}$$

for $\lambda \in (0,1)$ establishing the desired concavity. If you set $p = 1$ for the single-output case, the curve $0Y$ in Figure 9.5 depicts the revenue function for a nonconvex technology, $R(p,x)$. In that case, $\bar{R}(p,x)$ corresponds to $0\bar{A}Y$.

9.6 A Road Not Taken?

A reasonable reaction to these duality results might be as follows: *If one knows that self-interested, price-taking producers behave as though there exists a canonical technology, why not start with $\bar{T}$ instead of T?*

One reason is that economists originally conceptualized producers as maximizing the difference between $pf(x)$ and wx, and then reasoned forward. It was gradually established that the conditions required for this problem to have well-behaved solutions implied that a producer's supply curves slope upward in the output price and that input demands slope downward in their prices. Until *circa* 1970, most production analyses adopted that perspective.

A by-product of the Second World War was an increased interest in the mathematics of optimization. In the 1950s and 1960s, that interest brought new perspectives on and new tools for studying maximization and minimization problems. The realization of the importance of the connections between *dual optimization problems* of the type exemplified by

$$\max_y \{py - c(w,y)\}$$

and

$$\max_p \{py - \pi(p,w)\}$$

was an important outgrowth. So, for many years, economists just did not understand that many economic problems could be studied from a dual perspective.

So, history is a partial answer. But more important is the fundamental idea that model formulation best proceeds by first understanding the basics of the practical problem and then formulating a tractable analytic model.

For many economic problems, that means starting from a primal perspective. As important as mathematics is to economic analysis, its ultimate usefulness stems from the *extramathematical reasoning* that the economist attaches to the abstract mathematical objects.

For example, we've learned that economic behavior consistent with the laws of supply and demand implies the existence of a mathematical object that we've named $\bar{T}$ and interpreted as a canonical technology. $\bar{T}$'s existence, however, is a *mathematical consequence* of the existence of a positively homogeneous and convex function of variables (p, w) that we've called "prices." If those objects were, say, different-colored marbles, the mathematical object $\bar{T}$ would still exist. But its extramathematical interpretation differs. It assumes its peculiar meaning to us because we framed our model in terms of a set T interpreted as a technology. In their own way, the duality results confirm Le Tellier's observation: . . *plus nous avançons dans la connaissance de l'univers, plus il nous apparaît fondè sur des lois mathèmatiques.*[10]

9.7 Exercises

Exercise 42. **For an arbitrary $w > 0$ define the half space:*

$$\{x : wx \geq c(w, y)\}.$$

Draw a two-dimensional representation of that half space. Now take another $w' > 0$, define the half space it generates as

$$\{x : w'x \geq c(w', y)\},$$

and illustrate it visually on the same figure. Prove that their intersection,

$$\{x : wx \geq c(w, y)\} \cap \{x : w'x \geq c(w', y)\},$$

forms a convex set consistent with free disposability of input that contains $X(y)$ as a subset. Extend this reasoning to show that

$$\begin{aligned} X(y) &\subset \{x : wx \geq c(w, y) \ \textit{for all } w\} \\ &\equiv X^*(y), \end{aligned}$$

the dual input set.

[10] For a translation, see Chapter 1.

Exercise 43. **Prove that $X^*(y)$ defined in Exercise 42 satisfies free disposability of inputs (FDI) and is a convex set.*

Exercise 44. **Following the reasoning in Exercise 42, show that*

$$\begin{aligned} Y(x) &\subset \{y : py \leq R(p,x) \ \textit{for all } p\} \\ &\equiv Y^*(x), \end{aligned}$$

the dual output set.

Exercise 45. **Prove that $Y^*(x)$ satisfies free disposability of output and is a convex set.*

Exercise 46. **Prove that $\bar{c}(w,y)$ is positively homogeneous and concave as a function of w.*

Exercise 47. **Prove that $\bar{R}(p,x)$ is positively homogeneous and convex as a function of p.*

10
Distance Functions

10.1 Introduction

Our discussion, so far, has treated multiple-input, multiple-output versions of T using technology sets, input sets, and output sets. We have shown that each representation is equivalent to the others, and we have demonstrated how to use them to construct production, input-requirement, profit, cost, and revenue functions. We did not study numerical or *function* representations of multiple-input, multiple-output versions of T. But any reader of an intermediate microeconomics textbook will have encountered multiple-input, multiple-output technologies described by a *transformation function*, $t(x, y)$, that defines the technology set as

$$T \equiv \{(x, y) : t(x, y) \geq 0\}. \tag{10.1}$$

The provenance of $t(x, y)$ is often vague. But it usually satisfies some convenient mathematical properties.[1]

That perspective takes the transformation function, $t(x, y)$, as *the primitive (most basic) representation of the technology* and derives T from it. $T's$ properties follow from those of t(x,y). By contrast, our approach defines T, develops its properties, and then uses it to develop production functions and input-requirement functions. Thus, T is the primitive representation. We prefer that approach because technology sets are simpler, and more general, mathematical structures than transformation functions. They also have clear visual representations.

Still, function representations of T are important components of the production economist's toolkit. Practical applications often require manipulation of numerical data, and function representations link set-based concepts and empirical practice. They provide a cardinal means for summarizing the

[1] Some writers reverse the inequality in (10.1) to define the technology. This is a matter of convention, and the appropriate choice of sign depends on how one poses the properties of $t(x, y)$ that characterize the technology set.

Lectures on Neoclassical Production Economics. Robert G. Chambers, Oxford University Press.
 DOI: 10.1093/9780197817759.003.0011

information contained in T. This chapter uses T to deduce function representations of multiple-input, multiple-output technologies that we call *distance functions*.

10.2 Characteristics of a Function Representation

Chapter 3 showed that if T satisfies free disposability of output (FDO), then in the single-output case

$$f(x) \geq y \Leftrightarrow (x, y) \in T; \tag{10.2}$$

and if T satisfies free disposability of input (FDI), then in the single-input case

$$e(y) \leq x \Leftrightarrow (x, y) \in T. \tag{10.3}$$

We interpreted equivalence relations, (10.2) and (10.3), as saying that, respectively: FDO ensures that knowledge of the production function is equivalent to knowledge of the technology set, and that FDI ensures that knowledge of the input-requirement function is equivalent to knowledge of the technology set. (Recall that $A \Leftrightarrow B$ means that A implies B (written $A \Rightarrow B$) and B implies A ($B \Rightarrow A$), so that A and B are equivalent to one another.)

The production and the input-requirement functions express values in terms of real numbers. We take real-valuedness as the first of two defining characteristics of a *function representation of* T. The second echoes the equivalence relations (10.2) and (10.3). Knowing the function provides the same information as knowing T.

Definition 23. *A function representation of T is a real-valued function that characterizes T exhaustively so that knowledge of it is equivalent to knowing T.*

A real-valued transformation function, $t(x, y)$, that satisfies (10.1) is a function representation of T. But $t(x, y)$ being real-valued leaves unresolved the real units in which it expresses values. Are they apples, oranges, labor hours, units of capital, acres of land, widgets, ... ? And what do they measure?

To start answering these questions, consider Figure 10.1. It portrays T as all points on or below the curve $f(x)$ that traces out the graph of a production function. The vertical axis measures units of output, y, and the horizontal axis measures units of input, x. For input use x^*, the maximum producible output is $f(x^*)$ that corresponds to the point on $f(x)$ directly above x^*. For output y^*, the minimal input that can produce it is $e(y^*)$, falling directly below the point on $f(x)$ that has the same vertical height as y^*.

The production function measures the *vertical distance* between the point $(x^*, 0)$ and $(x^*, f(x^*))$. The input-requirement function measures the *horizontal distance* between $(0, y^*)$ and $(e(y^*), y^*)$. The different units arise from different perspectives on T. But both are real-valued. The production function describes how to put a fixed amount of the input, x, to its best use. The input-requirement function answers the related, but subtly different, question: How best to produce a fixed amount of output y?

Suppose that rather than viewing inputs and outputs separately, we evaluate the performance of a given *input-output bundle*, illustrated as (x^*, y^*) in Figure 10.1, relative to T. For example, does (x^*, y^*) involve *too much* of the input to produce y^*, or is *too little* production of the output resulting from x^*?

The *too much* question asks *whether* input use can be reduced from x^* and still produce y^*? Or can we *subtract from* x^* some amount, call it β, and still produce y^*? And if that's possible, the next natural question is *how much*? Or what is the largest real number that we can subtract from x^* and still produce y^*? Translated into math terms, the *how much* question seeks:

$$i(x^*, y^*) \equiv \max\{\beta \in \mathbb{R} : (x^* - \beta, y^*) \in T\}. \tag{10.4}$$

The smallest x in Figure 10.1 that can produce y^* is $e(y^*)$. Hence,

$$x^* - i(x^*, y^*) = e(y^*),$$

or $i(x^*, y^*) = x^* - e(y^*)$.

$i(x^* y^*)$ measures *the horizontal distance between* (x^*, y^*) *and* $(e(y^*), y^*)$. The latter falls on the *boundary of the technology set, T*. Therefore, $i(x^*, y^*)$ measures, in units of the input, how far (x^*, y^*) lies inside of T.

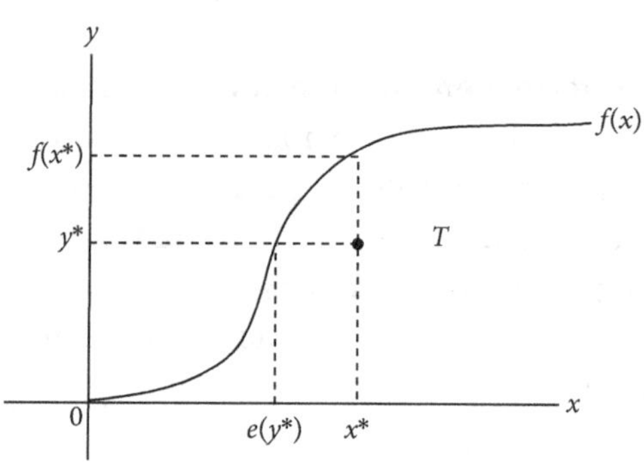

Figure 10.1 Production, Input-Requirement, and Distance Functions

Because $i(x^*, y^*)$ measures the horizontal distance between x^* and $e(y^*)$, adding any real number, γ, to x^* holding y^* fixed is the same as moving (x^*, y^*) parallel to the horizontal axis. If $\gamma > 0$, the move is to the right, and if $\gamma < 0$ the move is to the left. That movement, however, has no effect on $e(y^*)$, which is determined by the boundary of T. Therefore,

$$x^* + \gamma - i(x^* + \gamma, y^*) = e(y^*),$$

whence

$$\begin{aligned} i(x^* + \gamma, y^*) &= x^* + \gamma - e(y^*) \\ &= \gamma + i(x^*, y^*) \end{aligned}$$

Thus, the balancing change required in $i(x^*, y^*)$ simply corrects for the amount of the movement. This characteristic of $i(x^*, y^*)$ presages a defining characteristic of distance functions that we later call the *translation property*.

We answer the *too little* output question the same way. If y^* is *too little* production from x^*, one can hold the input constant but increase output by a positive amount, call it α, and stay in T. In Figure 10.1, that means moving due north from (x^*, y^*) parallel to the vertical axis. One also naturally asks by *how much*? Or in math terms, what solves

$$o(y^*, x^*) \equiv \max\{\alpha \in \mathbb{R} : (x^*, y^* + \alpha) \in T)\}? \tag{10.5}$$

Because $f(x^*)$ is the largest possible output for x^*,

$$y^* + o(y^*, x^*) = f(x^*)$$

or $o(y^*, x^*) = f(x^*) - y^*$ that we interpret as the *vertical distance between the boundary of* T, $(x^*, f(x^*))$, *and* (x^*, y^*). And an easy argument establishes that $o(y^*, x^*)$ satisfies a parallel version of the translation property expressed in output units

$$o(y^* + \gamma, x^*) = o(y^*, x^*) - \gamma$$

for all real γ.

The functions $o(y, x)$ and $i(x, y)$ are examples of constructs that we call *distance functions*. Using them, we can now say what $t(x, y)$ measures and in which units. Identifying $t(x, y)$ with $i(x, y)$,

$$t(x, y) \equiv i(x, y),$$

means that $t(x, y)$ measures the overuse in input units of x in producing y. If T satisfies FDI, this version of $t(x, y)$ is a function representation of the technology because

$$t(x, y) \geq 0 \Leftrightarrow x \geq e(y) \Leftrightarrow (x, y) \in T.$$

Identifying $t(x, y)$ using $o(y, x)$

$$t(x, y) \equiv o(y, x)$$

gives a measure of the underproduction in output units of y for input use of x. And if FDO applies,

$$t(x, y) \geq 0 \Leftrightarrow f(x) \geq y \Leftrightarrow (x, y) \in T.$$

10.3 Distance Functions for Inputs and Outputs

Even in the simplest cases, different perspectives give different representations of T. The production function, the input-requirement function, and the distance functions are all real-valued functions derived from T. Each communicates different information about the technology that reflects the perspective used to examine T. An important distinction between the measures lies in the assumptions that ensure each is a function representation of T. We invoked free disposability of inputs and free disposability of outputs. Both are subject to real-world counterexamples. Thus, in settings where different assumptions may prove appropriate, different function representations of T prove useful.

This section develops two function representations of multiple-input, multiple-output T. Both measure the distance that a given (x, y) lies from a frontier of the technology, and we call them *distance functions*. One measures in input terms and the other in output terms. Before developing them, we take a visual detour to illustrate the concept of *vector addition*.

10.3.1 A Visual Primer on Adding and Subtracting Vectors

Vector addition and *vector subtraction* are the *elementwise* extensions to real vectors of the concepts of addition and subtraction for real numbers. So, for example, if we take $x = (2, 1)$ and $y = (1, 2)$ in Figure 10.2, their sum equals

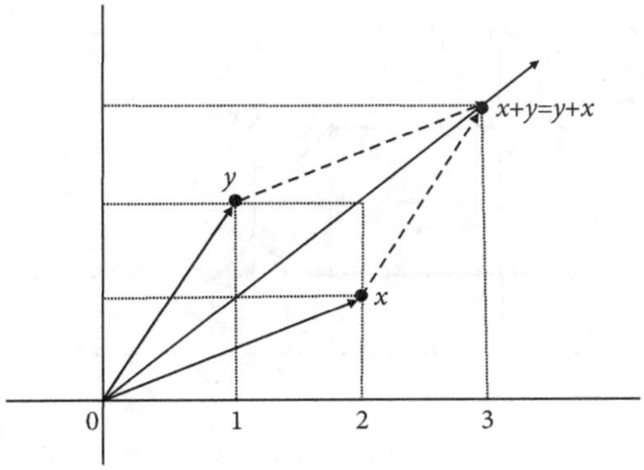

Figure 10.2 Adding and Subtracting Vectors

$x+y = (x_1+y_1, x_2+y_2) = (3,3)$. The generalization to higher dimensional vectors follows the same elementwise addition rule. For any two N-dimensional vectors x and y:

$$x + y = (x_1 + y_1, x_2 + y_2, \cdots, x_N + y_N).$$

To visualize, take $x = (2,1)$ and add $(1,2)$ to it. That operation moves one from $(2,1)$ to $(3,3)$. The dotted line segment connecting $(2,1)$ to $(3,3)$ that depicts this movement is the vector $y = (1,2)$ translated to take the *tip* of the vector $x = (2,1)$ as its origin. This exemplifies the *tip-to-tail (head-to-tail)* rule for vector addition: *To add y to x, draw the vector connecting the point x to the origin, and then place the tail of y to its tip to get the sum* $x + y = (3,3)$. Because addition is commutative, the order of addition does not matter, so that $x + y = y + x$. Therefore, taking $y = (1,2)$ as the first vector and placing x at its tip also results in $(3,3)$. The line segments connecting 0 to x, x to $x + y$, $x + y$ to y, and y to 0 (or vice versa) form a *parallelogram* that exemplifies the *parallelogram rule* for visualizing vector addition. The tip-to-tail and parallelogram rules are equivalent.

10.3.2 Input Distance Functions

Figure 10.3 depicts an input set, $X(y)$. Our initial focus is on x^o that belongs to $X(y)$. Starting at x^o, holding the second input constant at x_2^o and moving due west leads eventually to x^{oo} that is on the isoquant for y, $\bar{X}(y)$. Moving further west beyond x^{oo}, however, goes out of $X(y)$. The move from x^o to x^{oo} gives the largest amount of the first input that can be subtracted from x_1^o *while holding* x_2 *constant at* x_2^o *and staying in* $X(y)$. We write the operation of subtracting

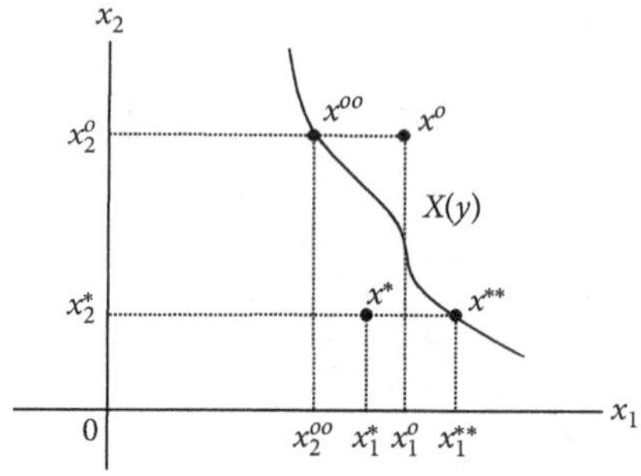

Figure 10.3 Input Distance Function Multiple Inputs

an arbitrary amount, β, from x_1^o while holding the second input constant at x_2^o in math terms as

$$(x_1^o, x_2^o) - (\beta, 0) = x^o - \beta e^1,$$

where $e^1 = (1, 0)$. Solving

$$x^o - \beta e^1 = x^{oo}$$

gives $\beta = x_1^o - x_1^{oo}$. This visual demonstration shows that $\beta = x_1^o - x_1^{oo}$ solves

$$I(x^o, y) \equiv \max\left\{\beta \in \mathbb{R} : x^o - \beta e^1 \in X(y)\right\} \quad (10.6)$$

When written for arbitrary x, $I(x, y)$ generalizes (10.4) from the single-input case to the two-input case. It is real-valued by definition. We now show that *it can be* a function representation of the technology, or in math terms

$$x \in X(y) \Leftrightarrow I(x, y) \geq 0. \quad (10.7)$$

Let $(x, y) \in T$ so that $x \in X(y)$. Because 0 is a real number, then $x - 0 \cdot e^1 \in X(y)$ satisfies the choice criterion for β in (10.6). Therefore, *the largest* β that satisfies $x - \beta e^1 \in X(y)$ can be no smaller than 0. This argument verifies that

$$x \in X(y) \Rightarrow I(x, y) \geq 0.$$

In words, if x can produce y, the distance function evaluated at (x, y), $I(x, y)$, must be nonnegative. To complete the equivalence relation claimed in (10.7), we must show that

$$I(x, y) \geq 0 \Rightarrow x \in X(y).$$

Or, in words, if the distance function is nonnegative, then x can produce y. By definition, $x - I(x, y)e^1 \in X(y)$. But $I(x, y) \geq 0$ implies that $x \geq x - I(x, y)e^1$. Therefore, *if $X(y)$ satisfies free disposability of inputs (FDI)*, we conclude that $x \in X(y)$. Or, in symbols

$$I(x, y) \geq 0 \Rightarrow x \in X(y).$$

Having gone both ways,[2] we conclude that: *If $X(y)$ satisfies FDI,*

$$x \in X(y) \Leftrightarrow I(x, y) \geq 0.$$

$I(x, y)$ is a function representation of the technology.

The illustration for $I(x^o, y)$ shows that moving x_1^o to the right or the left, while holding x_2 constant, only changes the respective distance function by the amount added to or subtracted from the first input. Thus, for γ an arbitrary real number,

$$I(x + \gamma e^1, y) = I(x, y) + \gamma.$$

Maurice Allais[3] introduced $I(x, y)$ and called it the *disposable surplus* of x_1. It measures the amount of the first input that the producer *can dispose of* but still be able to produce y. $I(x, y)$, which only allows x_1 to adjust, is a special case of measures that allow multiple inputs to vary.

Consider Figure 10.3. As drawn, moving from x^* that is outside of $X(y)$ in any direction to the northeast leads eventually to the isoquant for $y, \bar{X}(y)$. And moving from x^o in any direction to its southwest also leads to $\bar{X}(y)$. Movement to the northeast of a given vector, $\hat{x}$, is the same as adding to it a vector, g, to get $\hat{x} + g$ with $g \geq 0,\ g \neq 0$. Movement to the southwest adds a vector, h, to $\hat{x}$ with $h \leq 0,\ h \neq 0$. If g points to the northeast, $-g$ points to the southwest.

Let $g \geq 0,\ g \neq 0$ and consider the following function:

$$I^g(x, y) \equiv \max\{\beta \in \mathbb{R} : x - \beta g \in X(y)\}. \tag{10.8}$$

$I^g(x, y)$ gives the largest multiple of g that can be subtracted from x while staying in $X(y)$. It is a real number by definition. And, like $I(x, y)$, under the

[2] That is having shown that both directions of $\Leftrightarrow$, $\Rightarrow$ and $\Leftarrow$ are true.

[3] Allais was a French economist and physicist who was awarded the Nobel Memorial Prize in Economics in 1988.

assumption of free disposability of inputs, it characterizes $X(y)$. We show the latter using an argument that parallels the one used for $I(x, y)$.

We first show that $x \in X(y) \Rightarrow I^g(x, y) \geq 0$. If $x \in X(y)$, then $x - 0 \cdot g \in X(y)$ meets the criterion defining $I^g(x, y)$. As before, that shows

$$x \in X(y) \Rightarrow I^g(x, y) \geq 0.$$

To complete the equivalence relation, we must go the other way and show that

$$I^g(x, y) \geq 0 \Rightarrow x \in X(y).$$

Because $g \geq 0,\ g \neq 0$, this follows if $X(y)$ satisfies free disposability of inputs (FDI) because the definition of $I^g(x, y)$ requires that $x - I^g(x, y)g \in X(y)$ and $x \geq x - I^g(x, y)g$. Thus, we have shown the following:

- **Function Representation**: *If $X(y)$ satisfies FDI, $x \in X(y) \Leftrightarrow I^g(x, y) \geq 0$. $I^g(x, y)$ is a function representation of the technology.*

We have shown that adding an arbitrary real number, γ, to x in the single-input case or to x_1 in the two-input case changes $i(x, y)$ and $I(x, y)$ by γ. Both results are special cases of the more general:

- **Translation Property**

$$I^g(x + \gamma g, y) = I^g(x, y) + \gamma, \ \gamma \in \mathbb{R} \tag{10.9}$$

Figure 10.4 illustrates the Translation Property. There x^o falls in $X(y)$. The vector g contains positive amounts of both inputs. To find $I^g(x^o, y)$, draw a

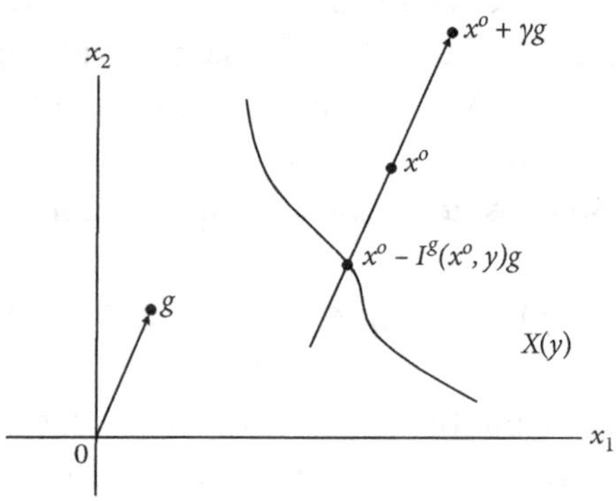

Figure 10.4 The *Translation Property*

line parallel to g through x^o and then move along it until it intersects $\bar{X}(y)$ (illustrated by $x^o - I^g(x^o, y)g$). Adding γg to x^o slides it along the line segment parallel to g by γ units of g to $x^o + \gamma g$. But it does not affect $X(y)$. Thus, the point of intersection between the line segment through x^o parallel to g and $\bar{X}(y)$ remains at $x^o - I^g(x^o, y)g$. Hence, the only change required to move from $I^g(x, y)$ to $I^g(x + \gamma g, y)$ is to add γ.

Here's the math argument:

$$
\begin{aligned}
I^g(x + \gamma g, y) &= \max\{\beta : x + \gamma g - \beta g \in X(y)\} \\
&= \max\{\beta : x - (\beta - \gamma)g \in X(y)\} \\
&= \max\{\beta - \gamma + \gamma : x - (\beta - \gamma)g \in X(y)\} \\
&= \max\{\beta - \gamma : x - (\beta - \gamma)g \in X(y)\} + \gamma \\
&= I^g(x, y) + \gamma
\end{aligned}
\tag{10.10}
$$

The first equality in (10.10) repeats the definition, and the second follows by collecting terms on g. The third adds 0 in the form of $\gamma - \gamma$ to the β in the objective function. The fourth follows by observing that for fixed γ maximizing $\beta - \gamma + \gamma$ requires maximizing $\beta - \gamma$. The final equality follows by replacing β in the definition of $I^g(x, y)$, which we can always do because $\beta - \gamma$ is a real number, and by taking the fixed γ outside of the maximization problem.

We call $I^g(x, y)$ a *distance function* or, sometimes for clarity's sake, an *input distance function.* We warn the reader, however, that this nomenclature is not standard. Other writers reserve the term *distance function* for different mathematical objects. And different writers use different terms for the concept that we define as $I^g(x, y)$. One encounters multiple aliases, including *a surplus function, a benefit function, a directional distance function, a directional input distance function*, and *an input-oriented directional distance function*, among others.

Semantics aside, two points are crucial. First, $I^g(x, y)$ is a *cardinal measure* expressed in quantities that can be meaningfully added, subtracted, or multiplied. That differentiates it, for example, from the *ordinal* utility functions of consumer theory that *can only rank alternative outcomes.* Thus, if $u(x)$ is a utility function, $u(x) > u(y)$ ensures that the consumer prefers x to y, but it does not mean that x is better than y by $u(x) - u(y)$ utils. By contrast, if $I^g(x^*, y) = 2I^g(x^o, y)$, x^* is twice as far (in units of g) from the isoquant for y as x^o. Because one is adding (or subtracting) units of a vector, g, that may seem unfamiliar. But one can always envision an input vector as a bundle of inputs, for example, g = (two units of labor, one unit of capital, one unit of land, three units of fertilizer).[4]

Second, because moving away from x in different directions leads to different regions of an isoquant, $I^g(x, y)$ varies with the choice of g. That observation prompted a convention in production economics of calling g the *direction* because it orients the way in which one moves away toward an isoquant.[5] That is an apt visual description of the movement. But it obscures g's economic role of providing a metric for measuring different aspects of $X(y)$. For that reason, we call g the *numeraire bundle* or, even more simply, the numeraire.

10.3.3 A Technical Difficulty*

The definition of $I^g(x, y)$ in (10.8) assumes that a well-defined largest value exists over the set of real numbers β satisfying

$$\{\beta \in \mathbb{R} : x - \beta g \in X(y)\}.$$

In practice, that definition is sensible for many production problems. But instances exist in which it is not. Take the case of a technology that consists of only one point, so that $T = \{(\hat{x}, \hat{y})\}$. That is, one and only one input-output bundle is technically feasible. It's now easy to imagine input-output combinations $(\bar{x}, \bar{y})$ for which $(\bar{x} - \beta g, \bar{y}) \neq (\hat{x}, \hat{y})$ for all real β. Because no β can satisfy the constraint, $I^g(x, y)$ is ill-defined. The mathematical convention that accommodates such outcomes assigns a value of $-\infty$ to $I^g(\bar{x}, \bar{y})$ in such cases. (Exercise 48 asks you to develop an illustration of this type of technical difficulty.)

10.3.4 A Distance Function for Output Sets

We can characterize $X(y)$ and, thus, T, satisfying free disposability of inputs (FDI) using an input-requirement function, a one-dimensional distance function, $i(x, y)$, the more general two-input $I(x, y)$, and the even more general $I^g(x, y)$. We also know that free disposability of outputs (FDO) ensures that the single-output production function, $f(x)$, and the one-dimensional distance function, $o(y, x)$, characterize T.

[4] Allais's original intent in introducing the disposable surplus measure was to define a cardinal welfare measure for an ordinal utility structure.

[5] Unfortunately, I am partly responsible for this.

A reasonable conjecture, therefore, is that a multiple-output analogue exists for $I^g(x, y)$ and that it characterizes $Y(x)$ if the technology satisfies FDO. This is indeed true. We sketch the argument here but leave the details to the reader as an exercise (see Exercise 49).

Figure 10.5 presents an output set, $Y(x)$, that satisfies FDO. The point y^o falls inside $Y(x)$. Let the $g > 0$ depicted represent a *numeraire output vector.* (To avoid notational clutter, we also use g to denote the output numeraire vector. The dimension of g and whether it contains inputs or outputs, however, varies with the context.) Moving from y^o in the direction of g brings one to the transformation curve for the output set.

Let $g \geq 0; g \neq 0$ and define the *(output) distance function* for (x, y) as

$$O^g(y, x) \equiv \max\{\alpha \in \mathbb{R} : y + \alpha g \in Y(x)\}. \tag{10.11}$$

It measures the largest multiple of the numeraire vector g that can be added to y while staying in $Y(x)$. One visualizes it as placing a vector parallel to g at the tip of y^o and proceeding along it to the transformation curve that bounds $Y(x)$. If, as for y^o in Figure 10.5, the movement is to the northeast, $O^g(y^o, x)$ is positive. If, as for y^*, the movement is to the southeast, $O^g(y^*, x)$ is negative.

Exercise 49 asks you to demonstrate:

$$O^g(y + \gamma g, x) = O^g(y, x) - \gamma, \ \forall \gamma \in \mathbb{R} \quad (\textit{Translation Property})$$

and *if T satisfies free disposability of output, then*

$$O^g(y, x) \geq 0 \Leftrightarrow y \in Y(x) \quad (\textit{Function Representation}).$$

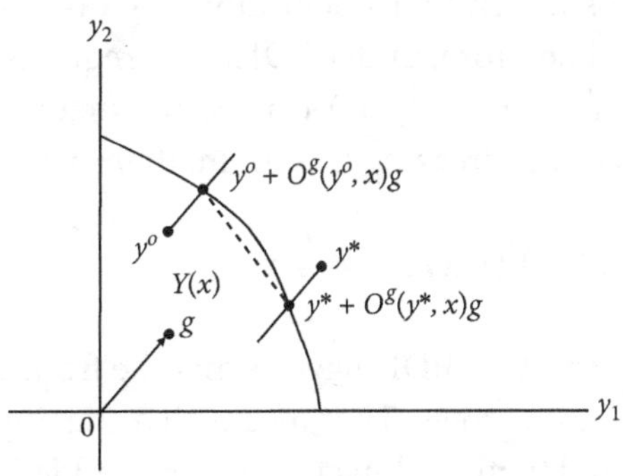

Figure 10.5 The Output Distance Function

It is more precise to write the *input distance function* when referring to $I^g(x, y)$ and the *output distance function* for $O^g(y, x)$. We opt instead for the simpler *distance function* whenever the adjective is clear from the context.

10.3.5 Distance Functions and the Canonical Assumptions

We now study the consequences of our five axioms (assumptions) for distance functions. Because we devoted an extensive discussion to developing $I^g(x, y)$ and only sketched $O^g(y, x)$, we change tack and focus the discussion on the latter, while leaving a more detailed treatment of the former to the reader. Let $g \geq 0,\ g \neq 0$ in all cases that follow in this subsection. Remember that g now represents a numeraire bundle of outputs.

T not Empty

As with the production and input-requirement functions, $T \neq \emptyset$ guarantees that distance functions are mathematical objects of legitimate economic interest. The reasoning is as before. Nonemptiness requires that an (x, y) exists that belongs to the technology set. Take that input-output bundle. If there exists no $\alpha > 0$ such that $y + \alpha g \in Y(x)$, $O^g(y, x) = 0$. Otherwise, for that bundle, $O^g(y, x)$ is given by (10.11). Thus,

- $T \neq \emptyset \Rightarrow \exists\ (x, y)$ such that $O^g(y, x) \geq 0$.

If we observe a multiple-input, multiple-output bundle, a distance function can be associated with it.

Free Disposability of Input

FDI requires that $Y(x) \subset Y(x')$ for $x' \geq x$. Increasing any input cannot make the output set smaller. By its definition, the distance function satisfies $y + O^g(y, x)g \in Y(x)$. Therefore, under FDI $x' \geq x$ requires that $y + O^g(y, x)g \in Y(x')$. But that implies that $O^g(y, x')$ can be no smaller than $O^g(y, x)$. The distance function is nondecreasing in x. In math terms,

- FDI $\Rightarrow O^g(y, x') \geq O^g(y, x)$ for $x' \geq x$.

Recall from Chapter 4 that FDI suggests that the frontier of $Y(x)$ shifts outward as the input bundle grows. That means that starting at any y belonging to $Y(x)$ one can proceed further along the vector αg added to the tip of y before encountering the transformation curve, $\bar{Y}(x)$. (Draw the illustration yourself.)

Thus, the distance between the frontier of the output set and y in the direction parallel to g cannot get smaller.

Free Disposability of Output

We know that FDO ensures that $O^g(y,x)$ is a function representation of the technology. That is its most salient technical consequence. But it is not the only one.

FDO requires that $y^o \leq y \in Y(x) \Rightarrow y^o \in Y(x)$. By definition, we know that $y + O^g(y,x)g \in Y(x)$. But that means that for $y^o \leq y$, $y^o + O^g(y,x)g \in Y(x)$, so that $O^g(y,x)$ satisfies the qualifying condition in (10.11) for (x, y^o). Therefore, $O^g(y^o,x)$ can never be smaller than $O^g(y,x)$. And thus, $y^o \leq y \Rightarrow O^g(y^o,x) \geq O^g(y,x)$.

- FDO $\Rightarrow O^g(y,x)$ is nonincreasing in y.

Under FDO, decreasing the output bundle always keeps one in the output set. Therefore, the distance between the smaller bundle and the frontier cannot be larger than the distance between the frontier and the larger bundle. (Draw the illustration yourself.)

$Y(x)$ Is a Convex Set

Consider two points in Figure 10.5: y^o that belongs to convex $Y(x)$ and y^* that does not.[6] By the definition $O^g(y,x)$, we know that $y^o + O^g(y^o,x)g \in Y(x)$ and $y^* + O^g(y^*,x)g \in Y(x)$. These latter points are illustrated by the respective intersections between the line segments through y^o and y^* parallel to g and the transformation curve $\bar{Y}(x)$.

Take the simple average of these two points of intersection. It corresponds to the point,

$$\frac{y^o + y^*}{2} + \frac{O^g(y^o,x) + O^g(y^*,x)}{2} g \in Y(x),$$

that falls midway between points of intersection on the dashed line segment that connects them. Convexity ensures that it lies inside $Y(x)$. It equals $\frac{y^o+y^*}{2}$ translated in the direction of g by the amount $\frac{O^g(y^o,x)+O^g(y^*,x)}{2}$. That translation satisfies the criterion in (10.11) for the candidate α. Thus,

[6] While $Y(x)$ being a convex set is consistent with convexity of T, as we noted in Chapter 4, convexity of $Y(x)$ is a slightly weaker restriction than convexity of T.

$$O^g\left(\frac{y^o + y^*}{2}, x\right) \geq \frac{O^g(y^o, x) + O^g(y^*, x)}{2}.$$

We can make the same argument for any other weighting factor $0 < \lambda < 1$. Therefore, we conclude that

- $Y(x)$ is a convex set $\Rightarrow O^g(y, x)$ is concave as a function of y, $O^g(\lambda y^o + (1 - \lambda)y^*, x) \geq \lambda O^g(y^o, x) + (1 - \lambda)O^g(y^*, x),\ 0 < \lambda < 1$.

No Free Lunch and No Fixed Costs

No free lunch (NFL) requires that zero input use cannot produce any positive output. That implies that the output set for zero input, $Y(0)$, cannot contain any $y \geq 0,\ y \neq 0$. That raises the practical difficulty that there may not exist a real α such that $y + \alpha g \in Y(0)$. In other words, the set of α's satisfying the condition required for a distance function may be the empty set, $\emptyset$. In that instance, following mathematical convention, we set $O^g(y, x) = -\infty$. No fixed cost (NFC), $(0, 0) \in T$ ensures that $O^g(0, 0) = 0$.

The Axioms and $I^g(x, y)$

We leave it to the reader to show the following (please see Exercise 51):

- $T \neq \emptyset \Rightarrow \exists\ (x, y)$ such that $I^g(x, y) \geq 0$.
- FDI $\Rightarrow I^g(x', y) \geq I^g(x, y)$ for $x' \geq x$ (nondecreasing in x).
- FDO $\Rightarrow I^g(x, y') \geq I^g(x, y)$ for $y' \leq y$ (nonincreasing in y).
- $X(y)$ is a convex set $\Rightarrow I^g(x, y)$ is concave as a function of x.
- NFC $\Rightarrow I^g(0, 0) = 0$.

10.4 All Numeraires Are Not Created Equal*

The idea of a numeraire percolates throughout economics. Its role and importance are phrased in different ways. We use the aphorism "only real prices matter." Another aphorism is "absence of money illusion." Both convey the idea that economic decisions only reflect relative valuations of commodities.

Because the numeraire determines the real units in which we measure abstract concepts such as value, economists often treat its choice as arbitrary. For valuation purposes, that is likely true. But the differences between $I^g(x, y)$ and $O^g(y, x)$ show that different numeraires can matter in practical settings.

This chapter focuses on two types of numeraire. One consists of an input bundle and another of an output bundle. For the former, FDI ensures that $I^g(x, y)$ is a function representation of the technology. FDO plays that role for $O^g(y, x)$.

Our motivation for examining those two alternatives is rooted in tradition rather substance. FDI and FDO are the natural generalizations of the assumptions upon which economic jargoneers rely when talking about production functions, marginal products, average products, and the like. They provide the analytic means required to discuss multiple-input, multiple-output production processes in familiar terms. This tradition is reinforced by the duality between profit-maximizing behavior in competitive markets and the canonical technology. After all, if canonical and noncanonical models give the same economic conclusions, why not abandon the latter in favor of the former on practical grounds? That dual connection, however, hinges on the assumption that producers maximize returns when they receive *positive* prices for outputs and pay *positive prices* for inputs.

Many (perhaps most) productive activities generate undesirable by-products. Even the mundane tasks of mowing one's lawn or vacuuming one's house generate noise that is distracting, if not downright distressing. To my knowledge, no active markets exist that offer positive prices for lawn mower noise. But there do exist noise-canceling devices for which one pays a *positive price* to ameliorate the noisy by-products of lawn mowers, leaf blowers, and other machinery. Instead of being paid to generate the output noise, one pays (in terms of time and foregone buying power for other items) to alleviate it. To those producers, the opportunity cost of the output noise is negative and not positive.

So, the canonical model has its limits. And we should ensure that its limits do not limit our ability to examine producer behavior. Thus, in choosing ways to represent the technology, we should be sensitive to assumptions that may be violated in practice. And inputs and outputs being positively priced is the linchpin to the observational equivalence of a noncanonical technology with one that exhibits FDI and FDO. Chapter 2 emphasizes that both FDI and FDO are subject to counterexamples. Thus, they may prove inappropriate modeling assumptions in some practical settings.

Here is an example. Consider a farmer who uses land, seed, an array of farm implements (tractors, etc.), labor, fertilizers, pesticides, and an array of environmentally determined inputs such as natural moisture and radiation to produce corn. We know that FDI is too strong an assumption for this farmer because too much fertilizer applied to a fixed amount of land can kill a corn plant. That would seem to rule out using $I^g(x, y)$ in modeling T. We might instead rely on FDO to specify an output distance function. But FDO is also implausible. Corn farmers produce undesirable by-products in the form of soil and nutrient runoff and CO_2 emissions whose remediation requires effort and thus violates FDO.

Is there a way out of this quandary, or are distance functions just analytic "toys" used to manipulate abstract economic models? The answer to the first question is yes, and the answer to the second is no. We can continue the illustration with the same example. Take the same farmer using the same inputs producing the same good and bad outputs. Because the manner in which we choose subscripts for inputs and outputs is arbitrary, choose input indices so that 1 corresponds to land.

Now consider the generalization (weakening) of FDI:

- **Free Disposability of Land (FDL)**: $(x, y) \in T \Rightarrow (x+\lambda e^1, y) \in T,\ \lambda \geq 0.$

Here $e^1 = (1, 0, \ldots, 0)$ is a vector of the same dimension as x so that $x + \lambda e^1 = (x_1 + \lambda, x_2, \ldots, x_N)$ augments the land input by the positive amount λ while holding all other inputs unchanged. FDL requires that increasing land use does not cause congestion. We leave it to the reader to judge its physical plausibility. For analytic purposes, its importance is that it is a weaker assumption than FDI. Assume for the purposes of argument that it is true.

Now (re)define

$$I(x, y) = \max\left\{\beta \in \mathbb{R} : x - \beta e^1 \in T\right\}$$

as the generalization of disposable surplus extended to the case of an arbitrary number of inputs. $I(x, y)$ now measures the *disposable surplus of land* in production, holding all other inputs and output constant.

Following the same line of argument used earlier shows that: *If T satisfies FDL, $x \in X(y) \Leftrightarrow I(x, y) \geq 0$ and $x \in X(y) \Leftrightarrow I^{e^1}(x, y) \geq 0$. The disposable surplus of land is a function representation of T.* We do not belabor the point, but it is apparent that similar arguments defining alternative distance functions for inputs that do not suffer from congestion (see Chapter 2) deliver function representations of T. Parallel arguments do the same for output distance functions defined for outputs that are reasonably construed as disposable.

The take-away messages are that the numeraire choice requires reasonable caution and that our specification of a flexible numeraire, g, facilitates exercising that caution for real-world applications. Failure of the canonical assumptions does not license ignoring their basic messages.

10.5 Exercises

Exercise 48. *Let $X(y) = \{(2,3)\}$ so that the input set has only a single point in it. (We do not assume that $X(y)$ satisfies FDI.) Let $x = (2,5)$ and $g = (1,1)$. Illustrate $X(y)$, x, and g on the real coordinate plane. Demonstrate that there exists no $\{\beta \in \mathbb{R} : x - \beta g \in X(y)\}$.*

Exercise 49. *Let $g \geq 0, g \neq 0$. Show that:*

$$O^g(y + \gamma g, x) = O^g(y, x) - \gamma, \forall \gamma \in \mathbb{R} \quad (\textit{Translation Property});$$

and if T satisfies free disposability of output, then

$$O^g(y, x) \geq 0 \Leftrightarrow y \in Y(x),$$

so that it is a function representation of T.

Exercise 50. *In economics, the term* distance function *seems to be traceable to Shephard (1953), who introduced it in the context of a single-output product function. Shephard's conceptualization had appeared earlier in other studies, under different names, in Konüs, 1939 and Debreu, 1951. And it has apparent roots in Minkowski's* Distanzfunktion, *used to characterize convex absorbing sets (Minkowski, 1911). We can write the generalization of Shephard's distance functions in terms of input sets as*

$$D(x, y) = \max\{\delta > 0 : x \in \delta X(y)\}$$

$D(x, y)$ measures how much $X(y)$ can be shifted radially outward (keeping the respective boundaries parallel to one another) while keeping x in radially expanded set. (a) Illustrate $D(x, y)$ for a multiple-input technology. (b) Prove that

$$D(x, y) = (1 - O^x(y, x))^{-1}.$$

(Hint: Note that the numeraire now takes $g = x$.)

Exercise 51. **Show the following:*

- $T \neq \emptyset \Rightarrow \exists\ (x, y)$ *such that* $I^g(x, y) \geq 0$.
- *FDI* $\Rightarrow I^g(x', y) \geq I^g(x, y)$ *for* $x' \geq x$.
- *FDO* $\Rightarrow I^g(x, y') \geq I^g(x, y)$ *for* $y' \leq y$.

- *$X(y)$ is a convex set* $\Rightarrow$ *$I^g(x, y)$ is concave as a function of x.*
- *NFC* $\Rightarrow$ *$I^g(0, 0) = 0$.*

Explain each result and illustrate it graphically.

Exercise 52. **Let $T = \{(x_1, x_2, y_1, y_2) : (x_1, x_2)$ can produce $(y_1, y_2)\}$ and assume that $(x_1, x_2, y_1, y_2) \in T \Rightarrow (x_1', x_2, y_1', y_2) \in T$ for $x_1' \geq x_1, y_1' \leq y_1$. In words, the first input and the first output are freely disposable, but the second input and the second output are not. Define the* surplus function *for T as*

$$s(x_1, x_2, y_1, y_2) = max\{\beta \in \mathbb{R} : (x_1 - \beta, x_2, y_1 + \beta, y_2) \in T\}.$$

Prove that: a) $s(x_1, x_2, y_1, y_2) \geq 0 \Leftrightarrow (x_1, x_2, y_1, y_2) \in T$; and b) $s(x_1 + \alpha, x_2, y_1 - \alpha, y_2) = s(x_1, x_2, y_1, y_2) + \alpha$ for $\alpha \in \mathbb{R}$.

11
Using Distance Functions

11.1 Introduction

Distance functions and their near mathematical relations play important roles in different areas of economics. This chapter studies two uses in analyzing production: developing cost and revenue functions; and measuring efficiency (inefficiency) and relative performance

11.2 Obtaining Cost and Revenue Functions

We first examine the use of distance functions to pose and solve cost minimization and revenue maximization as *nonlinear programming problems.* Then we use those results to derive *dual distance functions.* Those results provide another perspective from which to examine the duality linkage between quantity- (primal-) based representations of T and price- (dual-) based representations. We then illustrate the role that distance functions can play in providing a numerical basis for calculating shadow (virtual) prices for inputs or outputs.

We offer a caveat before proceeding. Chapters 5 through 9 provide in-depth discussions of cost functions, revenue functions, profit functions, and dual relations. The focus of the present discussion is on using distance functions to identify economic equilibria and on applying duality mappings. It complements rather than substitutes for Chapters 5 through 9. A sound grasp of the material in those chapters is essential to absorbing the implications of this discussion.

11.2.1 From $I^g(x, y)$ to $c(w, y)$

We maintain two assumptions in discussing cost minimization. The first, $X(y)$, is nonempty and ensures the existence of a meaningful cost function, $c(w, y)$. The second, free disposability of inputs (FDI), ensures that we can use $I^g(x, y)$ to frame the discussion.

Lectures on Neoclassical Production Economics. Robert G. Chambers, Oxford University Press.
 DOI: 10.1093/9780197817759.003.0012

Because FDI implies that $I^g(x, y)$ is a function representation of $X(y)$, $x \in X(y) \Leftrightarrow I^g(x, y) \geq 0$, we can write the cost-minimization problem as

$$\begin{aligned} c(w, y) &\equiv \min_x \{wx : x \in X(y)\} \qquad (11.1) \\ &= \min_x \{wx : I^g(x, y) \geq 0\}. \end{aligned}$$

The second equality in (11.1) is a special case of a *nonlinear program*. *Nonlinear programming* studies mathematical methods for solving optimization problems that involve nonlinear *objective functions* or nonlinear *constraint* functions.[1] Here the objective function, wx, is linear in x, and the constraint, $I^g(x, y) \geq 0$, is nonlinear. Other nonlinear programs that you may have encountered are the consumer utility maximization and the expenditure minimization problems. The methods used to derive $c(w, y)$ from $I^g(x, y)$ can be applied in the consumer context to derive the expenditure function from a distance-function representation of consumer preferences.

The definition of $I^g(x, y)$ ensures that

$$x - I^g(x, y)g \in X(y) \text{ for all } x. \qquad (11.2)$$

In words, taking an input bundle, x, calculating its associated distance function for y, $I^g(x, y)$, and using that result to calculate $x - I^g(x, y)g$, give a transformed input bundle that can produce y. We refer to this transformation of x into $x - I^g(x, y)g$ as the *translation of x into X(y) in the direction of g*, or the *translation transformation* for short.

Because $c(w, y)$ provides the cheapest way to produce y, expression (11.2) establishes that it must be a lower bound to the market value of any translated input bundle.

$$c(w, y) \leq wx - I^g(x, y)wg, \textit{ for all } w, x \qquad (11.3)$$

And because $X(y)$ is not empty, a cost-minimizing input bundle must exist. (There can be more than one, see Chapter 6.) Denote it by $x(w, y)$.

Our first result is:

- **Cost-minimizing input bundles require zero translation**: Let $x(w, y)$ solve problem (11.1). Then $I^g(x(w, y), y) = 0$.

The implication is that the translation of a cost-minimizing bundle, $x(w, y)$, into $X(y)$ is itself $x(w, y)$. Verifying this claim involves a proof by contradiction. Because $x(w, y) \in X(y)$, free disposability of inputs (FDI) requires that

[1] Standard references on nonlinear programming include Mangasarian, 1969; and Bertesekas, 2016.

$I^g(x(w,y),y) \geq 0$. Let that inequality be strict. Then $wx(w,y) > wx(w,y) - I^g(x(w,y),y)wg$. That strict inequality and expression (11.2) contradict the original assumption that $x(w,y)$ is the cheapest input bundle in $X(y)$.

Therefore, we know that if $X(y)$ is nonempty and satisfies FDI, the lower bound in (11.3) is "tight" and is achieved at cost- minimizing bundles, $x(w,y)$. That means that the cost function also minimizes the cost of all translations into $X(y)$. Thus,

$$\begin{aligned} c(w,y) &= \min_x \{wx - I^g(x,y)wg\} \\ &= \min_x \left\{ wg\left(\frac{w}{wg}x - I^g(x,y)\right)\right\} \\ &= wg \min_x \left\{\frac{w}{wg}x - I^g(x,y)\right\}. \end{aligned} \tag{11.4}$$

The second equality in (11.4) follows by collecting terms. The third follows because the solution to choosing x to minimize the product $wg\left(\frac{w}{wg}x - I^g(x,y)\right)$ for wg held fixed is the same as choosing x to minimize $\frac{w}{wg}x - I^g(x,y)$.

Besides providing an alternative way to compute $c(w,y)$, expression (11.4) emphasizes the role that g plays in analyzing optimal producer behavior. Because g contains at least one positive element and input prices are positive, $wg > 0$. The product of input prices and the numeraire bundles, wg, gives the *market value of the numeraire input bundle.*[2] That value provides a convenient numeraire for converting nominal prices into real terms.

Invoking the positive homogeneity (only real prices matter) property of cost functions and dividing both sides of (11.4) by wg then gives

$$c\left(\frac{w}{wg},y\right) = \min_x \left\{\frac{w}{wg}x - I^g(x,y)\right\}. \tag{11.5}$$

Problems (11.4) and (11.5) have the same solutions. The difference is that the former uses *nominal input prices* and the latter uses *real input prices.* (Remember, only real prices matter!) The normalizing factor is the market value of g.[3] To simplify notation, in the following let

$$v \equiv \frac{w}{wg}$$

[2] Notice, for example, that taking $g = (1,0,\ldots,0)$ is the same as taking w_1 as the numeraire price. It is the market value of one unit of the first input.

[3] Index numbers with which you may be familiar may include the producer price index or the consumer price index. Both measure the market value of the same bundle of goods in different time periods. The use of market bundles to create numeraires is standard and widespread.

be the vector of real-input prices expressed in units of the numeraire bundle g.

Chapter 8 posed the profit-maximization problem in three separate forms. The first cast it as maximizing the value of profit subject to (x, y) belonging to T. The second and third (equivalent) formulations recast it as the following nonlinear programs

$$\begin{aligned} \pi(p, w) &\equiv \max_x \{R(p, x) - wx\} \\ &\equiv \max_y \{py - c(w, y)\}. \end{aligned} \tag{11.6}$$

The first formulation involves maximizing the difference between a *nonlinear* function of x, $R(p, x)$, and a *linear* function of x, and the second involves maximizing the difference between a *linear* function of y and a *nonlinear* function of y, $c(w, y)$. Expression (11.5) has the same generic structure as (11.6), the difference between a linear and nonlinear form. What distinguishes (11.5) from (11.6) is that optimization involves minimization rather than maximization. We can, however, pursue a similar strategy to characterize a solution to (11.5).[4]

Let $x(v, y)$ solve (11.5). By the definition of a minimum, it must satisfy

$$vx - I^g(x, y) \geq vx(v, y) - I^g(x(v, y), y), \textit{ for all } x.$$

In words, all other values of x generate at least as expensive translations into $X(y)$ as $x(v, y)$. Adding $I^g(x(v, y), y)$ to both sides of this inequality gives:

$$I^g(x(v, y), y) + v\,(x - x(v, y)) \geq I^g(x, y) \textit{ for all } x. \tag{11.7}$$

Expression (11.7), in the language of Chapter 8, is a necessary and sufficient (if and only if) condition for $x(v, y)$ to be cost-minimizing. That is: if $x(v, y)$ solves (11.5), it must satisfy (11.7) (this is the only if part); and if $x(v, y)$ satisfies (11.7) it must solve (11.5) (this is the if part).[5]

The criterion characterizing the cost-minimizing solution is that the affine function of x,

$$I^g(x(v, y), y) - vx(v, y) + vx, \tag{11.8}$$

[4] Because minimizing $f(x)$ is equivalent to maximizing $-f(x)$, the notational changes involved in moving from minimization to maximization only require changing the directions of inequalities.

[5] For the calculus *cognoscenti*, we emphasize that expression (11.7) is a stronger condition than the first-order condition for minimization, the second-order condition, or the two combined.

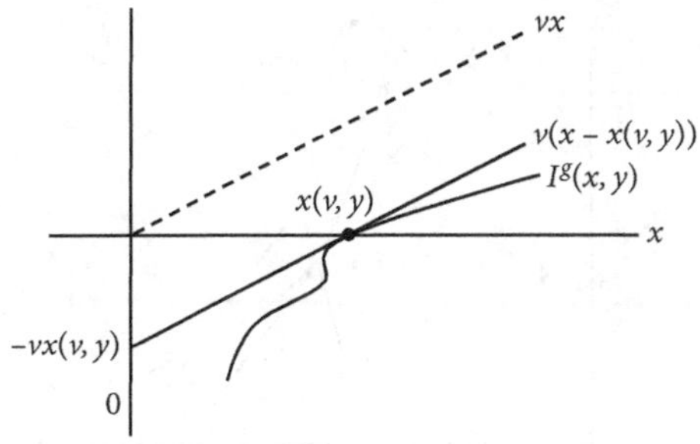

Figure 11.1 Necessary and Sufficient Condition for Cost Minimization

is greater than or equal to (*majorizes, dominates*) the distance function $I^g(x,y)$ for all possible values of x. *The graph of the distance function,* $I^g(x,y)$*, as a function of x must fall completely in the half-space on or below the graph of the affine function,* $I^g(x(v,y),y) + v\,(x - x(v,y))$*, of x.*

Figure 11.1 illustrates. The dotted line segment emanating from the origin depicts the *linear* function vx of x with slope of v. The *affine* line segment parallel to it, $I^g(x(v,y),y) + v\,(x - x(v,y))$, has intercept

$$I^g(x(v,y),y) - vx(v,y) = -vx(v,y)$$

and is illustrated by the solid line that parallels the dotted line segment. (Remember, we established above that $I^g(x(v,y),y) = 0$.)

Evaluating expression (11.8) and $I^g(x,y)$ at $x = x(v,y)$ shows that both equal zero. The bounding affine function and the distance function take the same value at the cost-minimizing point, $x(v,y)$. But everywhere else, the graph of $I^g(x,y)$ cannot go above the graph of the affine function (11.8). That affine function of x, $I^g(x(v,y),y) + v(x - x(v,y))$, must support the graph of $I^g(x,y)$ from above at the cost-minimizing solution, $x(v,y)$.

Because v (the vector of real prices) is the normal to that affine function, the requirement in (11.7) is (in part) that the slope of $I^g(x,y)$ be equated to v (a tangency condition). The same argument shows that we can illustrate the cost-minimizing solution, $x(v,y)$, in the two-input case as occurring at a tangency between a line segment with normal, v, and the zero level set for $I^g(x,y)$, $\{x : I^g(x,y) = 0\}$ as illustrated in Figure 11.2.

Figure 11.2 also helps to clarify how the "translation transformation" simplifies solving the cost-minimizing problem. Evaluating the function in (11.5) to be minimized,

$$vx - I^g(x,y),$$

at the input bundle depicted in Figure 11.2 as $x(v,y) + \gamma g$ gives

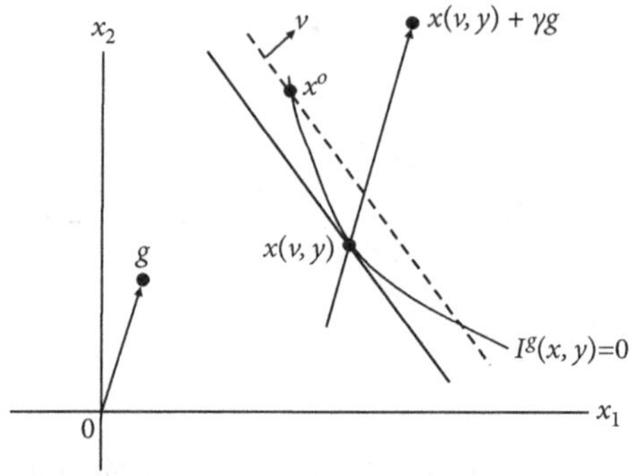

Figure 11.2 Cost-Minimizing Solutions Invariant to Translation

$$\begin{aligned} v\left(x(v,y)+\gamma g\right)-I^g(x(v,y)+\gamma g,y) &= vx(v,y)+\gamma-I^g(x(v,y)),y)-\gamma \\ &= vx(v,y)-I^g(x(v,y)),y) \\ &= c(v,y). \end{aligned}$$

The first equality follows by applying the Translation Property to $I^g(x(v,y)+\gamma g,y)$ on the left-hand side and noting that $vg = \frac{w}{wg}g = 1$. Because this argument works for *arbitrary* γ, it follows that if $x(v,y)$ solves the cost-minimization problem (11.5), so too must *any* translation of it in the direction of g (regardless of the size or sign of γ). That's true because *the translation transformation maps every input bundle onto the zero level set for* $I^g(x,y)$, $\{x : I^g(x,y)=0\}$. Instead of searching over all possible input bundles, the translation transformation, therefore, reduces the search to inputs translated into the level set $\{x : I^g(x,y)=0\}$.[6] Summarizing, we have shown that:

- **Cost-Minimizing Solutions Are Invariant to Translation**: Let

  $$x(v,y) \in argmin\{vx - I^g(x,y)\},$$

  then

  $$\begin{aligned} x(v,y) \in argmin\{vx - I^g(x,y)\} &\Leftrightarrow x(v,y)+\gamma g \\ &\in argmin\{vx - I^g(x,y)\} \text{ for all } \gamma. \end{aligned}$$

We now derive Shephard's Lemma from Chapter 6 using this formulation of the cost-minimization problem. The definitions of $c(v,y)$ and $x(v,y)$ require that for all v^* and v

[6] For those acquainted with Lagrangean multipliers and Lagrangean functions, this is an alternative approach to accommodating nonlinear constraints in nonlinear programs.

$$c(v^*, y) \leq v^* x(v, y) - I^g(x(v, y), y)$$

and

$$c(v, y) = vx(v, y) - I^g(x(v, y), y).$$

The inequality reminds us that what's cost minimizing for v need not be cost minimizing for $v^* \neq v$. The equality repeats the definition of $c(v, y)$ for this formulation of the problem. Subtracting the equality from the inequality, remembering that $I^g(x(v, y), y) = 0$, gives

$$c(v, y) + (v^* - v)x(v, y) \geq c(v^*, y) \tag{11.9}$$

for all v^* and v. Expression (11.9) repeats Shephard's Lemma from Chapter 6. One can recapture the cost-minimizing demand $x(v, y)$ as the slope of a hyperplane that supports the cost function from above at $(v, c(v, y))$.

We summarize this discussion in **C**:

- **C**: Let $X(y)$ satisfy FDI. Then $x(v, y)$ solves (11.5) if and only if the affine function of x, $v(x - x(v, y))$, supports the graph of $I^g(x, y)$ from above at $(x(v, y), I^g(x(v, y), y))$. Any solution to (11.5) forms the normal to a hyperplane that supports the graph of $c(v, y)$ from above at $(v, c(v, y))$.

11.2.2 From $c(w, y)$ to the Dual Distance Function $\bar{I}^g(x, y)$

Chapter 9 developed duality relationships between cost functions, revenue functions, profit functions, and T. The earliest duality demonstrations in economics used function representations of T that are special cases of our distance functions. We now develop a duality mapping that generates an input distance function from $c(w, y)$.

11.2.2.1 A Dual Input Distance Function

The positive homogeneity of $c(w, y)$ in w (only real price matters) ensures that dividing both sides of

$$c(w, y) \leq wx - I^g(x, y)wg \; \textit{for all } w, x$$

by $wg > 0$ and adding $I^g(x, y)$ transforms it into the equivalent form

$$I^g(x, y) \leq vx - c(v, y) \; \textit{for all } v, x. \tag{11.10}$$

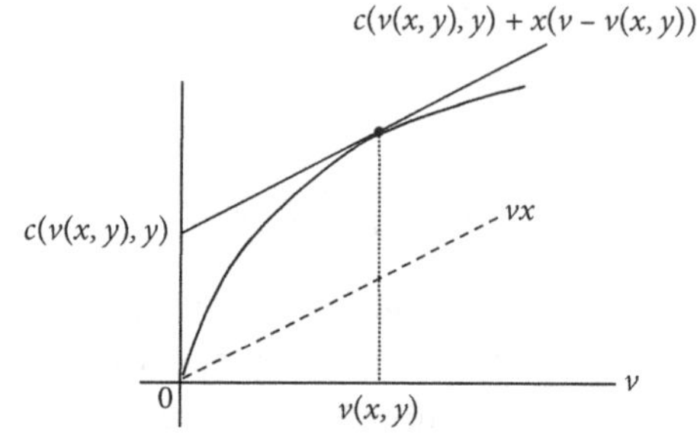

Figure 11.3 Solution to the Dual Distance Function Problem

The distance function bounds the difference between the real market value of the input bundle, vx, and the minimal real cost of producing y, $c(v, y)$, from below. Because expression (11.10) holds for all possible v, it must also satisfy:

$$I^g(x,y) \leq \bar{I}^g(x,y) \equiv \min_v \{vx - c(v,y)\}. \tag{11.11}$$

We call $\bar{I}^g(x,y)$ a *dual (input) distance function* and the difference between $I^g(x,y)$ and $\bar{I}^g(x,y)$ $I^g(x,y) - \bar{I}^g(x,y) \leq 0$, a *duality gap*.

Write solutions to (11.11) as $v(x,y)$. As minimizing solutions, they must satisfy

$$vx - c(v,y) \geq v(x,y)x - c(v(x,y),y) \textit{ for all } v,$$

or in equivalent form

$$c(v(x,y),y) + x(v - v(x,y)) \geq c(v,y) \textit{ for all } v. \tag{11.12}$$

Inequality (11.12) completely characterizes solutions to (11.11). It requires that the affine function of v, $c(v(x,y),y) + x(v - v(w,y))$, with normal x support the cost function from above at $(v(x,y), c(v(x,y),y))$. See Figure 11.3 for an illustration.

Expression (11.12) evokes the same principles as expression (11.9) and Shephard's Lemma. The difference is that x in (11.12) is evaluated at an arbitrary input level and $v(x,y)$ that solves (11.11), while expression (11.9) is evaluated at $x(v,y)$, the cost-minimizing solution v and arbitrary v. They are *dual* versions of the same inequality principle.

To illustrate, solve (11.11) for $x = x(\hat{v}, y)$, the cost-minimizing bundle for $\hat{v}$. By (11.12), any solution, $v(x(\hat{v},y),y)$, must satisfy

$$c(v(x(\hat{v},y),y) + x(\hat{v},y)(v - v(x(\hat{v},y),y)) \geq c(v,y) \text{ for all } v. \tag{11.13}$$

Comparing (11.9) evaluated at $v = \hat{v}$ and (11.13) shows that $x(\hat{v}, y)$ must be cost minimizing for both $\hat{v}$ and $v(x(\hat{v}, y), y)$. That may seem to imply that $\hat{v} = v(x(\hat{v}, y), y)$. For sufficiently restrictive versions of $X(y)$, it does. More generally, conditions (11.9) and (11.13) require that *both* $\hat{v}$ and $v(x(\hat{v}, y), y)$ support $X(y)$ at $x(\hat{v}, y)$. If $\hat{v} \neq v(x(\hat{v}, y), y)$, that is possible if the isoquant is "kinked" at $x(\hat{v}, y)$. (For more details, please consult Chapter 6.) But if the isoquant is suitably smooth at $x(\hat{v}, y)$, then $\hat{v} = v(x(\hat{v}, y), y)$.

Regardless of the number of solutions, these arguments show that the problem posed in (11.11) seeks the input price vectors for which the given x is cost minimizing. Because we chose $\hat{v}$ arbitrarily in this illustration, the principle applies for all possible choices of v and $x(v, y)$. The duality mapping "inverts" the cost-minimizing input-demand functions to obtain as *price-dependent* demands, $v(x, y)$, the real prices at which a cost-minimizing producer would demand x.[7]

By the definition of $\bar{I}^g(x, y)$, it must be true for all x^* and x that

$$\bar{I}^g(x, y) \leq v(x^*, y)x - c(v(x^*, y), y)$$

and

$$\bar{I}^g(x^*, y) = v(x^*, y)x^* - c(v(x^*, y), y).$$

The inequality reminds us that even though $v(x^*, y)$ solves (11.11) for x^*, it may not solve it for other x. The equality repeats the definition of $\bar{I}^g(x^*, y)$. Subtracting the equality from the inequality gives

$$\bar{I}^g(x^*, y) + v(x^*, y)(x - x^*) \geq \bar{I}^g(x, y) \ \textit{for all } x. \qquad (11.14)$$

Comparing expressions (11.14) and (11.7) reveals that they are dual versions of one another. Evaluating (11.7) at $v(x, y)$, we find that a solution for problem (11.11) gives

$$I^g(x(v, y), y) + v(x, y)\,(x - x(v(x, y), y)) \geq I^g(x, y)\ \textit{for all } x,$$

which shows that $x(v(x, y), y)$ must be cost-minimizing for $v(x, y)$. Just as (11.11) and (11.9) convey the same information, so too do (11.14) and (11.7).

Solutions to (11.5) and (11.11) satisfy the same criteria and convey this information. We summarize this discussion by stating I, which is dual to condition C:

[7] Because the convention in economics is to plot consumer demand functions with price on the vertical (dependent) axis and quantity on the horizontal (independent) axis, any reader with a background in microeconomics will have encountered price-dependent demand functions.

- **I**: Let $X(y)$ satisfy FDI. Then $v(x,y)$ solves (11.11) if and only if the affine function of v, $c(v(x,y),y) + x(v - v(x,y))$, supports the graph of $c(v,y)$ from above at $(v(x,y), c(v(x,y),y))$. Any solution to (11.11) forms the normal to a hyperplane that supports the graph of $\bar{I}^g(x,y)$ from above at $(x, \bar{I}^g(x,y))$.

11.2.2.2 Properties of $\bar{I}^g(x,y)$

The dual distance function, $\bar{I}^g(x,y)$, is nondecreasing in x and satisfies the Translation Property. We leave the monotonicity demonstration to the reader. Here's a simple argument for the Translation Property. Let γ be an arbitrary real number. Then

$$\begin{aligned} \bar{I}^g(x+\gamma g, y) &= \min_v \{v(x+\gamma g) - c(v,y)\} \\ &= \min_v \{vx + \gamma - c(v,y)\} \\ &= \min_v \{vx - c(v,y)\} + \gamma \\ &= \bar{I}^g(x,y) + \gamma \quad (\textit{Translation Property}) \end{aligned} \tag{11.15}$$

The first equality follows by the definition, and the second by multiplication and the fact that $vg = 1$. The third equality follows by the fact that the minimal value of $vx - c(v,y) + \gamma$ for γ held fixed is achieved by minimizing the difference $vx - c(v,y)$. And the fourth follows by the definition.

As a nondecreasing function satisfying the translation property, $\bar{I}^g(x,y)$ shares the characteristics of an input distance function generated by a nonempty input set consistent with the free disposability of inputs (FDI). Therefore, we can interpret the elements of its upper contour set

$$X^*(y) \equiv \{x : \bar{I}^g(x,y) \geq 0\}$$

as belonging to a *dual input set* satisfying FDI. Moreover, because $\bar{I}^g(x,y) \geq I^g(x,y)$ for all (x,y), we observe that

$$x \in X(y) \Rightarrow I^g(x,y) \geq 0 \Rightarrow \bar{I}^g(x,y) \geq 0 \Rightarrow x \in X^*(y)$$

so that

$$x \in X(y) \Rightarrow x \in X^*(y)$$

Any element of $X(y)$ also has to belong to $X^*(y)$. Thus, $X(y)$ must be contained within $X^*(y)$ so that $X(y) \subset X^*(y)$.

The reverse implication that $x \in X^*(y) \Rightarrow x \in X(y)$ is not always true. $X^*(y)$ can contain input bundles that cannot produce y. The reasoning echoes that of Chapter 9. Because $\bar{I}^g(x,y)$ is the minimal value of a function, $vx - c(v,y)$, that is affine in x, it must be concave as a function of x. We demonstrated versions of that characteristic of optimal value functions in Chapters 6, 7, 8, and 9. Hence, we leave its graphical illustration to you as an informal exercise. Instead we give a simple algebraic proof. Let $v^* \equiv v(\lambda x^o + (1-\lambda)x', y)$ denote the solution to (11.11) for $\lambda x^o + (1-\lambda)x'$, $0 < \lambda < 1$. Then, by definition,

$$\begin{aligned} v^* x^o - c(v^*, y) &\geq \bar{I}^g(x^o, y) \\ v^* x' - c(v^*, y) &\geq \bar{I}^g(x', y). \end{aligned}$$

Multiplying the first by λ, the second by $1-\lambda$, adding, and using the definition of v^* as a minimizer give

$$\bar{I}^g(\lambda x^o + (1-\lambda)x', y) \geq \lambda \bar{I}^g(x^o, y) + (1-\lambda)\bar{I}^g(x', y), \quad 0 < \lambda < 1. \tag{11.16}$$

Expression (11.16) shows that $\bar{I}^g(x,y)$ is concave as a function of x. Concavity of the dual distance function implies that $X^*(y)$, the dual input set, is a convex set. (See Exercise 53.) To develop $\bar{I}^g(x,y)$, we did not require a convex $X(y)$. But $X^*(y)$ must be convex. Therefore, the two input sets can differ, and it is possible that $X(y) \neq X^*(y)$.

The following, however, is true:

- **Dual Cost and Distance Functions**: Let $X(y)$ be a convex set that satisfies free disposability of inputs (FDI). Then $X^*(y) = X(y)$, and[8] another.

$$\begin{aligned} c(v,g) &= \min_x \{vx - I^g(x,y)\} \\ I^g(x,y) &= \min_v \{vx - c(v,y))\} \end{aligned}$$

A dual distance function that is recaptured from $c(w,y)$ only reflects input bundles in $\bar{X}(y)$ that are consistent with cost minimization. And so, if the input set is nonconvex (contains "dimples"), a cost minimizer avoids them in favor of cheaper input bundles. Because points falling in "dimples" cannot be cost minimizing, $\bar{I}^g(x,y)$ yields a dual approximation to the original input set that

[8] When the cost and distance functions satisfy these conditions, they are *concave conjugates* of one another.

replaces them with a *convexified* version of $X(y)$ that envelops the "dimples." $X^*(y)$ and $X(y)$ give the same cost- minimizing solutions. From an economic perspective, *they are observationally equivalent.* But they can differ. On the other hand, if $X(y)$ is convex and satisfies FDI, we can recapture $I^g(x, y)$ from $c(w, y)$ as its dual distance function.

11.2.3 From $O^g(y, x)$ to $R(p, x)$ to $\bar{O}^g(y, x)$

We now sketch analogous approaches: for deriving the revenue function, $R(p, x)$, from the output distance function, $O^g(y, x)$; and for using $R(p, x)$ to derive a dual (output) distance function, $\bar{O}^g(y, x)$. The switch to an output setting changes the notation and the specifics of the argument, but not the principles. We, therefore, summarize the results but leave derivations to the reader.

Let $Y(x)$ be nonempty and satisfy free disposability of output (FDO). Our maintained structure differs. But the difference only reflects the change in focus from inputs to outputs. Let $g \geq 0, \;\; g \neq 0$. We remind the reader that g now represents a *numeraire output bundle.* Its dimension and components differ from the input numeraire.

The revenue function is an (upper) bound for the value of all output bundles translated into $Y(x)$ in the direction of g. That is,

$$y + O^g(y, x)g \in Y(x) \;\Rightarrow\; R(p, x) \geq py + O^g(y, x)pg \textit{ for all } p, y.$$

Let

$$q = \frac{p}{pg}$$

be the vector of real output prices expressed in units of the value of the numeraire bundle. Using an argument analogous to that for the input distance functions gives

$$R(q, x) = \max_y \{qy + O^g(y, x)\}. \tag{11.17}$$

Denote solutions to (11.17) by $y(q, x)$. We leave it to the reader as an exercise (see Exercise 54) to establish and discuss

- **R**: Let $Y(x)$ be nonempty and satisfy FDO. Then $y^* \in y(q, x) \Leftrightarrow O^g(y^*, x) - q(y - y^*) \geq O^g(y, x)$ *for all* y and $y^* \in y(q, x) \Leftrightarrow R(\hat{q}, x) \geq R(q, x) + y^*(\hat{q} - q)$ *for all* $\hat{q}, q$.

Just as the revenue function is an upper bound to $py + O^g(y,x)g$ for all y, p, $O^g(y,x)$ is a *lower* bound to the difference between maximal revenue and observed revenue. That is,

$$y + O^g(y,x) \in Y(x) \Rightarrow R(p,x) - py \geq O^g(y,x)pg \text{ for all } p, y.$$

Thus,

$$O^g(y,x) \leq \bar{O}^g(y,x) \equiv \min_q \{R(q,x) - qy\}, \tag{11.18}$$

Denoting solutions to (11.18) by $q(y,x)$, we have:

- **O**: Let $Y(x)$ be nonempty and satisfy FDO. Then $q^* \in q(y,x) \Leftrightarrow R(q^*,x) + y(\hat{q} - q^*) \leq R(\hat{q},x)$ *for all* $\hat{q}$ and $q^* \in q(y,x) \Leftrightarrow \bar{O}^g(y,x) - q^*(\hat{y} - y) \geq \bar{O}^g(\hat{y},x)$ *for all* $\hat{y}$.

The demonstration of **O**, and a discussion of why, in general, $\bar{O}^g(y,x) \neq O^g(y,x)$ are left to the reader.

Finally, we have

- **Dual Revenue and Distance Functions**: Let $Y(x)$ be a convex set that satisfies free disposability of output (FD0). Then $O^g(y,x) = \bar{O}^g(y,x)$, and

$$\begin{aligned} R(q,x) &= \max_y \{qy + O^g(y,x)\} \\ O^g(y,x) &= \min_q \{R(q,x) - qy\}. \end{aligned}$$

11.2.4 Shadow Prices and Distance Functions

The dual statements **C-I** and **R-O** are the core economic results that support eliciting *shadow (virtual) prices* from function representations of the technology. Shadow price definitions vary, but perhaps the simplest definition is that a commodity's shadow price is one that would convince an individual to choose the commodity. Shadow prices assume particular importance in welfare and benefit-cost analyses when economists attach monetary values to goods or services that are not traded in active markets. Oftentime, those shadow prices are determined by calculating consumer valuation of the items.

Our treatment, in principle, is the same, but we derive shadow prices using knowledge of T and not preferences. The focus, therefore, is on producer valuation of inputs and outputs. As elsewhere, we use a numeraire vector to convert nominal values to real values. (We continue to denote the numeraire as g regardless of whether it contains inputs, output, or a mix of the two.)

The criterion used to define a shadow price is that it is consistent with *optimal behavior*. So, for example, if $\hat{v}$ (denominated in normalized units) is to be a shadow price for $\hat{x}$, $\hat{x}$ must be an *optimal choice* when $\hat{v}$ is the market price. In this discussion, we only treat the following: *shadow prices of inputs* for individuals producing a predetermined level of y, and *shadow prices of outputs* for individuals using a predetermined level of x. The definition of optimality maintained in the former is *cost minimization* and *revenue maximization* in the latter. Even though we restrict attention to these two cases, the same principles apply to other settings. (See Exercise 58.)

We say that: *$\hat{v}$ represents a shadow price vector for $\hat{x}$ in producing y* if

$$I^g(\hat{x}, y) + \hat{v}(x - \hat{x}) \geq I^g(x, y) \text{ for all } x;$$

and *$\hat{q}$ represents a shadow price vector for $\hat{y}$ in using x if*

$$O^g(\hat{y}, x) - \hat{q}(y - \hat{y}) \geq O^g(y, x) \text{ for all } y.$$

The rationales are that $\hat{x}$ would be cost minimizing (optimal) for producing y if real input prices were $\hat{v}$, and $\hat{y}$ would be revenue maximizing (optimal) for x if real input prices were $\hat{q}$. Moreover, if T is convex, the shadow input prices represent solutions to (11.11) for the input vector $\hat{x}$, and the shadow output prices represent solutions to (11.18) for the output vector $\hat{y}$. Thus, the former can be thought of as price-dependent demands and the latter as price-dependent supplies (marginal cost) that can be derived directly from a function representation of the technology.

So even though we have derived and treated distance functions as function representations of T, they also provide a natural means for measuring values even in the absence of market prices. These values *are obtained as the normals (slopes) for hyperplanes that support the appropriate distance function.*

That definition of shadow price differs from the definition often encountered in practice that only requires that a shadow price vector be the normal for a tangent hyperplane, in this instance, to a distance function. Ours is more stringent in that it requires the tangency to be associated with the hyperplane supporting the graph of the relevant distance function. Under the assumption that T is canonical, the definitions are the same. Otherwise, they are not. (See Exercise 59.)

11.3 Measuring Efficiency and Relative Performance

For firms operating in a competitive market setting, judging relative performance reduces to comparing cost, revenue, or profit. For example, if two firms face the same market price constellation (p, w) but realize different profits, one can meaningfully call one *more profitable* than the other.

While many firms operate in competitive markets, others do not. For example, providers of basic services or utilities such as electricity, water, sewage, and waste remediation are often operated by public authorities. Similarly, some U.S. states and some Canadian provinces restrict sales and marketing of alcoholic beverages to publicly managed "alcoholic beverage stores (ABS)" or "package stores."

We now show how distance functions provide an objective means for measuring and comparing relative performance when profit-seeking does not motivate production choices. We assume that $X(y)$ and $Y(x)$ are nonempty. Other assumptions are detailed when needed.

11.3.1 Efficient Sets and Distance Functions

Chapter 4 defines the *isoquant* for $X(y)$ as

$$\bar{X}(y) \equiv \{x \in X(y) : \lambda x \notin X(y) \text{ for } \lambda \in (0, 1)\}, \tag{11.19}$$

and the *transformation curve* for $Y(x)$ as

$$\bar{Y}(x) \equiv \{y \in Y(x) : \lambda y \notin Y(x) \text{ for } \lambda > 1\}, \tag{11.20}$$

and interprets them, respectively, as a lower boundary for $X(y)$ and an upper boundary for $Y(x)$.

Because $\bar{X}(y)$ and $\bar{Y}(x)$ bound production sets, a natural conjecture is that they represent *technically efficient* sets of points. Whether the conjecture is true depends upon the definition of *technical efficiency*. For example, a well-established tradition relies on the $\geq$ ranking and defines $y^o \in Y(x)$ *as technically efficient if there exists no other* $y^* \in Y(x)$ *such that* $y^* \geq y^o$ *and* $y^* \neq y^o$. According to this criterion, technical efficiency for "o" requires that there exist no other member of the output set that contains at least the same amount of all outputs as "o" and strictly more of at least one.

Given that interpretation, y^o depicted in Figure 11.4 is not technically efficient but y^* is. Thus, belonging to a transformation curve does not imply

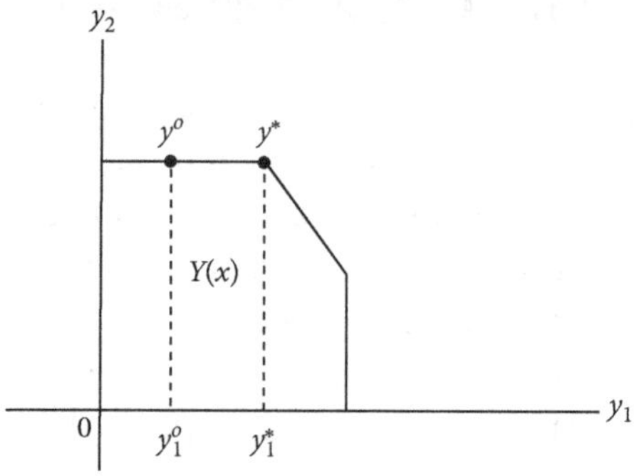

Figure 11.4 Are Points on the Transformation Curve Efficient?

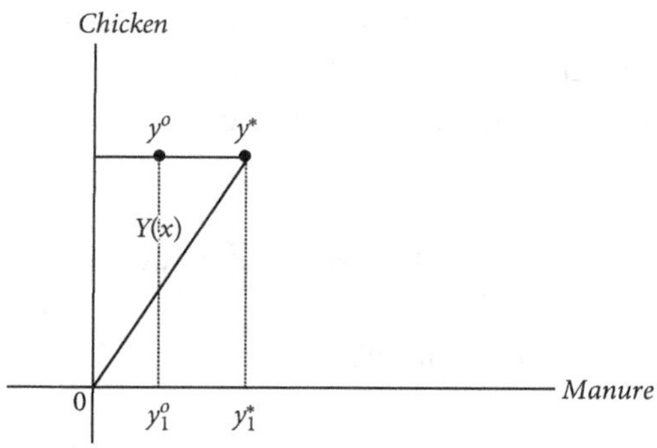

Figure 11.5 Undesirable Outputs and Efficiency

technical efficiency in this sense. Parallel arguments show that belonging to an isoquant may not guarantee technical efficiency.

How does reimagining and relabeling Figure 11.4 as in Figure 11.5 affect that argument? Now the second output is chicken, and the first is a by-product of chicken production, manure. Is it more efficient to generate more or less manure for a given level of chicken production? Answers to that question vary according to personal values, societal conventions, and the economic context.

For a chicken producer, manure might be a waste product that requires remediation. In that case, y^o might seem more efficient than y^*. Manure might also be a product to be sold to other producers searching for nitrogen nutrients. Then the original judgment seems valid. Or, it might be both: something that has value in limited amounts to some producers but that otherwise demands treatment.

We do not argue that Figure 11.4 and Figure 11.5 are realistic. But *as different thought experiments*, they demonstrate that defining technical efficiency can involve more than isolating an isoquant, a transformation curve, or relying upon the $\geq$ ranking. Boundaries or boundary points, as mathematical objects, are just surfaces (sets of points) or points that separate members of the set from its complement. Whether they are efficient depends upon the extramathematical interpretation that we attach to that boundary.

Being mindful of such issues, we offer notions of technical efficiency that can be adapted to accommodate different production settings and different assumptions about input and output disposability.

Definition 24. *Let* $x \in X(y)$. *x is g-*efficient for *y if there exists no* $\alpha > 0$ *such that* $x - \alpha g \in X(y)$.

Definition 25. *Let* $y \in Y(x)$. *y is g-*efficient for *x if there exists no* $\beta > 0$ *such that* $y + \beta g \in Y(x)$.

Visually, *x is g-efficient* if starting at $x \in X(y)$ *any* tiny movement in the direction of $-g$ leaves the input set. For y to be g-efficient for x, any movement away from y in the direction of g moves outside of $Y(x)$. To illustrate, y^* is $(1, 0)$-efficient for y in Figures 11.4 and 11.5, but y^o is not. Both y^* and y^o are $(0, 1)$-efficient.

Our definitions depend upon the vectors g. They change when g changes and, so, they are *path-dependent.* (As elsewhere, we adjust the definition of g according to whether we operate with inputs or outputs.) The underlying premise is that movements in the g direction in the case of outputs and in the $-g$ direction for inputs improve efficiency or are "good" or "desirable" in an appropriate sense. But because it's path-dependent, what is appropriate can be adjusted to accommodate different contexts.

We write the set of g-efficient inputs for y in symbol form as

$$X^g(y) \equiv \{x \in X(y) : x \text{ is g-efficient for } y\} \tag{11.21}$$

and call it the *g-efficient input set for y*, or more simply, the *efficient input set* when there can be no confusion. We write the set of g-efficient outputs as

$$Y^g(x) \equiv \{y \in Y(x) : y \text{ is g-efficient for } x\}, \tag{11.22}$$

and call it the *g-efficient output set for x.*

The definitions of $I^g(x, y)$ and $O^g(y, x)$ imply that distance functions are function representations of $X^g(y)$ and $Y^g(x)$, respectively. (We leave the proof of the following equivalence relations to you as an exercise.)

- **EX:** $x \in X^g(y) \Leftrightarrow I^g(x, y) = 0$.
- **EY:** $y \in Y^g(x) \Leftrightarrow O^g(y, x) = 0$.

11.3.2 Relating Technical Efficiency to Economic Efficiency

Chapter 5 showed that profit-maximizing producers do not locate on an iso-profit line that passes inside of the technology set, T. Similar conditions were deduced for revenue maximizers and cost minimizers. Using **EX, EY** and our results on $I^g(x, y)$ and $O^g(y, x)$ evaluated at cost-minimizing input bundles and revenue-maximizing bundles, we formalize this principle as:

- **Cost minimization requires technical efficiency**: Let $X(y)$ be nonempty and satisfy free disposability of inputs (FDI) and $g \geq 0, g \neq 0$. Then x is cost minimizing for (w, y) only if $x \in X^g(y)$.
- **Revenue maximization requires technical efficiency**: Let $Y(x)$ be nonempty and satisfy free disposability of outputs (FDO) and $g \geq 0, g \neq 0$. Then y is revenue maximizing only if $y \in Y^g(x)$.

Identifying technically efficient input bundles or output bundles, therefore, logically precedes cost minimization and/or revenue maximization. Exercise 63 asks you to extend this observation to profit-maximizing demand and supplies.

For canonical technologies, the dual forms of the input and output distance functions emphasize the connection between economically optimal points and technical efficiency. For example, under FDI and convexity

$$I^g(x, y) = \bar{I}^g(x, y) = v(x, y)x - c(v(x, y), y).$$

Hence, $x \in X^g(y) \Rightarrow v(x, y)x = c(v(x, y), y)$, so that x is *cost minimizing at its shadow prices*. If $x \in X^g$ is inefficient, its dual formulation requires that its shadow prices be chosen to make the departure from cost minimization as small as possible. Thus, another interpretation of $\bar{I}^g(x, y)$ is that it finds the real prices for which x is as close as possible to being the cheapest input bundle capable of producing y. Parallel arguments under FDO and convexity give the interpretation of $\bar{O}^g(y, x)$ as choosing the shadow output prices that make y as close to revenue maximizing as possible.

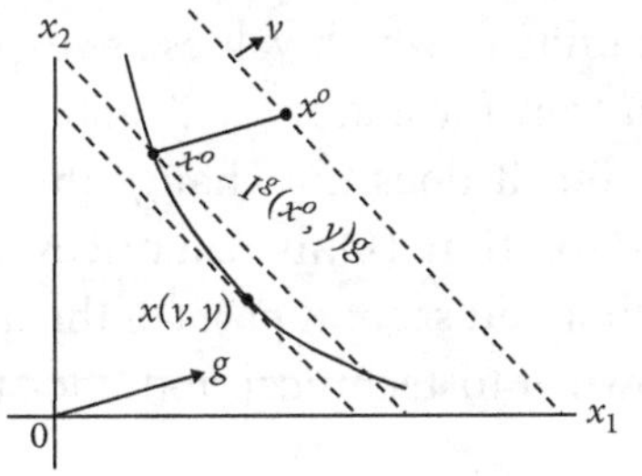

Figure 11.6 Cost Inefficiency and Technical Inefficiency

The concepts of g-efficiency apply regardless of the market setting. When markets are competitive and observed prices are available, it's easy to link technical efficiency measures expressed in terms of shadow price values to measures of *economic efficiency* expressed in terms of observed cost, revenue, or profit.

We illustrate for the case where producers minimize the cost of producing y. But the same principles apply for revenue maximization and profit maximization. Take $x^o \in X(y)$ and $g > 0$ as depicted in Figure 11.6. The g-inefficiency of x^o is measured by $I^g(x^o, y)$ that equals the length of the line segment that connects x^o to its translation transformation $x^o - I^g(x^o)g$ divided by the length of g. As illustrated, x^o lies inside $X(y)$ by $I^g(x^o, y)$ units of g.

The translation transformation of x^o, $x^o - I^g(x^o, y)g$, is not cost minimizing for the input price vector depicted by the dashed isocost line segments with normal v. Instead, cost minimization occurs at $x(v, y)$. The difference between the real cost of x^o and minimal real cost, $vx^o - c(v, y)$, is positive and decomposes as

$$(vx^o - I^g(x^o, y)) + (I^g(x^o, y) - c(v, y)).$$

(One arrives at this decompostion by the simple device of adding zero in the form of $-I^g(x^o, y) + I^g(x^o, y)$ to the cost difference $vx^o - c(v, y)$ and collecting terms. Remember $vg = 1$, so that the real value of $vI^g(x, y)g$ is $I^g(x, y)$.)

The first component of the decomposition, $vx^o - I^g(x^o, y)$, measures the real cost of operating at x^o rather than at its technically efficient translation transformation for g. The second component, $I^g(x^o, y) - c(v, y)$, measures the real cost difference between operating in $X^g(y)$ but away from the cost-minimizing solution. This has led to a convention of referring to the first component as *technical inefficiency* and the second as *allocative or price inefficiency*.

These measures depend upon the choice of g and vary with g. Holding w constant, changing g changes the value of the numeraire bundle, wg, and thus the real economic units in which values are expressed. Changing g also changes the translation transformation of x^o and thus the efficient point to which x^o is compared. But it does not change the slope of the isocost line or the cost- minimizing solution. (Only real prices matter.) Thus, the points compared in both the first and second parts of the decomposition vary with g, so that the breakdown into technical and allocative inefficiency is also path-dependent.

A similar analysis applies for an arbitrary $y^o \in Y(x)$. In place of parallel restatements, we leave the demonstration to the reader as Exercise 64.

11.3.3 Judging Relative Performance

Because $I^g(y,x)$ and $O^g(y,x)$ measure efficiency, they also provide the means to compare relative performance over time, place, or both and time and place.

Figure 11.4 provides easy examples. Both y^o and y^* belong to $\bar{Y}(x)$ and $y^* \geq y^o$ and $y^* \neq y^o$. Hence, one can meaningfully say that y^* is *larger* than y^o. It's also meaningful to say that y^* is *more (1,0)-efficient* than y^o because it belongs to $Y^{(1,0)}(x)$ and y^o does not. Matters are more ambiguous when comparisons are based on $Y^{(0,1)}(x)$. Both y^o and y^* belong to $Y^{(0,1)}(x)$, so it's questionable to label y^* as the "more efficient" even though it is the larger of the two.

Comparisons between producers not operating on a transformation curve or isoquant are even more problematic. Figure 11.7 illustrates with y^o and y^*. As drawn, $O^{(1,0)}(y^*,x) < O^{(1,0)}(y^o,x)$, so that y^* is closer to $Y^{(1,0)}(x)$. But the situation reverses for $g = (0,1)$, and $O^{(0,1)}(y^*,x) > O^{(0,1)}(y^o,x)$, and thus the latter is closer to $Y^{(0,1)}(x)$.

Changing the "yardstick" changes the outcome of the comparison. This path dependence is an inherent difficulty in developing scalar-valued measures of multiple-dimensional (vector) performance.

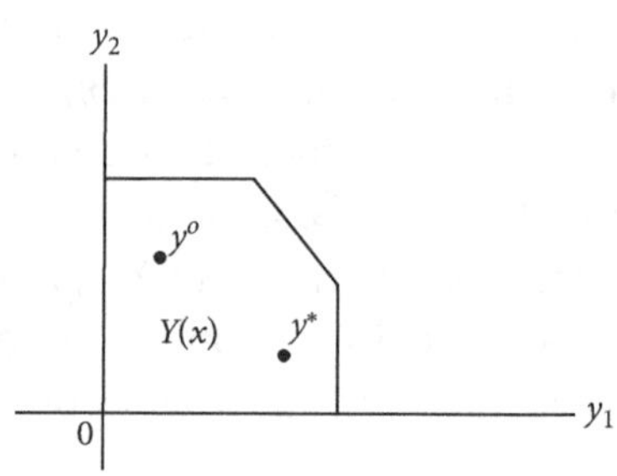

Figure 11.7 More or Less Efficient?

A simple thought experiment illustrates the generic problem. Pick a pastime that you enjoy. Then ask yourself and a fellow *aficiniado*: Who is or was the greatest practitioner of that pastime? Surely, you will not be surprised to encounter a difference in opinion. Differences are the norm, and not the exception, in such comparisons. Measuring performance of activities with multiple dimensions requires the ability to rank the relative importance of the activities as well as real measures of them.

Different tacks can be taken to resolve such dilemmas. For example, some advocate averaging across different yardsticks. Not surprisingly, however, little to no agreement exists on which averaging method or which yardsticks to include. Others advocate picking a traditional yardstick and basing all comparisons on it.

Our view is that permitting and accommodating different perspectives enhances the ability to compare performance. Therefore, we offer path-dependent relative performance measures. As a first step, we offer weaker notions of input and output disposability that permit inputs or outputs to be *disposable* in only a single direction.

Definition 26. *Let $g \geq 0, g \neq 0$ denote a vector of outputs. $Y(x)$ exhibits* g-disposability of outputs: *if $y \in Y(x) \Rightarrow y - \lambda g \in Y(x)$ for all $\lambda \geq 0$ and $y - \lambda g \geq 0$.*

Definition 27. *Let $g \geq 0, g \neq 0$ denote a vector of inputs. $X(y)$ exhibits* g-disposability of inputs: *if $x \in X(y) \Rightarrow x + \lambda g \in X(y)$ for all $\lambda \geq 0$.*

Using arguments developed in Chapter 10, we find it's easy to establish that the appropriate version of *g*-disposability ensures that $O^g(y, x)$ and $I^g(x, y)$ provide function representations of $Y(x)$ and $X(y)$. (Exercise 65 asks you to verify this claim.) Relying on that fact, we then define two notions of relative efficiency:

Definition 28. *Let $Y(x)$ satisfy g-disposability. Then y^* is more g-efficient than y^o if $O^g(y^*, x) \leq O^g(y^o, x)$.*

Definition 29. *Let $X(y)$ satisfy g-disposability. Then x^* is more g-efficient than x^0 if $I^g(x^*, y) \leq I^g(x^o, y)$.*

Our conditional judgments about relative *g*-efficiency translate into comparing the relative distances (in the direction *g*) of different points to an appropriate frontier of a technology set. While the choice of which measure to use remains subjective, the measures themselves are real-valued and therefore can be meaningfully compared, added, and subtracted.

11.4 Exercises

Exercise 53. *Let* $\bar{I}^g(\lambda x^o + (1-\lambda)x', y) \geq \lambda \bar{I}^g(x^o, y) + (1-\lambda)\bar{I}^g(x', y), \quad 0 < \lambda < 1.$ *Show that* $X^*(y)$ *is a convex set.*

Exercise 54. **Verify statement* ***R*** *with a formal argument, illustrate the results visually, and explain them intuitively. Be sure to include a discussion of McFadden's Lemma (see Chapter 7).*

Exercise 55. **Verify statement* ***O****, with a formal argument, illustrate the results visually, and explain them intuitively.*

Exercise 56. **Let* $v(x, y)$ *denote a solution to (11.11). Prove that*

$$\left(v(x^o, y) - v(x^*, y)\right)\left(x^o - x^*\right) \leq 0.$$

Explain the economic meaning.

Exercise 57. **Let* $q(y, x)$ *denote a solution to (11.18). Prove that.*

$$\left(q(y^o, x) - q(y^*, x)\right)\left(y^o - y^*\right) \geq 0.$$

Exercise 58. **Let* T *be a convex set that satisfies free disposability of output. For observed* $(x, y) \in T$*, derive the shadow input and output prices based on the profit-maximizing optimality criterion. Explain.*

Exercise 59. *Oftentimes, one encounters empirical applications that identify the normal to a hyperplane tangent to* $I^g(x, y)$ *as defining shadow prices. Figure 11.8 illustrates one such case for* $\hat{x}$*. Is* $\hat{v}$ *illustrated there a shadow price? Explain your reasoning.*

Exercise 60. *For* $x \in X(y)$*, prove that*

$$x \in X^g(y) \Leftrightarrow I^g(x, y) = 0.$$

Exercise 61. *For* $y \in Y(x)$*, prove that*

$$y \in Y^g(x) \Leftrightarrow O^g(y, x) = 0.$$

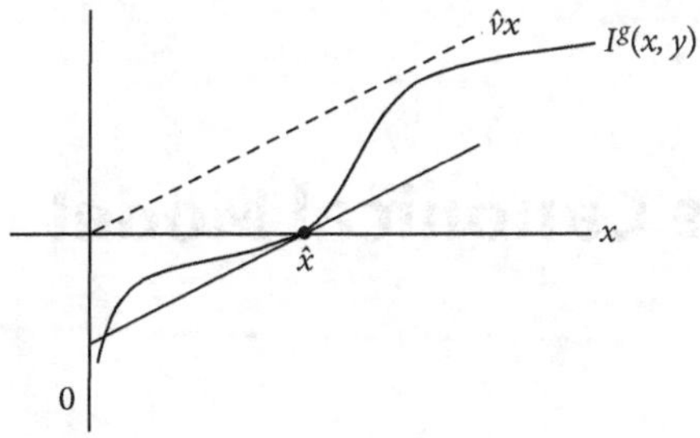

Figure 11.8 Shadow Price or Not?

Exercise 62. *What are $Y^{(0,1)}(x)$ and $Y^{(1,0)}(x)$ in Figure 11.3? Explain why they are the same or why they differ.*

Exercise 63. *Let $(x^*(p,w), y^*(p,w))$ solve*

$$\max_{(x,y)}\{py - wx : (x,y) \in T\}.$$

Prove that $x^*(p,w) \in X^g(y^*(p,w))$ and $y^*(p,w) \in Y^g(x^*(p,w))$.

Exercise 64. *Using $O^g(y,x)$ and $R(p,x)$, develop a decomposition of real revenue inefficiency for g*

$$R(q,x) - qy^o$$

for $y^o \in Y(x)$. Illustrate it graphically.

Exercise 65. *a) Let $Y(x)$ satisfy Definition 26. Prove that*

$$y \in Y(x) \Leftrightarrow O^g(y,x) \geq 0.$$

b) Let $X(y)$ satisfy Definition 27. Prove that

$$x \in X(y) \Leftrightarrow I^g(x,y) \geq 0.$$

Exercise 66. **Let $Y(x)$ satisfy Definition 26 with $g \geq 0, g \neq 0$. Prove that*

$$R(q,x) = \max_{y}\{qy : y \in Y^g(x)\}.$$

12
Beyond the Canonical Model

12.1 Introduction

The canonical technology is a cornerstone of an analytic edifice that houses the theories of producer behavior, consumer behavior, market equilibrium, public economics, and economic growth. Each of those theories, in turn, sustains an empirical literature that enriches our understanding of how economies operate and that supports public decision making.

Even so, the canonical-technology model has limits. At various points in our discussion, we have glimpsed some consequences of relaxing its assumptions. We now turn to a more systematic treatment that focuses on relaxing convexity and free disposability of inputs and outputs. We choose those properties because familiar counter examples to each exist. Nonempty T and no free lunch, however, seem physically evident. Goods and services are produced and require the transformation of other goods or services. And besides stating a physical principle, our version of no fixed cost is also a statement about the decision setting. Producers are free to do nothing. No fixed cost (NFC) does not rule out examining either cost or revenues that are fixed in the short run. Both can exist. In fact, they motivate our consideration of $c(w, y)$ and $R(p, x)$, which are short-run concepts—the former because input decisions are made *holding output constant* and the latter because output decisions are made *holding input constant.*

Our derivations of $f(x)$, $I^g(x, y)$, and other representations of T detail the specific consequences for each representation of imposing free disposability of inputs, free disposability of output, and convexity. Relaxing those properties reduces to observing that those specific properties do not apply and to avoiding their use whenever appropriate. Such inferences are straightforward and so are well left to the reader. Therefore, we frame our discussion using the duality results of Chapter 9. Producers who maximize profit for predetermined input and output prices act *as if* they face a canonical technology. *For modeling purposes*, no generality is then lost by assuming one. But matters change when fixed prices do not exist or if producers can manipulate them. We examine some consequences of each exception to these assumptions.

Lectures on Neoclassical Production Economics. Robert G. Chambers, Oxford University Press.
 DOI: 10.1093/9780197817759.003.0013

12.2 Nonpriced Outputs or Inputs

12.2.1 Nonpriced Outputs

Consider a simple version of T. Let there be two outputs y_1 and y_2, and assume that $p = (0, p_2)$ with $p_2 > 0$. Chapter 8 shows that profit maximization requires that supplies $y^*(p, w) = (y_1^*(p, w), y_2^*(p, w))$ satisfy

$$c(w, y_1, y_2) \geq c(w, y_1^*(p, w), y_2^*(p, w)) + 0(y_1 - y_1^*(p, w)) + p_2(y_2 - y_2^*(p, w))$$

for all y_1, y_2. Evaluating this expression at $y_2 = y_2^*(p, w)$ gives

$$c(w, y_1, y_2^*(p, w)) \geq c(w, y_1^*(p, w), y_2^*(p, w)) + 0(y_1 - y_1^*(p, w)) \text{ for all } y_1.$$

The graph of the affine function of y_1, $c(w, y_1^*(p, w), y_2^*(p, w)) + 0(y_1 - y_1^*(p, w))$, must support the graph of the cost function, $c(w, y_1, y_2^*(p, w))$, from below in $(y_1, \$)$ space. Because the slope of that affine function is zero, $y_1^*(p, w)$ satisfies

$$c(w, y_1, y_2^*(p, w)) \geq c(w, y_1^*(p, w), y_2^*(p, w)) \text{ for all } y_1.$$

The producer chooses the optimal supply of the zero-priced output to minimize the cost of producing it and $y_2^*(p, w)$.

This inequality must hold for all y_1, so it must hold when $y_1 = 0$. Thus, profit maximization in the face of a 0 price for the first output requires that

$$c(w, 0, y_2^*(p, w)) \geq c(w, y_1^*(p, w), y_2^*(p, w)). \tag{12.1}$$

Profit maximization requires that $(0, y_2^*(p, w))$ must be at least as costly to produce as $(y_1^*(p, w), y_2^*(p, w))$. Expression (12.1) is consistent with FDO only if $y_1^*(p, w) = 0$ or

$$c(w, 0, y_2^*(p, w)) = c(w, y_1^*(p, w), y_2^*(p, w)),$$

moving from zero production of y_1 to positive production is costless.

Together, the assumptions of a zero-priced y_1 and a canonical T and expression (12.1) suggest that a rational firm won't produce y_1. Nevertheless, we observe situations—pollution or undesirable outputs—where firms produce outputs that fetch a zero price.

Consider a farmer producing corn, y_2, and nitrogen emissions, y_1. The emissions can be runoff into the ecosystem and/or nitrous oxide emissions into the atmosphere. Let the farmer's inputs be x_1, nitrogen fertilizer, and x_2, an aggregate of the remaining inputs that we call *effort*. Historically, active markets for nitrogen emissions were nonexistent, and emissions were unpriced. But they occurred. If T does not require emissions to be freely disposable, then expression (12.1) with $y_1^*(p, w) > 0$ is no longer problematic. We can explain such outcomes as positive emissions lowering the cost of producing corn. Or, perhaps better, as reducing emissions requiring diverting effort from corn production to remediation.

Chapters 10 and 11 suggest a simple modification to canonical T that accommodates this setting. Replace FDO with g-disposability. For example, if $Y(x)$ satisfies g disposability for $g = (0, 1)$: (a) an output distance function representation of $Y(x)$ exists; and (b) the marginal cost of y_1 can be either positive or negative.

Upon identifying this lacuna in the canonical model, however, the early environmental-economics literature pursued another path. Its ubiquity, persistence, and problematic nature merit closer scrutiny. The solution was to treat emissions as a freely disposable "input" to be incorporated into a "production function" for the good output, y_2. In this specification, corn production obeys

$$y_2 = n(x_1, x_2, y_1),$$

with all function arguments freely disposable, so that

$$(x_1^o, x_2^o, y_1^o) \geq (x_1, x_2, y_1) \Rightarrow n(x_1^o, x_2^o, y_1^o) \geq n(x_1, x_2, y_1).$$

Keeping $p_1 = 0$, profit maximization now requires that $(x^*(p, w), y^*(p, w))$ satisfy

$$\begin{aligned} & p_2 n(x_1^*(p, w), x_2^*(p, w), y_1^*(p, w)) - w_1 x_1^*(p, w) - w_2 x_2^*(p, w) \\ & \geq p_2 n(x_1, x_2, y_1) - w_1 x_1 - w_2 x_2 \end{aligned}$$

for all (x_1, x_2, y_1, y_2). And, in particular,

$$p_2 \left(n(x_1^*(p, w), x_2^*(p, w), y_1^*(p, w)) - n(x_1^*(p, w), x_2^*(p, w), 0) \right) \geq 0. \qquad (12.2)$$

Because the "input," y_1, is freely disposable in the "production" of y_2, this resolves the dilemma raised by expression (12.1). It provides an economic rationale for the farmer to produce a positive amount of y_1 that commands a zero market price.

Unfortunately, this "cure" creates difficulties. To illustrate, measure both x_1 and y_1 in units of nitrogen mass. Start with a situation where, say, 75% of the nitrogen applied escapes into the environment so that $y_1 = .75x_1$.[1] Corn production is then $n(x_1, x_2, .75x_1)$. Free disposability of the emissions "input," however, requires that $n(x_1, x_2, x_1) \geq n(x_1, x_2, .75x_1)$. *Even if all the nitrogen applied escapes into the environment, corn output is no lower than if 25% were transformed into corn.* Moreover, because both are freely disposable, *fertilizer application and the "input" emissions must be production substitutes. That is, holding x_2 and y_2 constant, lowering fertilizer application requires an increase in emissions to maintain production feasibility.* Both implications beggar belief.

Free disposability of the "input" y_1 also requires

$$(x_1, x_2, y_1, y_2) \in T \Rightarrow (x_1, x_2, \infty, y^2) \in T.$$

In words, producing any finite amount of y_2 using a finite amount of the "inputs" (x_1, x_2, y_1) implies that the same production can be had by permitting infinitely large emissions holding the nitrogen applied and effort constant. If nitrogen application is held constant, what is the source of the arbitrarily large emissions that this specification requires to be technically feasible? In effect, "reverse congestion" exists. Arbitrarily large amounts of emission are costlessly available.

These implausible implications reflect *material-balance* concerns. The rough idea behind material balance accords with the laws of thermodynamics. Matter can neither be created nor destroyed; it can only be transformed from one form to another. Nitrogen runoff or nitrous oxide emissions depend importantly upon the nitrogen applied. If nitrogen is not applied or already in the soil, it can't be emitted. The emissions-as-input specification violates this principle.

We've identified situations where standard abstractions are problematic. Treating emissions as either a freely disposable output or as a freely disposable "input" has paradoxical implications. Both appear too strong for some practical settings. More to the point, farmers clearly have incentives to control nitrogen emissions. After all, they apply nitrogen to promote the growth of corn. *Nitrogen that percolates into the environment is nitrogen not embodied in more corn.* Because the farmer pays for nitrogen fertilizer, what escapes into the environment wastes valuable resources. The farmer should prefer that more nitrogen rather than less be embodied in corn growth. But controlling

[1] This may seem a high emissions rate, but estimates of the amount of nitrogen fertilizer applied that end up in the air, soil, or water run as high as 80%.

emissions carries a cost in terms of effort diverted from other productive activities. If, in the zero-price setting, expression (12.1) holds, *those costs outweigh the cost savings associated with wasted fertilizer at the observed margin.* Whether they will elsewhere depends importantly on the physical setting.

12.2.2 Nonpriced Input

Let there be two inputs x_1 and x_2. Assume that $w = (0, w_2)$ with $w_2 > 0$. We continue to refer to x_2 as the input aggregate, effort, but we now take x_1 to be a natural resource that the producer accesses for free. In this setting, a profit-maximizing producer chooses $x^*(p, w) = (x_1^*(p, w), x_2^*(p, w))$ to satisfy

$$R(p, x_1^*(p, w), x_2^*(p, w)) + 0(x_1 - x_1^*(p, w)) + w_2(x_2 - x_2^*(p, w)) \geq R(p, x_1, x_2)$$

for all x_1, x_2. Evaluating this expression at $x_2 = x_2^*(p, w)$ gives

$$R(p, x_1^*(p, w), x_2^*(p, w)) + 0(x_1 - x_1^*(p, w)) \geq R(p, x_1, x_2^*(p, w))$$

for all x_1. Profit maximization requires that the revenue function evaluated at $x_2^*(p, w)$ treated as a function of x_1, $R(p, x_1, x_2^*(p, w))$, must be everywhere bounded from above by the affine hyperplane of x_1

$$R(p, x_1^*(p, w), x_2^*(p, w)) + 0(x_1 - x_1^*(p, w))),$$

whence

$$R(p, x_1^*(p, w), x_2^*(p, w)) \geq R(p, x_1, x_2^*(p, w)).$$

A profit maximizer chooses the "free" natural resource to maximize the joint revenue realized from it and $x_2^*(p, w)$.

Because 0 is one possible level of use for the natural resource, profit maximization now requires:

$$R(p, x_1^*(p, w), x_2^*(p, w)) \geq R(p, 0, x_2^*(p, w)).$$

Unlike the analogous output case, profit maximization with $x_1(p, w) > 0$ is compatible with the canonical model's FDI condition. That, however, does not mean that zero-pricing of a resource is not problematic from a social perspective. Evidently, the resource's social value is positive (otherwise we would not call it a resource). Therefore, a profit-maximizing producer uses more of it than if it were priced at its social value (Chapter 8). The economic problems associated with improperly pricing a resource remain. But they raise no difficulties for reasoning based on the canonical model of T.

12.2.3 Lessons from Relaxing FDI and FDO

Allowing local conditions for "equilibrium results" to dictate global assumptions about T can be problematic, if not outright misleading. It can yield models that counter physical reality and that pave the route to future *paradoxes.*

Addressing a model assumption that generates paradoxical results requires more than simply changing the sign of a marginal effect or renaming physical entities. That's the stuff of jargoneers. A more cautious approach follows Occam's Razor. Lacking more detailed knowledge, choose the simplest alternative assumption that addresses the perceived paradox. For our simple examples, that translates into relaxing free disposability of y_1.

Having made that point for *the current examples*, we caution that the appropriate model adjustment depends on the context. No single modification works in all circumstances. Canonical, in our semantics, connotes familiar or "standard." Thus, adjustments to the canonical model required by the departures from that setting must depend upon the nature of the departures. For example, we identified material-balance concerns as reasons for questioning the standard natural resource and environmental economics modeling of a bad output. And we suggested that nitrogen emissions and fertilizer applications should vary together. But we did not impose that criterion. That raises the question of when and how to incorporate experienced-based knowledge into our economic models. That is the essence of the craft of being a good applied production economist. And the best generic answer seems to be: "It depends".

12.3 Producers Can Manipulate Market Prices

This discussion assumes that you have been introduced to the theories of monopolistic, monopsonistic, oligopolistic, oligopsonistic, and game-theoretic behavior. Our focus here, therefore, is not on optimal producer behavior in those settings. Instead, it's on how a canonical technology prescribes producer behavior.

We've learned that we can characterize the economic behavior of input-price-taking producers using a cost function that is nondecreasing, positively homogeneous, and concave in w and that it satisfies Shephard's Lemma (Chapter 6). Chapter 7 gives parallel results for output-price-taking producers and the revenue function. Those results manifest fundamental economic behavior for price-taking, cost-minimizing, and revenue-maximizing producers. They do not arise from restrictions that we have placed on T.

Imposing convexity and disposability on T, however, lets us describe $c(w,y)'s$ behavior as a function of output and $R(p,x)'s$ behavior as a function of x. Free disposability of output and convexity imply that $c(w,y)$ is nondecreasing and convex in y. And free disposability of input and convexity imply that $R(p,x)$ is nondecreasing and concave in x.

We have also learned that profit-maximizing, price-taking producers make economic decisions characterized by a profit function, $\pi(p, w)$, that is monotonic, positively homogeneous, and convex in (p,w). Moreover, such profit functions imply the existence of observationally equivalent dual cost and dual revenue functions that are consistent with a canonical technology (Chapter 9).

That nexus between profit-maximizing behavior and a canonical T makes the latter a "reductionist" model for analyzing price-taking, profit maximizers. It reduces analyzing producer behavior to simple marginal principles to characterize economic exchange. The notion of a cost (input-requirement) function exhibiting a positive and nondecreasing marginal cost is one example. So, too, is a revenue (production) function exhibiting positive but decreasing marginal revenue of the inputs. These restrictions are not essential to developing the standard theory of producer behavior, but they provide a convenient platform for analyzing it.

That's an attractive property *for a model.* Its parsimony permits abstract analysis using easily grasped principles. But like all models, a canonical T is an abstraction. Departures from it are expected and are not paradoxical. Moreover, those departures can have important behavioral consequences when the paradigm of profit-maximizing, price-taking producers poorly approximates reality. Then a failure to recognize the reductionist nature of canonical T hinders our ability to analyze economic behavior.

We investigate further by examining two settings. One is relevant to an input-price-taking producer who may be able to manipulate p. The other is relevant to an output-price-taking producer who may be able to manipulate w. A producer with monopoly power in output markets is a special case of the former, and a producer with monopsonistic power in inputs markets is a special case of the latter.

12.3.1 The Cost Function and Economies of Size

Figure 12.1 depicts a cost function for a single-output canonical technology. Suppose that a firm has determined that $2y^o$ is the optimal amount to produce a good. How should it produce it? To be concrete, should the firm produce $2y^o$ at a cost of $c(w, 2y^o)$ in a single "plant"? Or should it set up two identical "plants" and produce y^o in each? As Figure 12.1 shows, splitting into two "plants" incurs a cost of $2c(w, y^o)$ to produce $2y^o$. That is less than $c(w, 2y^o)$, the cost of producing $2y^o$ in a single plant. The firm saves by setting up two "plants" rather than one. (Here we emphasize that the canonical model exhibits no fixed setup costs.)

Asking the same question about y^o shows that the producer also saves cost by splitting production of y^o into two "plants" of *size* $\frac{1}{2}y^o$. In short, the canonical model predicts that firms reduce cost by splitting production of *size* y into smaller "plants."

This potential gain from splitting operations is a consequence of the *increasing marginal cost* associated with a canonical T. Increases in output cost more at the margin as the *size (level)* of output grows. In the single-output case, that means that *unit (average) cost*, $\frac{c(w, y)}{y}$, is increasing in y. We illustrate unit cost as the slope of a line segment connecting the origin, 0, and the point $(y, c(w, y))$ on the graph of the cost function. We call increasing unit cost *diseconomies of size.*

A reverse argument applies if the cost function is nondecreasing and *concave* as a function of output. Then, output increases cost less at the margin as output grows. (See Figure 12.2.) Unit cost is decreasing in y. The cost function then exhibits *economies of size.* The producer has an incentive to centralize production *even in the absence of fixed costs.* And it is often argued that this facilitates monopolization.

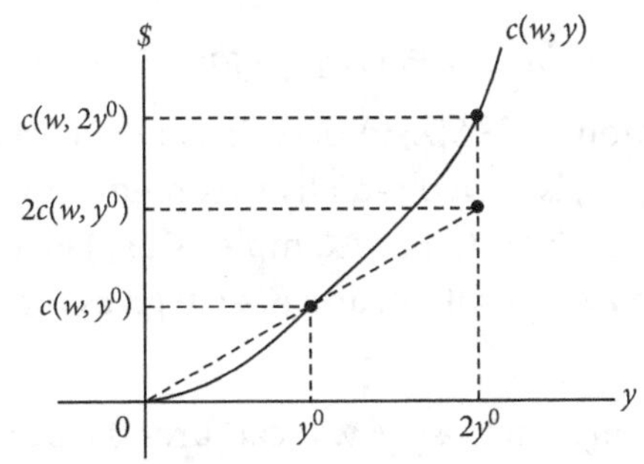

Figure 12.1 Canonical Model and Diseconomies of Size

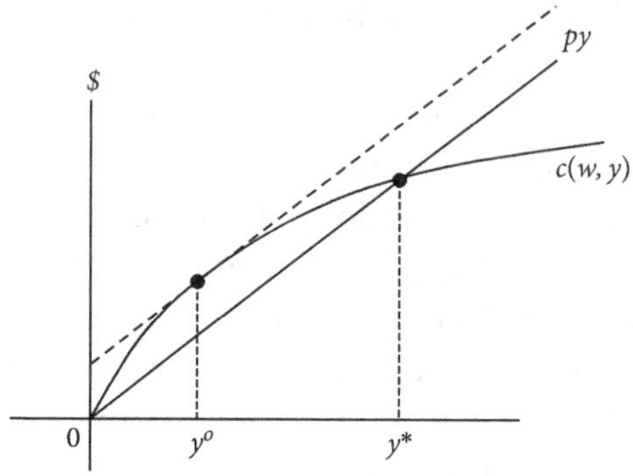

Figure 12.2 Economies of Size

Figure 12.2 provides an illustration. Let py represent revenues derived from output for a given market price. Applying the "price equals marginal cost rule" suggests that a price-taking firm would operate at y^o. But profit there is negative. A price-taking producer does better by operating at y^* where zero profit is made. Moreover, increasing production beyond y^* generates increasingly large positive profits. At that price, production would be unboundedly large if $c(w, y)$ depicts cost behavior. Unboundedly large production, however, implies that the firm can influence p unless market demand is perfectly inelastic. That suggests a potential conflict with assuming that p is fixed to the producer.

The dividing line between economies of size and diseconomies of size occurs where the firm neither gains nor loses by centralizing. Unit cost remains constant as output varies. Cost then exhibits *constant returns to size.*

Similar reasoning applies in the multiple-output case. But unit cost, $\frac{c(w,y)}{y}$, is ill defined when y is an M-dimentional vector (bundle) of outputs $y = (y_1, \ldots, y_M)$. Some extra notation helps clarify.

Let

$$S(\lambda; y) \equiv c(w, \lambda y) \; for \; \lambda \geq 0$$

Treated as a function of λ, $S(\lambda; y)$ describes how costs vary as the output bundle, $y = (y_1, \ldots, y_M)$, is varied radially (keeping output ratios unchanged) while operating a single "plant." For example, $S(2; y)$ gives the cost associated with producing $2y$ in a single plant, and $S(\frac{1}{2}; y)$ gives the cost associated with cutting y by half.

We call $\frac{S(\lambda; y)}{\lambda}$ the *ray unit cost of y*. It captures the per unit cost of producing λ units of the fixed output bundle, y. (The term "ray" here recognizes that it depicts how costs vary as one proceeds out the ray connecting the origin in output space and the point y in output space. Thus, the cost of one unit of that bundle is $c(w, y)$.)

Exercise 69 asks you to show that, *treated as a function of* λ, $S(\lambda; y)$ *is non-decreasing and convex with* $S(0; y) = 0$ *if* T *is canonical.* Then, the graph of $S(\lambda; y)$ assumes a similar shape to Figure 12.1 but now plotted over the $(\lambda, \$)$ coordinate plane. We now pose the same question for $y = (y_1, \ldots, y_M)$ that we posed in Figure 12.1 for a single-output, y. Does a firm save cost by producing $2y$ in two plants, each of size y, rather than doing it in a single plant? The monotonicity and convexity of $S(\lambda; y)$ ensure that

$$S(2; y) \geq 2S(1; y) \geq 2(2(S(\frac{1}{2}); y)).$$

And inductive argument shows that successively splitting the output bundle lowers ray unit cost for y for canonical T.

This reasoning motivates:

Definition 30. *Let* $\lambda > 0$. *The technology exhibits* diseconomies of size *at* (y, λ) *if ray unit cost is increasing in* λ; *and* economies of size *at* (y, λ) *if ray unit cost is decreasing in* λ.[2]

Definition 30 describes *local* properties of $c(w, y)$. They depend upon the output bundle, y, and the number of its units, λ. (Implicitly, they also depend upon w.) Thus, $c(w, y)$ can exhibit diseconomies of size at some output levels but economies of size for others. As an example, Figure 12.3 depicts the graph of $S(\lambda; 1)$ derived from the "lazy-S shaped production function" of Chapter 4. It exhibits economies of size at low-output levels but diseconomies of size at higher levels.

Definition 30 accommodates canonical and noncanonical technologies. Exercise 70 asks, for example, that you plot the graph of ray unit cost, $\frac{S(\lambda; 1)}{\lambda}$, associated with Figure 12.3 in $(\lambda, \$)$ space. The result is a U-shaped curve evocative of the "U-shaped average cost" familiar from intermediate microeconomics. Its bottom occurs where the slope is zero. That's often a knife-edge case. The slope of the ray unit cost curve switches from negative to positive. There, $c(w, y)$ exhibits neither diseconomies nor economies of size for that λ. We, therefore, say it exhibits *constant returns to size.* But to the right or left, matters differ.

[2] Many authors rely on a differentiably smooth technology to develop a calculus-based measure, the *elasticity of size,* in place of our notion of a ray unit cost. Then the appropriate definition becomes as follows: the technology exhibits diseconomies, constant returns, or economies of size as that elasticity is less than, equal to, or greater than one.

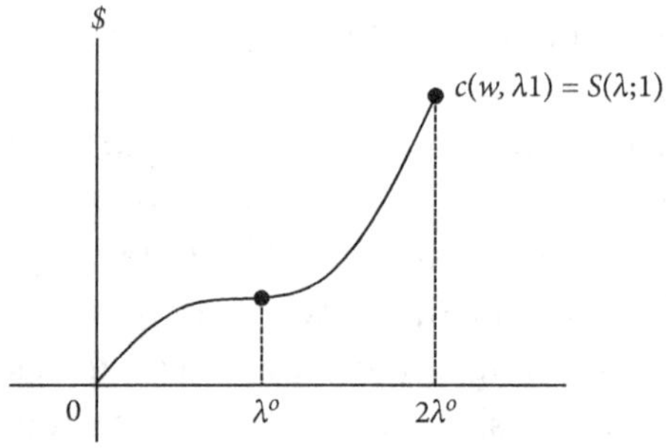

Figure 12.3 Variable Economies of Size

A canonical technology admits only two cases: diseconomies of size and constant returns to size. The latter, if globally true, occurs when the cost function is positively homogeneous as a function of y. That is,

$$c(w, \mu y) = \mu c(w, y) \text{ for all } y \text{ and } \mu > 0,$$

A cost function exhibiting constant returns globally admits only two possible outcomes for $\pi(p, w)$: $\pi(p, w) = 0$ or $\pi(p, w) = \infty$ (Exercise 71). The former corresponds to an equilibrium condition for the marginal firm. The latter rules out any reasonable equilibrium at those prices.

12.3.2 The Revenue Function and Economies of Scale

The treatment here mirrors that of the cost function for a noncanonical T. Rather than make parallel statements, we opt for a terser style that leaves it to the reader to draw the accompanying illustrations and to provide intuitive explanations. (Please, don't skip this step!)

Let there be a single input, x, and $R(p, x)$ denote its revenue function. Assume a canonical technology. We start with a simple question. If $2x$ has been identified as the optimal input level, is the firm better off locating that $2x$ in a single "plant" of "scale" $2x$ or in setting up two identical plants of scale x? The principle of diminishing marginal returns now ensures that

$$2R(p, x) \geq R(p, 2x).$$

A firm now generates more revenue by operating two plants of scale x than by operating a single plant of scale $2x$. An inductive argument shows that a firm gains by splitting plants of a given scale into smaller scale operations.

So, a canonical technology ensures that revenue gains associated with input increases become smaller at the margin as input usage grows. And that implies that the *unit (average) product of x*, $\frac{R(p,x)}{x}$ decreases as x increases. We call that *diseconomies of scale.*

If, however, T is not canonical and $R(p,x)$ is increasing and convex in x, the unit product of x grows with x. We call this *economies of scale. Constant returns to scale* occurs when unit product stays constant as x varies.

To extend the argument to the multiple-input case, $x = (x_1, \ldots, x_N)$ defines

$$P(\mu; x) \equiv R(p, \mu x) \text{ for } \mu \geq 0.$$

$P(\mu; x)$ describes maximal-revenue behavior as the scale of the operation varies along the ray in input space given by $\mu x = (\mu x_1, \ldots, \mu x_N)$. Defining $\frac{P(\mu;x)}{\mu}$ for $\mu > 0$ as *ray unit product for x and μ* motivates:

Definition 31. *Let $\mu > 0$. The technology exhibits diseconomies of scale at (x, μ) if the ray unit product is decreasing in μ; and economies of scale at (x, μ) if the ray unit cost is decreasing in μ.*

Size vs. Scale

Some writers use *size* and *scale* interchangeably, or use one to the exclusion of the other. And many call *economies of size (scale)* increasing returns to size (scale) and *diseconomies of size (scale)* decreasing returns to size (scale). We preserve the distinction to emphasize that *size* pertains to movements in output space and *scale* to movements in input space. Thus, size and scale capture distinct phenomena and give different perspectives on the economic consequences of relaxing the canonical assumptions. The "economies" vs. "diseconomies" jargon seems more evocative of the economic consequences of noncanonical T than "returns."

12.3.3 Lessons from Relaxing Convexity

Noncanonical technologies are not irrelevant for competitive markets, but they are penumbral. Their nonconvex regions reside in shadows cast by competitive producer behavior.

Outside of that context, however, nonconvexities can explain observed economic phenomena. For example, if a nonconvex T permits economies of size to persist globally (over all output ranges), firms can generate arbitrarily large profits by expanding production beyond the output where revenue overtakes cost. And once a firm's output becomes so "large," it is no longer sensible to assume or to believe that it cannot affect prices, p, received.

Known limitations of the canonical model motivated our extended discussions of the consequences of each of the five basic assumptions for different physical (*primal*) representations of T. Production functions, input sets, and distance functions are tools to investigate producer behavior that can be used in different market settings and under different assumptions on T. The canonical model's limits also motivate our "constructive approach" to modeling T that starts with a bedrock assumption. Our approach is that T is nonempty—a feasible input-output exists. And from there, a version of T should be constructed that captures the economic essence of the problem faced.

While modifying the canonical model is often merited, we recommend reasoned relaxation of its assumptions. Different aspects of it may prove useful in modelling some settings but not others. The earlier discussions of economies of size and economies of scale make this point elliptically by framing them in terms of cost and revenue functions.

Taking a step back illustrates the point. Let money returns from producing y be given by the real-valued function $r(y)$. The price-taking producer is the special case, $r(y) = py$. So, too, is the traditional monopolist case, $r(y) = p(y)y$, as are other market structures. The following argument applies regardless of the specific form of $r(y)$.

Assume that the firm *cannot* influence input prices. Cost for input use of x is given by the linear function of x, wx. You can envision this intuitively as a situation where a firm is "big" or "dominant" in the market for its product but is a "small" player relative to the overall economy with which it must compete for resources.

A profit maximizer now solves:

$$\Pi(w) \equiv \max_{(x,y)}\{r(y) - wx : (x, y) \in T\}. \qquad (12.3)$$

$\Pi(w)$ is maximal possible profit from y given input prices, w. It is a *profit function*. But to avoid confusion with $\pi(p, w)$, which is associated with a different market setting, we avoid that jargon here.

We note that we can reformulate this problem as

$$\max_{y}\{r(y) - c(w, y)\}.$$

The reasoning, which we leave it to you to formalize, is simple and has been used before. Let (x^*, y^*) solve (12.3); then it must be true that

$$wx^* = \min_x\{wx : (x, y^*) \in T\}.$$

Producers minimize the cost of producing the optimal y taking w as fixed. That rationalizes decomposing the original problem into two stages. First, study the optimal choice of x for given y and then study y. Our earlier discussion of economies and diseconomies of size applies, without change, to this problem setting.

Now we make some points we glided over earlier. By Chapter 11, $c(w, y)$ generates a dual (input) distance function, $\bar{I}^g(x, y)$, that induces a convex dual input set $X^*(y)$. $X^*(y)$ inherits some characteristics of a canonical T—nonpositive and diminishing marginal rate of technical substitution—but not others. For example, to ensure that $X^*(y)$ exhibits FDO, we must assume that $c(w, y)$ is nondecreasing in y. Some lessons learned in the "canonical" context can be applied in other contexts but not all.

Let $(x(w), y(w))$ denote solutions to (12.3) and consider two input price constellations w^o and w'. Following the discussion in Chapters 6, 7, and 8,

$$\begin{aligned} r(y(w^o)) - w^o x(w^o) &\geq r(y(w')) - w^o x(w') \\ r(y(w')) - w' x(w') &\geq r(y(w^o)) - w' x(w^o) \end{aligned}$$

Adding and rearranging give

$$(w^o - w')(x(w^o) - x(w')) \leq 0. \tag{12.4}$$

Profit maximization still requires that input demands vary inversely with their prices even if the firm can manipulate marginal returns from varying y.

Because $\Pi(w) = r(y(w)) - c(w, y(w))$, these expressions imply that

$$\Pi(w^o) \geq \Pi(w') + x(w')(w' - w^o)$$

for all (w', w^o). $\Pi(w)$ when graphed as a function of w in the $(w, \$)$ coordinate plane must be supported from below by the affine function of w

$$\Pi(w') + x(w')(w' - w).$$

Normals to hyperplanes supporting $\Pi(w)$ must be (minus) profit-maximizing demands for the relevant w, generalizing Hotelling's Lemma and Shephard's Lemma. An easy argument shows that $\Pi(w)$ is convex in w.

We now claim that any firm solving the problem posed in expression (12.3) behaves as if it faced a "quasi-canonical" T that is nonempty, has convex input sets, and exhibits free disposability of inputs.

$$x(w) = x(w, y(w))$$

where $x(w, y)$ continues to denote a cost-minimizing demand for y. Input demand behavior in w is decomposable into two components: one that describes optimal input adjustment within $X^*(y)$ and another that corresponds to input adjustment driven by movement across input sets. The first component is exhaustively characterized by $c(w, y)$. Lacking specific knowledge about $r(y)$, specific predictions cannot be made about the precise nature of the later adjustment. But expression (12.4) assures us that each input demand will be nonincreasing in its input price. Remnants of the predictions from the canonical framework remain.

12.4 Exercises

Exercise 67. *For the cost structure depicted in Figure 12.1, show graphically that unit cost is increasing in y.*

Exercise 68. *Let $c(w, y)$ denote the cost of producing a single output. Assuming that $c(w, 0) = 0$ and that $c(w, y)$ is concave in y, prove that unit cost is nonincreasing in y.*

Exercise 69. *Let T be a canonical technology. Show that $S(\lambda; y)$ is nondecreasing and convex as a function of λ with $S(0; y) = 0$. Illustrate the result visually.*

Exercise 70. *For $S(\lambda; 1)$ illustrated in Figure 12.3, graph ray unit cost, $\frac{S(\lambda;1)}{\lambda}$ as a function of $\lambda > 0$ in the coordinate plane.*

Exercise 71. *Prove that if T is canonical and exhibits constant returns to size for all y that either $\pi(p, w)$ equals zero or ∞ (infinity).*

Exercise 72. *Let T be a canonical technology. Show that $P(\mu; x)$ is nondecreasing and concave as a function of μ with $P(0; x) = 0$. Illustrate the result visually.*

Exercise 73. *Depict $P(\mu; 1)$ for a lazy-S-shaped production function. Derive $\frac{P(\mu; 1)}{\mu}$ as a function of $\mu > 0$ in the coordinate plane and illustrate it.*

Exercise 74. **Let T be canonical and exhibit constant returns to scale for all x. Prove that either $\pi(p, w) = 0$ or $\pi(p, w) = \infty$ for this technology. Compare this technology to the one described in Exercise 71.*

Exercise 75. **It is often argued that a competitive market for outputs cannot arise when T exhibits economies of size for all y and that a competitive market for inputs cannot arise if T exhibits economies of scale for all x. Do you agree or disagree. Explain your answer.*

Exercise 76. **Let producer expenditure on an input bundle, x, be given by the real-valued function $v(x)$. The competitive case corresponds to $v(x) = wx$ and the monopsonistic case to $v(x) = w(x)x$, where $w(x)$ is the price-dependent supply of x. Prove that:*

a) $\max_{(x,y)}\{py - v(x) : (x, y) \in T\} = \max_{x}\{R(p, x) - v(x)\}$; *and*
b) if $(x(p), y(p)) \in argmax\{py - v(x) : (x, y) \in T\}$, *then* $(p^o - p')(y(p^o) - y(p')) \geq 0$.

Discuss the solution of this problem in detail.

Bibliography

Asimov, I. (1951). *Foundation.* New York: Doubleday.

Bertesekas, D. (2016). Belmont, MA: Athena Scientific.

Chambers, R. G. (2021). *Competitive Agents in Certain and Uncertain Markets.* New York: Oxford University Press.

Debreu, G. (1951). The coefficient of resource utilization. *Econometrica 19*, 273–92.

Einstein, A. (1920). *Relativity: The Special and General Theory.* London: Methuen and Co. Ltd.

Fishburn, P. C. (1972). *Mathematics of Decision Theory.* The Hague: Mouton.

Konüs, A. A. (1939). The problem of the true cost of living. *Econometrica 7*, 10–29.

Le Tellier, H. (2020). *L'anomalie.* Paris: Éditions Gallimard.

Mangasarian, O. (1969). *Nonlinear Programming.* New York: McGraw-Hill.

Minkowski, H. (1911). *Theorie der Konvexen Korper, Insbesondere Begrundung ihres Oberflachenbegriffs.* Leipzig: Gesammelte Abhandlungen II.

Moreau, J. (1962). Fonctions duales convexes et points proximaux dans un espace hilbertien. *Comptes Rendus de l'Académie des Sciences de Paris A255*, 2897–99.

Rockafellar, R. (1970). *Convex Analysis.* Princeton, NJ: Princeton University Press.

Shephard, R. W. (1953). *Cost and Production Functions.* Princeton, NJ: Princeton University Press.

Index